# A Framework for Geodesign
## Carl Steinitz

## Changing Geography by Design

Redlands, California

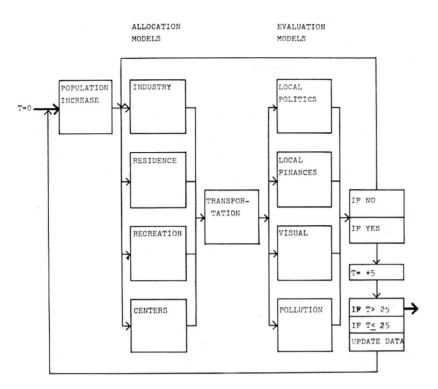

**Figure 1.17: The structure of the study's models.** | Source: C. Steinitz and P. Rogers. *A Systems Analysis Model of Urbanization and Change: An Experiment in Interdisciplinary Education.* Cambridge, MA: MIT Press, 1970.

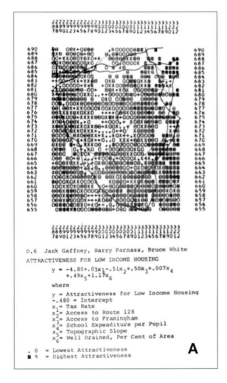

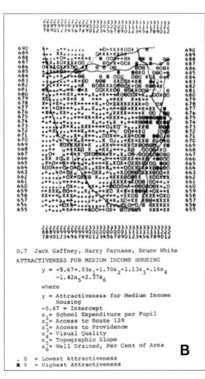

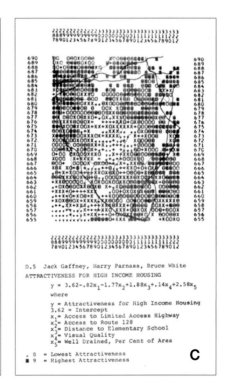

**Figures 1.18A, B, and C: Attractiveness for new low-income housing (A), for new middle-income housing (B), and for new high-income housing (C).** | Source: C. Steinitz and P. Rogers. *A Systems Analysis Model of Urbanization and Change: An Experiment in Interdisciplinary Education.* Cambridge MA: MIT Press, 1970.

## Change

While we were certainly aware of computer-based allocation models at that time, we deliberately had our students conduct the change model (the phase that changed the geography of the region) by hand, so that they would be as engaged as possible in the process. They made the allocations based on a smaller 250-meter grid, guided by the computer-generated evaluation maps (figure 1.19).

These unit-areas of change were represented by a color-coded cards for the land use to be allocated. The population model established the demand for each land-use type in a time stage and then student teams, each representing different land uses, engaged in the verbal and physical process of competing for the most attractive locations, much in the way that an

agent-based change model would function. They first simulated a future trend through the several time stages.

## Impact

The students then assessed the consequences of the trend changes with the several impact models. These impacts were visualized by overlaying colored pins and notes on the causal changes.

## Feedback

The students then interpreted the impacts and decided whether changes in the trend's land-use pattern of any stage were required.

**Figure 1.19:** Allocating change from new development and conservation.

## Change, impact, decision

Lastly, they re-allocated the changes by design, producing results measured to be environmentally superior and meeting the criteria for development (figure 1.20).

This Boston study was published in 1970 as *A Systems Analysis Model of Urbanization and Change: An Experiment in Interdisciplinary Education* (MIT Press), and led directly to a multi-year study of the growth of Boston funded by the National Science Foundation.[12]

These early experiences were highly influential in shaping my academic career and the framework for geodesign described in this book, and which I will detail through some selected case studies. There are others listed in the bibliography. One graduate student of mine during those early years was Jack Dangermond, who later founded the company that made the first commercially successful computer graphics mapping program. Today his firm, Esri, is the largest company in the world making and distributing GIS and related tools for others to use in geodesign.

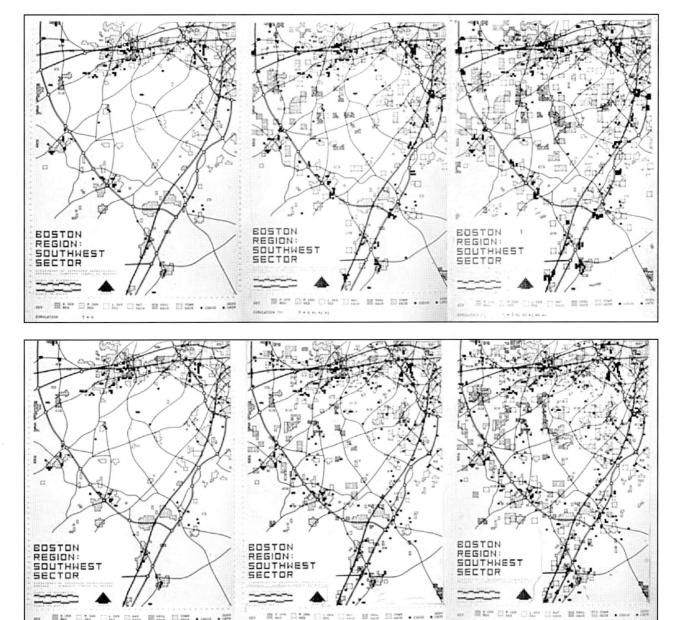

**Figure 1.20:** Trend growth (top three images) and improved growth (bottom three images). The top three maps show the growth of the southwest sector of Boston after 5, 15, and 25 years according to the trend. The bottom three maps show the growth as it was improved after several stages of feedback. | Source: C. Steinitz and P. Rogers. *A Systems Analysis Model of Urbanization and Change: An Experiment in Interdisciplinary Education.* Cambridge MA: MIT Press, 1970.

## Notes

1. H. A. Simon, *The Sciences of the Artificial* (Cambridge, MA: MIT Press, 1969).

2. C. Steinitz, "A Framework for Theory Applicable to the Education of Landscape Architects (and Other Environmental Design Professionals)," *Landscape Journal* 9 (1990): 136–43.
　Revised version in *Process Architecture* 127 (1995). (English and Japanese.).
　Revised version in *GIS Europe* 2 (1993): 42–45.
　Revised version in *Planning* (2000). (Chinese.)
　Revised version in *Environmental Planning for Communities: A Guide to the Environmental Visioning Process Utilizing a Geographic Information System (GIS)* (Cincinnati, OH: US Environmental Protection Agency Office of Research and Development, 2002).
　Revised version in chapter 3 of C. Steinitz, H. Arias, S. Bassett, M. Flaxman, T. Goode, T. Maddock, D. Mouat, R. Peiser, and A. Shearer, *Alternative Futures for Changing Landscapes: The San Pedro River Basin in Arizona and Sonora* (Washington, D.C.: Island Press, 2003).

3. H. A. Murray and C. Kluckhohn. *Personality in Nature, Society, and Culture* (New York: Knopf, 1953).

4. C. Steinitz, "Landscape Planning: A History of Influential Ideas," *Journal of the Japanese Institute of Landscape Architecture,* (January 2002): 201–8. (In Japanese.)
　Republished in *Chinese Landscape Architecture* 5: 92–95 and 6: 80–96. (In Chinese.)
　Republished in *Journal of Landscape Architecture (JoLA)* (Spring 2008): 68–75.
　Republished in *Landscape Architecture* (February 2009): 74 –84.

5. W. H. Manning. "A National Plan Study Brief," *Landscape Architecture* 13 (July 1923): 3–24.

6. I. L. McHarg, *Design with Nature* (Garden City, NY: Natural History Press, 1969).

7. N. Chrisman, *Charting the Unknown: How Computer Mapping at Harvard Became GIS* (Redlands, CA: ESRI Press, 2006).

8. K. Lynch, *The Image of the City* (Cambridge, MA: MIT Press, 1960).

9. C. Steinitz, "Meaning and the Congruence of Urban Form and Activity," *Journal of the American Institute of Planners* 34, no. 4, (July 1968): 223–47.

10. C. Steinitz, "The DELMARVA Study," (Proceedings, Council of Educators in Landscape Architecture, St Louis, MO, July 1968).

11. C. Steinitz and P. Rogers, *A Systems Analysis Model of Urbanization and Change: An Experiment in Interdisciplinary Education* (Cambridge, MA: MIT Press, 1970) [N. Dines, J. Gaffney, D. Gates, J. Gaudette, L. Gibson, P. Jacobs, L. Lea, T. Murray, H. Parnass, D. Parry, D. Sinton, S. Smith, F. Stuber, G. Sultan, T. Vint, D. Way, B. White]
　Japanese edition, Tokyo, Orion Press.1973.

12. C. Steinitz, H. J. Brown, P. Goodale, with P. Rogers, D. Sinton, F. Smith, W. Giezentanner, and D. Way, *Managing Suburban Growth: A Modeling Approach. Summary.* (Of the research program entitled The Interaction between Urbanization and Land: Quality and Quantity in Environmental Planning and Design.) (National Science Foundation, Research Applied to National Needs (RANN) Program Grant ENV-72-03372-A06. Cambridge, MA: Landscape Architecture Research Office, Graduate School of Design, Harvard University, 1978.)

# CHAPTER 2

# The context for geodesign

WHAT DO THE DESIGN OF a suburban subdivision in Phoenix, a forest preserve for Mozambique, a street in central London, a park in Brisbane, and a new city near Beijing have in common? Maybe a lot, or maybe nothing at all. It depends upon the lens through which you look. The ways in which a society thinks about its geography, and how it can or could be changed, significantly affect the approaches and methods it chooses to make those changes, if it decides to change anything at all.

## Geography matters

The "geographic context" is the area being studied during a geodesign project. A place has its own processes that geodesign will encompass, and the people of that place often have decision making power. They also have cultural knowledge that informs the criteria by which current and proposed environments are evaluated. Decisions are frequently made in group discussions using a common language of evaluative, descriptive adjectives. However, words such as "old," "crowded," "dry," "hot," "historically significant," "too expensive," and the like are not defined the same way in cities around the world, such as Beijing, Phoenix, Cairo, Kyoto, Lagos, or Sao Paolo. Rural regions also have great variety. Where you are really matters. Geodesign is applicable anywhere and everywhere, but rarely in the same ways.

## Scale matters[1]

At what scale should geodesign be applied? "Scale" refers mainly to the lens through which we look at the geographic study area, and the level of detail that we consider important or choose to ignore. A *larger* scale means a closer, more detailed view. At what scales should we design the geography? At the very local project level? At the regional level? At the national and global level? At all levels? Simultaneously? And if so, how?

Let me start by describing some of these scalar relationships as I see them, albeit in a very simplified manner. There is one planet earth. There are many nations, many regions, and many watersheds. And there are too-many-to-count individual places, projects, and people. The magnitude of these numbers is very different, and that fact is very important. There is one earth, but there are billions of places and people.

Concepts relevant for geodesign extend along a scalar continuum, and the extremes of these ranges are very different from one another (figure 2.1). At the global level, we tend to think and perhaps act for all of humanity. We work with both general and singular principles, hoping to make global laws and treaties that nations and their people can agree upon. These are based largely in the sciences, especially physics and chemistry, ecology, and biology, because the subjects of those disciplines

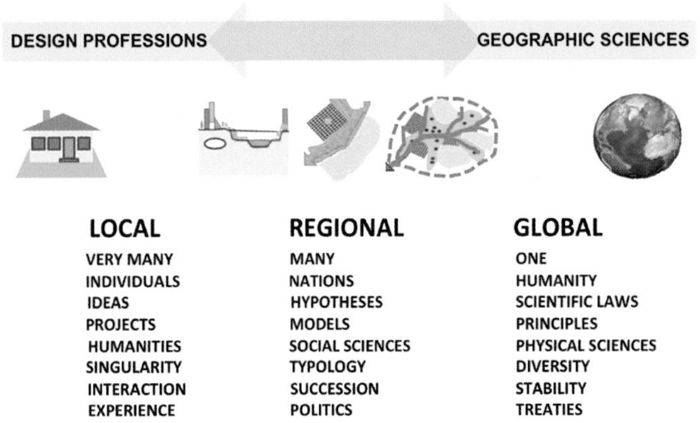

| DESIGN PROFESSIONS | | GEOGRAPHIC SCIENCES |
|---|---|---|
| **LOCAL** | **REGIONAL** | **GLOBAL** |
| VERY MANY | MANY | ONE |
| INDIVIDUALS | NATIONS | HUMANITY |
| IDEAS | HYPOTHESES | SCIENTIFIC LAWS |
| PROJECTS | MODELS | PRINCIPLES |
| HUMANITIES | SOCIAL SCIENCES | PHYSICAL SCIENCES |
| SINGULARITY | TYPOLOGY | DIVERSITY |
| INTERACTION | SUCCESSION | STABILITY |
| EXPERIENCE | POLITICS | TREATIES |

**Figure 2.1:** Scale matters when defining related phenomena. Geodesign themes and their characteristic concepts are horizontally linked according to the scale at which they are most relevant. To the left of this diagram are individual local characteristics. The middle list shows regional characteristics, and on the right are global characteristics. | Source: Carl Steinitz.

span continuously across the earth. They ignore regional and local political boundaries (or they should). I think the general aim of global studies is to understand change in order to stabilize it, something consistent with word "sustainable." This characterizes the objectives of the Kyoto Conference, the Rio Conference, Johannesburg, and others. A global perspective is extremely important because it lends its relevant scale to issues such as global warming, loss of biodiversity, and public health.

I often work at the mid-level, regional scale in my teaching, research, and consulting. As part of a collaborating team, we often focus on watersheds or city-regions. Instead of all humanity, we work one at a time with specific cultures. We recognize that there are differences between rich and poor, Mexican and Arizonian, older people and contemporary teenagers. Instead of formulating laws we learn about existing ones. We work with processes and hypotheses. We look for patterns and typologies. We generate, compare, and present alternatives. When asked, we make recommendations. In addition to the physical and ecological sciences, we emphasize the social sciences: politics, economics, and sociology. Instead of seeking stability we try to understand the dynamics of change, but we don't know exactly where it's going. We deal with politics, with legitimately conflicting views, and aim for possible consensus.

At the most local level, situations are very numerous and highly differentiated. Instead of considering all humanity or large cultural regions, you are dealing with individuals or groups. The client is frequently a municipality, a nongovernmental organization, or a business. During the geodesign project you come to know and interact with the stakeholders and individual people of the place. Instead of global principles and regional information, the data that you focus on are specific to that place. In practice, when you work with individuals and local groups rather than global principles and regional information, you are more likely to produce innovative ideas that become evident in the resulting plans and designs. It's very rare to invent new ideas at the global and regional levels.

What is particularly prominent and important at the local level are its people, and all their means of individual expression which contribute to its distinction: its arts and culture, the literature of the place, its food and music, and how it looks and feels. These features and characteristics are apparent in many local landscapes. Instead of privileging global singularity or regional typologies, at the local level we should recognize diversity and its advantages. Instead of studying stability, or broad patterns of change, we should study interactions. We should study exactly where species, including people, go to *do* things and how they relate to each other. And instead of attending global conferences and reporting to regional legislatures, we should

interact directly with citizens. The best way to do this is to live there, to be part of it. Geodesign at this level is not abstract; it can be the daily reality for the people of that place.

Thus it should be clear that designs for global, regional, and local aspects of the environment are very different from one another. Each scale or level requires a different style of working, a different kind of knowledge, and different professional and practical experiences, albeit with fuzzy boundaries and frequently overlapping concerns. The great scientist Galileo (1564–1642) was correct when he said "….many devices which succeed on a small scale do not work on a large scale."[2]

There are other relationships among these scalar lists. First of all, the diversity of the local feeds the centrality of the global. People create new ideas and new ways of thinking. This influences nations, which then influence global policy. In time, the global returns to influence nations and regions, as it should. And nations and regions should also then influence individuals. Environmentalist David Brower (1912–2000), founder of Friends of the Earth, once said that we should "think globally, act locally." We can also say: "Think locally, act globally." Unfortunately, most people, including designers, think locally and act locally.

But there are also risks inherent in these relationships. The more the world moves to globalization and the more we *all* believe we really know something, the potentially worse off (in my culturally determined opinion) it may be in the long-term because the world becomes more uniform and more authoritarian. From an ecological perspective, I doubt this is good because it is not necessarily diverse, changing, and self-renewing.

However, when the global and regional concepts are less emphasized, the more attention can be focused on local and individual interests. This may be better in the long run for some of us, but it will be more chaotic. And it may be more unfair, because we have rich countries and poor countries, big countries and small countries, modern people and traditional people. So if you see the world as the sum of many very local places, you may also regard it as very complicated; difficult to understand, coordinate, and plan for; and inequitable.

So we come to a dilemma. If you think only globally, you and your plans—and geodesign—can become authoritarian. And if you think only locally, things become chaotic and unfair. This is a major dilemma and problem for geodesign. The balancing concept, the thing that allows people to act locally, *and* nationally, *and* globally, is the idea of risk. Risk provides a useful tension, both in geodesign and in other aspects of decision making.

What is the risk of being more centrally authoritarian, or of being more decentralized and diverse? If something is a risk to everybody, then it belongs in the global list of figure 2.1 and demands a global policy. Global warming is a prime example, as is the threat to biodiversity. If something is a cultural risk, it affects us regionally. Conservation of languages and cultural landscapes belong at this middle scale where regional policy should dominate. And when something is a risk to an individual's rights, such as the right to creative ideas and their expression, it belongs in the inner circle and should not be hindered.

So, at what scale, or scales, should we act? It is relatively easy to "think locally" and "act locally." It is a much greater challenge to understand the earth and its global processes, and then still act locally. At the same time, having a local idea and then trying to change the world with it is also very difficult.

Geodesign will not be limited to any particular scale of application, but my experiences lead me to suggest that we consider improving education, research, and action in the middle range, from larger geographic areas to watersheds and regions. This scale is especially complex because it is influenced by both global and local issues. Even so, it can be very satisfying to work at a regional level, cutting across those circles and blurring their distinctions. I hope that this level of collaborative action is what attracts many of those interested in geodesign, and in changing geography by design.

## Size matters[3]

There are real differences between the extremes of the sizes at which geodesign is likely to be applied. As the size of the geographic study area increases, you have a very high risk of harmful impact if you make a mistake, or a poor or wrong decision. Thus the concept of risk dominates work on projects of larger size (figure 2.2), and we are challenged to minimize it. Why? Simply put, when the geography is large, more people and lots of money are likely to be involved. Many changes

become possible and the larger decisions become very important. The benefits can be great, but the risks are serious. At smaller sizes the relative risks decrease. For example, I really don't care so much if my neighbour has a modern or a traditional house (although I prefer the modern). There's little risk to me in either case. However, I do care greatly if I don't have drinking water. That's a very important risk.

When risks are great, serious analyses are needed and they become more necessary as the size of projects increases. Greater risk is why the geographic sciences will have greater influence on geodesign at larger sizes. As size increases, we rely more on the sciences to provide us with data and models so that we understand the processes occurring within the study area. For example, we can easily see if an individual building site is in a flood-prone area, but this is not the case if you are working with a large regional watershed. If we are designing a new city in that watershed, we must employ much more complicated and formal design strategies that interact with hydrological models. At larger sizes, the idea that you can go from one simple design concept diagram directly to its implementation on the ground is foolish; it doesn't work.

There is also a large difference in general public knowledge associated with project size. As sizes decrease and become more local and nearer to home and daily life, public knowledge about the project is likely to be naturally greater.

However, larger areas also require more public education and understanding (figure 2.3). The greater risks associated with larger sizes require a greater role for the geographic sciences and imply increasing scientific complexity. Yet this contributes to an inverse relationship with public understanding. Larger geodesign projects will inevitably require extra clear communication and a high degree of trust among the scientists, the collaborating designers, and the people of the place.

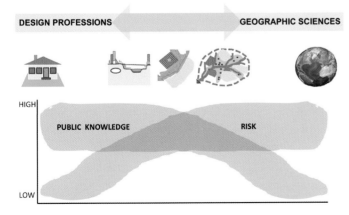

**Figure 2.2: As the size of geodesign projects changes, public knowledge and risk are inversely related.** | Source: Carl Steinitz.

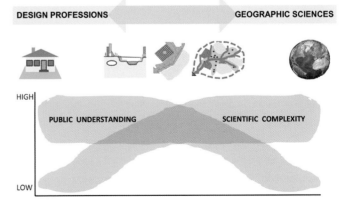

**Figure 2.3: As the size of geodesign projects changes, public understanding and scientific complexity are inversely related.** | Source: Carl Steinitz.

Every geodesign activity is necessarily filled with decisions to be made at every stage of the project. As the size of a geodesign project increases, centralized decisions will dominate over decentralized ones (figure 2.4). People usually understand their own house and may understand their neighborhood, but many people are less familiar with problems in their city or region, unfortunately. In a democracy, informing the public requires clarity and transparency in both assessment and presentation.

Project sizes affect the roles that decision makers play. During large projects, important design decisions are usually made by experts, and both elected and unelected people. Elected people (usually) are government officials, and unelected people in these cases could be heads of companies or banks or other entities involved with geodesign projects. These larger decisions are not normally made by popular vote. However, in smaller size geodesign projects, everybody may have a direct voice in the decisions.

Centralized decisions become more important as project sizes increase, in order to minimize social, economic, and ecological risk, and so on, and still achieve possible project benefits (figure 2.5). As sizes become larger, geodesign becomes more supply-based, focused on conserving existing resources and with a "defensive" strategy or attitude. First you need to understand the geography, the ecology, and the cultural values, then you have to establish priorities for conservation and you must be prepared to explain and defend those priorities. With larger size projects, design processes often emphasize conservative strategies and allocation, deciding what goes where *or where not.*

As the size of geodesign projects gets smaller, strategies are naturally more "offensive." The push of the market, the client-decision maker, and changes related to development set the requirements that drive the project.

The largest geodesign studies such as those of regional watersheds frequently emphasize strategies of conservation and development, and focus on *allocation.* Large projects have a design emphasis on tactics and *organization,* or how different elements relate to each other. Smaller size projects emphasize details and *expression,* what something looks and feels like. These emphases in design are very different and relate both to size and scale.

Clearly, size, scale, and geography matter, especially for geodesign. Galileo was right. Many methods, processes, and ideas that work at one scale or size or geography will not work at another.

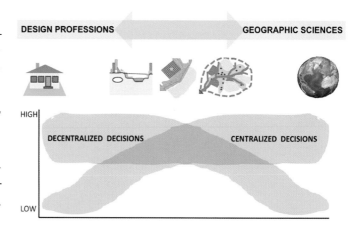

**Figure 2.4:** As the size of geodesign projects changes, centralized and decentralized decisions are inversely related. | Source: Carl Steinitz.

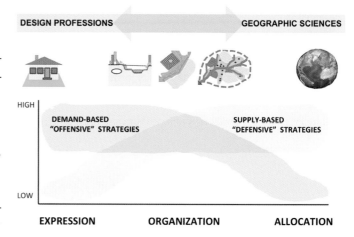

**Figure 2.5:** As the size of geodesign projects changes, the emphases on supply-based and demand-based geodesign strategies are inversely related. | Source: Carl Steinitz.

## Notes

1. Edited from C. Steinitz, "From Project to Global: On Landscape Planning and Scale," *Landscape Review* 9, no. 2 (2005): 117–27.

2. Galileo Galilei, *Dialogues Concerning Two New Sciences,* translated by Henry Crew and Alfonso de Salvio (New York: McGraw Hill Book Co., 1914).

3. Edited from C. Steinitz, "On Scale and Complexity and the Need for Spatial Analysis," Specialist Meeting on Spatial Concepts in GIS and Design; Santa Barbara, California; December 15–16, 2008.

# PART II

# A framework for geodesign

It is evident that there can be no such thing as *The Geodesign Process* (singular). Geodesign cannot have a singular methodology as long as its approaches, principles, and methods are applied to projects that range across size, scale, culture, content, and time. Yet the collaboration required for geodesign requires organization, *and organization requires a framework*. Thus, we need a framework for geodesign as a *verb*, for the asking of questions, for choosing among many methods, and for seeking the best possible answers.

Part II presents a framework for geodesign seen mainly as a process and as a verb, rather than a theory for geodesign as a noun. This framework, developed over many years and experiences, addresses six different questions and types of models common to geodesign projects. I present the components of this framework in chapter 3, and in chapters 4, 5, and 6 I elaborate on their characteristics and explain how they can be used.

# CHAPTER 3

# Questions and iterations

A CLEAR FRAMEWORK AROUND WHICH TASKS can be identified and linked is essential for collaboration in a large geodesign effort. For more than thirty years I have worked with and refined a general framework for the design professions that I first published in 1990.[1] This framework for geodesign consists of six questions that are asked (explicitly or implicitly) at least three times during the course of *any* geodesign study. These questions have sub-questions that are modified as needed by the geodesign team. The answers to those questions are models, and their content and levels of abstraction are particular to the individual case study. Some modeling approaches can be general, but data and model parameters are local to the people,

place, and time of the study, as are the geodesign actions whose consequences are being studied.

The framework for a particular geodesign study will be shaped by its many participants, and especially by the issues and requirements posed by the people of the place, along with other relevant people and institutions (figure 3.1). However, frequently these stakeholders do not agree, and these tensions are a common catalyst for a geodesign study. The stakeholders will likely want to be in close contact with the geodesign team at all stages of the work. The proposed designs must reflect their priorities, and in the case of disagreement among the stakeholders, alternatives will need to be developed. The geodesign

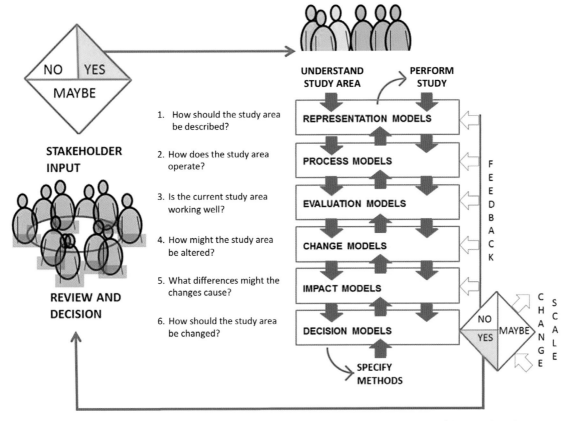

Figure 3.1: The stakeholders, the geodesign team, and the framework for geodesign. | Source: Carl Steinitz.

team also maintains a responsibility to consider alternatives beyond those already known and imagined. All of the products and results, including alternative designs and the assessments of their impact, will need to be presented for stakeholder review and their many decision processes.

This framework does not suggest a singular linear process, but one which has several iterative "loops" and feedback possibilities. Deviations certainly occur during the reality of geodesign projects, but following the organized sequence of these questions provides beneficial structure to any geodesign activity.

## The six questions of the framework

These key questions are the following:

1. *How should the study area be described in content, space, and time?* This question is answered by **representation models**, the data upon which the study relies.
2. *How does the study area operate?* What are the functional and structural relationships among its elements? This question is answered by **process models**, which provide information for the several assessment analyses of the study.
3. *Is the current study area working well?* This question is answered by **evaluation models**, which are dependent upon the cultural knowledge of the decision-making stakeholders.
4. *How might the study area be altered?* By what policies and actions, where and when? This question is answered by **change models**, which will be developed and compared in the geodesign study. These also generate data that will be used to represent future conditions.

5. *What differences might the changes cause?* This question is answered by **impact models**, which are assessments produced by the process models under changed conditions.
6. *How should the study area be changed?* This question is answered by **decision models**, which, like the evaluation models, are dependent upon the cultural knowledge of the responsible decision makers.

## The three iterations through the framework

Over the course of the geodesign study, each of these six primary questions and their subsidiary questions are asked three times. In the first iteration through the sequence (figure 3.2), they are asked rapidly, beginning with question 1 as it defines the context and scope of the work. In this first iteration we treat these as *WHY* questions for the project. In the second iteration, the same six primary questions are asked in reverse order from 6 to 1. This identifies and defines the methods of study, the *HOW* questions. And in the third iteration, they are asked again in the original order of 1 to 6 as we implement the study method and address the *WHAT, WHERE, and WHEN* questions.

It is important to emphasize that designing is not just proposing changes, as question 4 alone might suggest. Whether explicitly or implicitly, *all six questions* must be satisfied throughout *all three iterations* of the framework for a geodesign study to be complete. Decisions by the stakeholders may then lead to implementation of change.

## The first iteration: The *WHY* questions

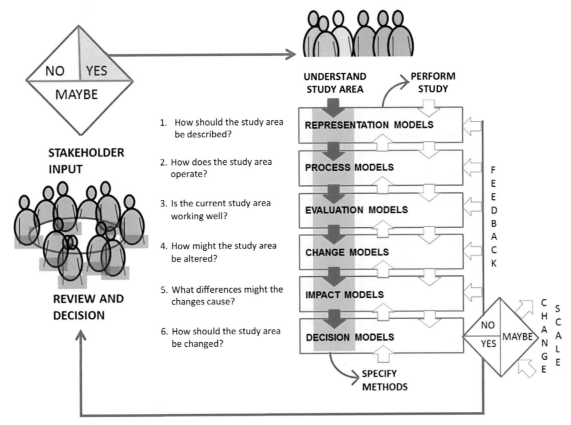

**Figure 3.2:** The first iteration, the *WHY* questions. In this iteration, the questions are asked in numerical order, from 1 to 6 as indicated by the green arrows moving downward in the figure. The answers to this round of questions provide the geodesign team with essential information to understand the context of the study. | Source: Carl Steinitz.

The objective of the first iteration is to understand the geographic study area and the scope of the study. So in this iteration, the six questions, asked in order from 1 to 6, are intended to answer *WHY* the study is to happen. The geodesign team will consider past and present descriptions and representations of the region and develop a general knowledge of how the landscape works in that place. Through this first iteration the geodesign team comes to understand the problems, issues, opportunities, and constraints of the place, the objectives of the geodesign application, and the relevant content and scale(s) of possible change. Possible changes and their potential types of impacts will be identified. The answers to the six questions also lead to an understanding of how the decision-making processes may operate for this particular geodesign activity.

Some typical initial questions that might be posed during this first iteration include the following:

1. Representation:
   Where is the study area? How should it be defined?
   What are its physical, ecological, economic, and social geographies?
   What are its physical, ecological, economic, and social histories?
2. Process:
   What are the area's major physical, ecological, economic, and social processes?
   How are they linked to each other?
3. Evaluation:
   Is the area seen as attractive? Why? Why not? By whom?
   Is the area developing or declining? In what ways?
   Are there current environmental or other "problems" in the area? Which? Where?
4. Change:
   What major changes are foreseen for the region?
   Are they related to growth or decline?
   Are the pressures for change being driven from the inside or the outside of the area?

5. Impact:

Are anticipated changes seen as beneficial or harmful? To whom?

Are they seen as serious? As irreversible?

6. Decision:

What is the main purpose of the geodesign study? Public action? Economic profit? Scientific advancement?

Who are the major stakeholders? Are they public or private?

Are "positions" known? Are they in conflict?

Are there legal and implementation-related aspects that must be considered?

Are there any binding limitations that must guide the activities of the geodesign study?

In any geodesign study, choices must be discussed and decisions made in order to narrow and define the scope of the geodesign application, define its methods and carry them out to a favorable decision. This is the primary focus of the first iteration through the framework.

## The second iteration: The *HOW* questions

The aim of the second iteration is to choose and clearly define the methods of the study, the *HOW* questions. In this stage, the framework is used in reverse order, working from question 6 to question 1 (figure 3.3). This reversal of the regular sequence of conducting a study is crucial to designing a set of potentially useful methods. In this way, geodesign becomes decision-driven rather than data-driven.

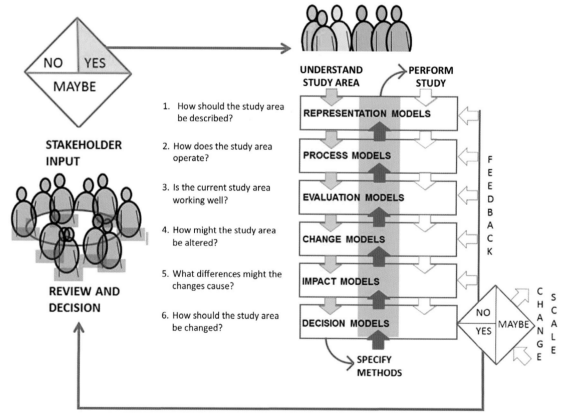

**Figure 3.3:** The second iteration, the *HOW* questions. In this iteration, the six primary questions are asked in reverse numerical order, from 6 to 1, as indicated by the green arrows moving upward. The answers to this round of questions provide the geodesign team with an agreed-upon methodology for the study. | Source: Carl Steinitz.

Some typical questions that might be posed during this second iteration include the following:

6. Decision:

    How will decisions be made? By whom?

    What do the decision makers need to know?

    What are their bases of evaluation? Scientific evaluations? Cultural norms? Legal standards? Are there issues of implementation such as cost, phasing, and choice of technology?

    Are there issues of public communication? Of visualization?

5. Impact:

    Which impacts of possible changes are most important?

    Which impacts must be must be assessed by law or regulations?

    How complex must the impact assessment be?

    How much, where, when, and to whom are these seen as "good" or "bad"?

4. Change:

    Who defines the assumptions and requirements for change? How?

    Which scenarios for change are selected? Toward which time horizon(s)? At what scale(s)?

    Which issues are beyond the capabilities of the geodesign team and study models?

    Which change model(s) are to be applied? Are the outcomes to be designed, or simulated, or both?

3. Evaluation:

    What are the measures of evaluation? In ecology? In economics? In politics? In peoples' visual preferences?

2. Process:

    Which process models should be included?

    How complex should the models be?

    At what scale(s) should they operate?

    At what time horizon(s)?

1. Representation:

    Where—exactly—is the study area? How is it bounded (and why?)

    Which data are needed? For which geography? At what scale? At which classification? For which times? From what sources? At what cost? In which mode of representation?

Designing the methodology for a geodesign study involves complex decisions, often drawing on the experience and judgment of the entire geodesign team. Understanding how public and private decisions to alter or conserve the landscape are made within that geodesign context is a basic element of a geodesign methodology. The requirements for the study must be understood and ranked in importance. The geodesign team must specify the impacts that the decision makers and their constituents will consider. Using their professional and scientific expertise, the geodesign team will need to consider the several ways of designing, and decide in which way they will achieve and propose strategies for change. They decide how to assess evaluations of existing conditions and investigate the structural and functional processes of the study area, and they then specifying appropriate models and their data needs. Only then can the team identify requirements for data acquisition and appropriate means of representation.

In addition to the six questions within the framework, I have also found these additional overarching questions relevant to making methods choices for any kind of geodesign study. While these questions are not explicitly part of the framework I have been describing, their answers provide additional information that a geodesign team will need to do its best work.

- Who should participate and how? Local residents? Political leaders? Corporate directors? Outside experts?

- What are the tradeoffs between faster results and rapid action versus possibly better research but delayed decisions?

- Will the study end with a single "product" or will it develop a continuing decision support process?

- What is the appropriate cost of the study? How much time, money, and basic research are needed?

## The third iteration: The *WHAT, WHERE, and WHEN* questions

1. How should the study area be described?

2. How does the study area operate?

3. Is the current study area working well?

4. How might the study area be altered?

5. What differences might the changes cause?

6. How should the study area be changed?

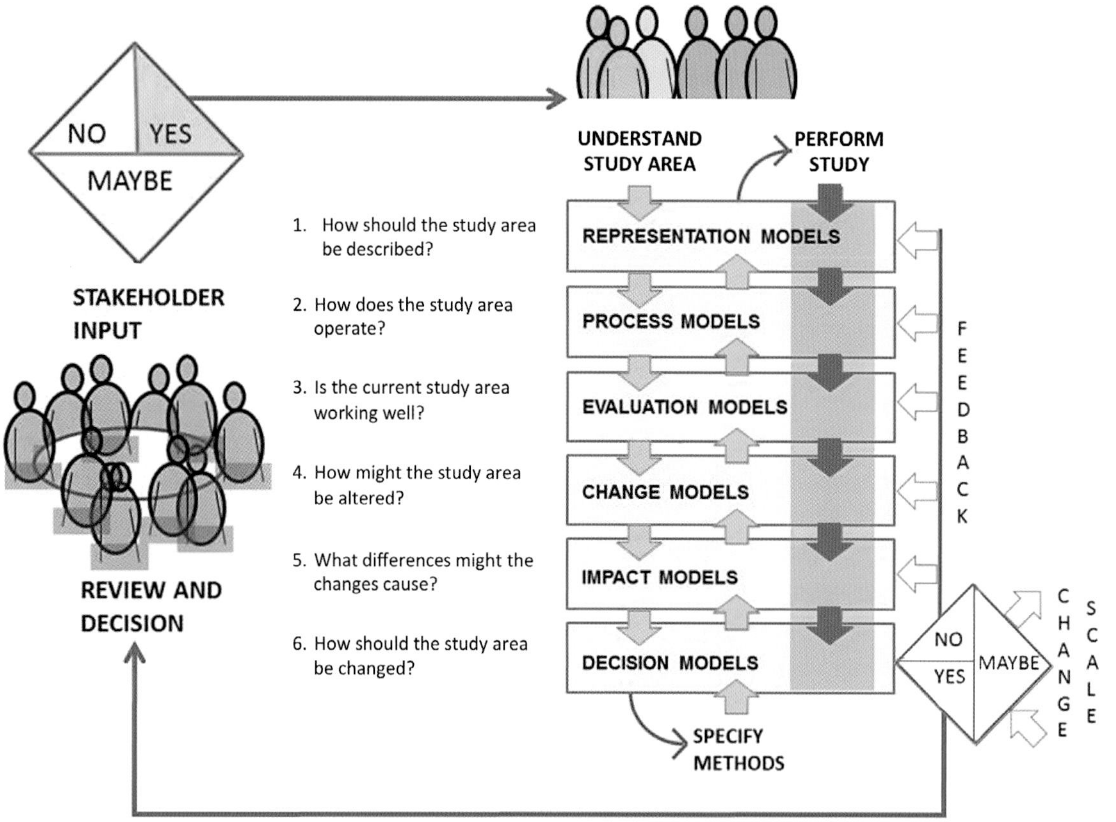

**Figure 3.4:** The third iteration: the *WHAT, WHERE, and WHEN* questions. In this iteration, the questions are again asked in numerical order, from one to six as indicated by the green arrows moving downward in the figure as the geodesign team carries out the study. | Source: Carl Steinitz.

The third iteration through the framework carries out the methodology designed by the geodesign team in the second iteration (figure 3.4). During this round we ask the *WHAT, WHERE, and WHEN* questions as we implement the study and provide results. In this third stage, the framework is again used from top to bottom, from questions 1 to 6, through models of representation, process, evaluation, change, impact, and decision.

During this third iteration of the framework, data become a central concern. We now identify and gather the data necessary for the study, organize them within an appropriate technology, and begin to represent them in a format useful for the study purposes. Once the relevant data are organized for the process models, the models are implemented and the resulting information helps us develop a baseline from which to assess both the existing study area and the impacts of future change. We design and/or simulate a range of alternative future states of the study area and comparatively assess their impacts. Decision makers can then better understand the potential consequences of their decisions and subsequent future changes. Some of the

many activities that need to be accomplished during this stage are listed here.

1. Representation models

   Obtain the needed data.

   Organize them in an appropriate technology.

   Visualize the data over space and time.

   Organize them to be shared among the members geodesign team.

2. Process models

   Implement, calibrate, and test the process models.

   Link them to each other as appropriate.

   Link them to the expected change models.

3. Evaluation models

   Evaluate past and present conditions.

   Visualize and communicate the results.

4. Change models

   Propose and/or simulate future changes.

   Represent them (as data).

   Visualize and communicate them.

5. Impact models

  Assess and compare the impacts of each change model via the process models.

  Visualize and communicate the results.

6. Decision models

  Compare the impacts of the change models and decide:

  *No*, which requires feedback, or

  *Maybe*, which may require further study at a different size or scale, or

  *Yes*, which leads to presentation to the stakeholders for their decision and possible implementation.

Once a geodesign team has worked its way through the three iterations of the framework questions, there can be three possible decisions as an outcome: *No*, *Maybe*, or *Yes* (figure 3.5).

Reaching a *No* implies that the study result does not satisfy the geodesign team and is not likely to meet the requirements of the decision makers. Then any or all of the six steps are subject to feedback and alteration: we can seek more or better data, an improved process model, altered criteria and re-evaluation, redesign of the proposed changes, mitigation of impacts, and (possibly) education of the decision makers. Plus, at any point in the framework, new inputs of different types and from different sources may be received, leading to a revisiting of decisions. This makes geodesign particularly nonlinear in its application.

If the team's decision is a *Maybe* or perhaps a contingent *Yes* decision, it may also trigger a change in the scale, size, or time frame of the study (figure 3.6). Shifting the scale of the project may lead to either larger or smaller geodesign activities, and the structure and content of several model types may require modifications. Nevertheless, the study will again proceed through the six questions of the framework and continue until the geodesign team achieves a positive (*Yes*) decision.

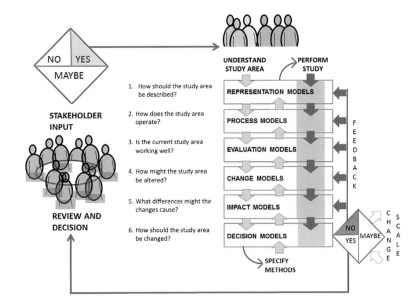

**Figure 3.5:** Decisions of *No*, *Maybe*, or *Yes* must be made by the geodesign team. If *No*, feedback can occur at any stage and leads to a revisiting of the questions and models. | Source: Carl Steinitz.

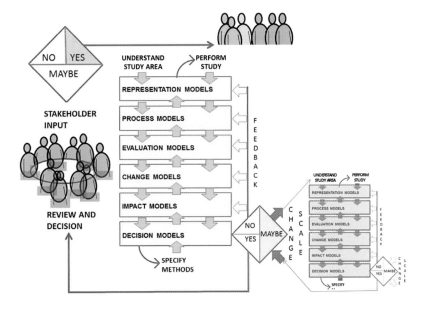

**Figure 3.6:** If a *Maybe* decision is reached after the framework has been followed, the size and scale of the geodesign study may be shifted up or down, and then the framework, its questions, and models will be revisited. | Source: Carl Steinitz.

If a *Yes* decision is reached by the geodesign team once the framework has been followed, the resulting study or proposed project is poised for presentation to the stakeholders for their review towards implementation and action (figure 3.7).

Decision making is the responsibility of the region's stakeholders, from the individual to the highest levels of government. In order to make decisions, questions must be asked and answered, and options for choice must be framed and deliberated. The decision makers (and there may be many layers of decision making) also have the choices of *No*, *Maybe*, or *Yes* (figure 3.8). A *No* may trigger the end of the study. A *Maybe* will likely be treated like feedback and require changes in the geodesign methods or their results. A *Yes* decision implies implementation and updating for future representation models.

Implementation of agreed-upon designs is not necessarily automatic or immediate, especially for larger and longer-term projects. In whatever ways the geography changes (and it may be via continuous geodesign study), there will be forward-in-time changes to new representation models. Future generations are likely to seek changes in *their* geography and see the implemented consequences of the geodesign team's study as part of their data, and so the cycle continues for generations of people of that place. All geographies, designed or otherwise, are always in a state of change.

When repeated and linked over scale and time, the questions of the framework may be the organizing basis of a very complex and ongoing study. The result may be a 2-, 3-, or 4-dimensional study, at a range of scales. Regardless of complexity, the same questions are repeated in any future projects. However, the answers, models, methods, and results, and the ways by which they were developed and applied will continue to vary.

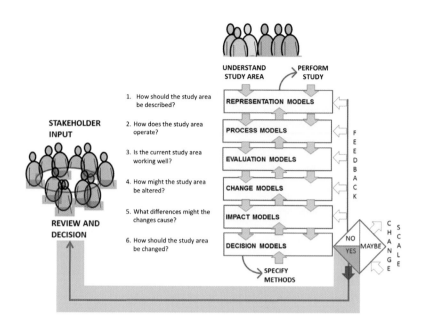

**Figure 3.7:** A *Yes* decision by the geodesign team implies completion and subsequent presentation to the stakeholders for their review and decision. | Source: Carl Steinitz.

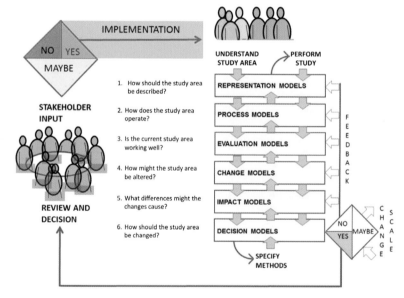

**Figure 3.8:** Review and a *Yes* decision may lead to implementation. | Source: Carl Steinitz.

# The framework in practice

At first glance, the framework may appear to be excessively linear. Yet while the framework's questions and models are purposely presented in an orderly and sequential manner, *the framework is normally not linear in its application,* and the route through any study is not straight forward (figure 3.9). A geodesign team can experience many entry ways into a study, including some idiosyncratic ones. In some cases we may receive inspiration from the place (genius loci), see the solution immediately, or present the client with a preconception. Furthermore, there will always be unanticipated issues, false starts, dead ends, and serendipitous discoveries along the way.

Variations to the framework are best executed by experienced professionals who have developed sophisticated internalized responses to the framework's questions. In other words, individuality, creativity, and invention in geodesign are most likely to succeed when well prepared for and applied in a clearly organized framework. Paraphrasing the eminent scientist Louis Pasteur (1822–1895), "Fortune favors the prepared mind."[2]

When designing the methodology for a geodesign study and carrying it forward to a decision, a symbiotic relationship develops between the geographic sciences, the design professions, information technologists, and the stakeholder clients. The degree to which their influences vary depends on which of the six questions is being addressed at that time. Questions 1, 2, and 3 refer mainly to the past and the existing conditions of the study's particular geographic context. The geographic sciences tend to dominate during this phase in their use of both (1) representation models and (2) process models. It is at this point that factual conditions for geodesign must be established as a baseline for evaluation and as a reference for change. The responsibility for (3) evaluation models is more diffuse. The design professions can provide more local, functional, and sensory understanding that incorporate local cultural knowledge and values.

Questions 4, 5, and 6 of the framework concern the future more than the past and present. Change models (4) will require the greatest contribution from the design professions, largely because of their education and experience in "synthesis." The geographic sciences have a major role with the impact models (5), which assess the proposed changes. Decision models (6) are ultimately the responsibility of the decision makers but in reality all may participate. Again, one hopes that there is (or was) a shared set of values among the collaborating scientists, designers, information technologists, and the people of the place.

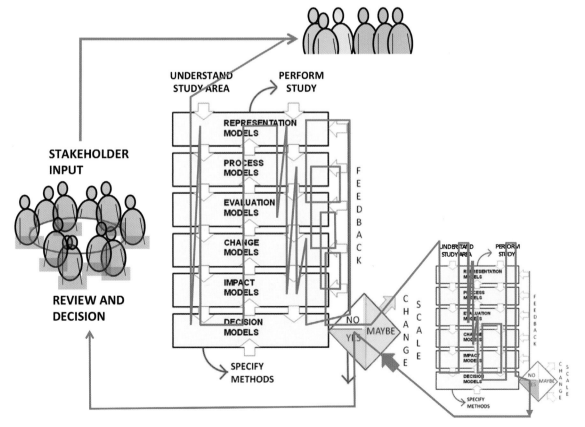

**Figure 3.9:** In practice and application, the framework for geodesign is never linear. Instead it can be flexible to accommodate the inevitable and unanticipated events that occur during any study. | Source: Carl Steinitz.

I contend that even with the inevitable unanticipated events, a typical geodesign project passes through the three iterations of the six questions of the framework, explicitly or implicitly, at least once before a *Yes* decision towards implementation can ever be reached. Choosing from the start to deliberately deviate from this type of framework may lead to poor and costly decisions and unhappy stakeholders or clients.

A framework is useful only if it is seen to be useful by those who work with it. This framework can be a valuable aid to the organization of large and complex geodesign problems. It has been used by me and others in professional practice, academic studies, academic and professional workshops, and in organizing and carrying out large, applied research programs. Some of these are described in the case studies later in this book.

## Notes

1.  C. Steinitz, "A Framework for Theory Applicable to the Education of Landscape Architects (and Other Environmental Design Professionals)," *Landscape Journal* 9 (1990): 136–43.

    Revised version in *Process Architecture* 127 (1995). (English and Japanese.)

    Revised version in *GIS Europe* 2 (1993): 42–45

    Revised version in *Planning* (2000). (Chinese.)

    Revised version in *Environmental Planning for Communities: A Guide to the Environmental Visioning Process Utilizing a Geographic Information System (GIS).* Cincinnati, OH: US Environmental Protection Agency Office of Research and Development, 2002.

    Revised version in chapter 3 of *Alternative Futures for Changing Landscapes: The San Pedro River Basin in Arizona and Sonora* by C. Steinitz, H. Arias, S. Bassett, M. Flaxman, T. Goode, T. Maddock, D. Mouat, R. Peiser and A. Shearer. Washington, D.C.: Island Press, 2003.

2.  Louis Pasteur, Lecture, University of Lille, December 7, 1854.

# CHAPTER 4

# The first iteration through the framework: Scoping the geodesign study

GEODESIGN PROJECTS ARE INITIATED in ways similar to other design or research projects. A stakeholder or decision maker, from the private or public sector, might approach a design professional or a geographical scientist and describe the need for a study or project. Sometimes a geodesign study starts within the process of a funded research program. In other situations, the idea for a geodesign study might be initiated by a potential member of the geodesign team. Regardless, a decision is made to pursue the opportunity, frequently on the basis of only a preliminary and general description of the geographic study area, people, and issues which will be the foci of the project.

The purpose of the first pass through the framework is to gain increased knowledge about the study area and the people of the place, and a collective understanding of the scope of the project so we can answer the WHY questions. Every geodesign study will have its unique conditions. The framework must be adapted to the particular issues and questions raised by the problem at hand. No two geodesign studies are totally alike and choices must be made. This is why scoping the study during the first iteration is so important.

The need for thorough scoping reminds me of the story about the two petitioners in court. They were arguing over an orange. The judge held the orange in his hand while the two petitioners each insisted that she needed it. Unable to decide between them, the judge cut the orange in two, giving half to each petitioner. Both went away very unhappy. Later, the judge found out that one had wanted the peel while the other had wanted the juice.

Moral: *Find out what the question is before you propose an answer.*

Collaboration among the participants is a key and fundamental characteristic of a geodesign study, and it must be coordinated from the beginning. This presents a "chicken and egg" problem. Which geographic scientists, which design professionals, and who else should participate? Preliminary decisions will need to be made by the leader of the geodesign team, knowing that initial ideas and people may change, and that his or her role may not even continue as project leader.

At this early point in the process while the team is being assembled, there is often a temptation to rush and collect data for the project. Such efforts should be strongly resisted and discouraged. Data collection is not the first step, as much as some participants might like it to be. Geodesign should be decision-driven, not data-driven. Before data are gathered, for use in a GIS or otherwise, other issues for the study must be better understood (figure 4.1).

**Figure 4.1:** Data collection should *not* be the first step of a geodesign project. Geodesign is not data-driven, it is decision-driven. | Source: Carl Steinitz.

First, the geodesign team must identify which issues and decisions are most likely to eventually change the geographic context for the better. These become the *WHY* questions that we ask during the first iteration through the framework (figure 4.2). Now is when we focus on understanding the people, geography, and issues that catalyzed the study in the first place, and also our roles in designing for those changes.

This phase of the project should be accomplished while working within the study area, if at all possible. Ideally a well-prepared site visit by the entire preliminary geodesign team occurs, guided by the client stakeholders and the people of the place. These people obviously vary, and are not likely to be in full agreement. If they were, they would likely have known what to do and might not have called upon the geodesign team for support in the first place. The initiating stakeholders could be private citizens, a corporation, a local or national government, or a nongovernmental organization. Moreover, they may represent themselves or have their interests represented by an advisory group or a committee. Regardless, these people are significant. They are likely to have a deeper personal knowledge of the study area than the members of the geodesign team. It is also likely that meetings will be held with them at intervals throughout the duration of the project, so establishing trustful

relationships from the beginning is important. However, they should not be the only groups that are consulted during the first iteration of the framework.

## Questions 1 through 6 and their related models

It is not uncommon for the geodesign team to begin the project knowing relatively little about the geographic study area and the people of the place. Initially, the team must rely on publically accessible media, publications, the Internet, and the people who made the initial contact. Often the six questions are posed during a series of meetings with interested parties, in a social context. I encourage asking the six framework questions and their many implied sub-questions in an ordered sequence, although this is adaptable to the specific context and social circumstances (figure 4.2).

Occasionally a geodesign project involves initial research related to the scoping of the study. Most of the questions are amenable to more formal research methods, and in that situation there would be a preliminary use of the framework as part of the scoping process. Specifying the research methods

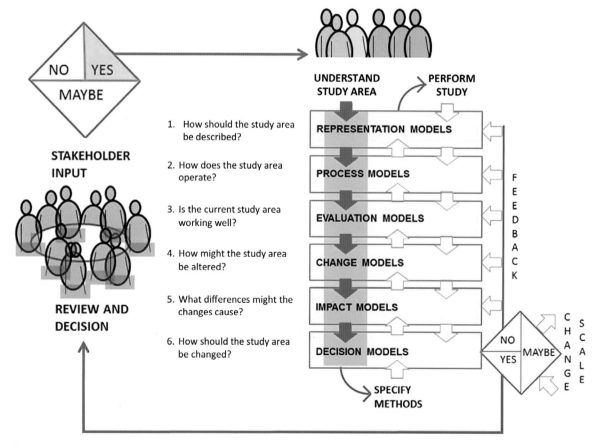

1. How should the study area be described?
2. How does the study area operate?
3. Is the current study area working well?
4. How might the study area be altered?
5. What differences might the changes cause?
6. How should the study area be changed?

**Figure 4.2: Identifying the study context and content; *WHY* are we doing it?** | Source: Carl Steinitz.

would be done during the second framework iteration, and carrying out the research becomes the third iteration. In any case, achieving a general and mutual understanding of the scope of the geodesign study is the most important outcome of the first iteration.

In this section I will expand on some of the typical and initial sub-questions that can be asked in the first iteration of the framework. I am purposely altering some from the prior overview chapter to demonstrate that they are adaptable. I will also review issues that are particularly germane to each of the types of models associated with the six framework questions.

### 1. *How should the study area be described in content, space, and time?*

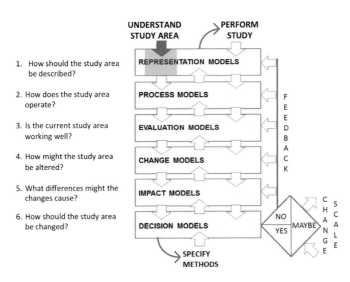

**Figure 4.3: Representation.** | Source: Carl Steinitz.

The representation models require that we understand what the appropriate study area should be for the geodesign project, and this is a deceptively complex question. All too often this is based on governmental jurisdictions or private property boundaries. Using such predetermined administrative boundaries may be convenient to obtain consistent data, but ignoring the adjacent areas means overlooking their conditions, possible interactions or relationships, and any consequences that may result from such interactions. Geodesign studies are likely to involve processes that take place over different geographical units, including watersheds, view-sheds, transport zones, sewer service areas, political boundaries, and the like. The study team would be wise to base their work on an area that includes several nested geographies, each appropriate to the process being modeled. This approach recognizes broader and otherwise overlooked relationships, reducing some of the study risks and increasing the likelihood of better results. Of

course it also adds cost and complexity, especially with regards to data from multiple jurisdictions that are likely to have different internal definitions, formats, and management systems. So this question must be probed early in the first iteration as it greatly influences the study methodology, schedule, and budget. Ultimately, the decision makers must agree with the appropriateness of the study region.

Representation model questions might include the following:

- Where are the boundaries of the study area's major systems?
- What is the area's physical, economic, and social geography?
- What is its physical, economic, and social history?
- Are there prior plans and designs for this geographic study area?
- Are there existing (digital) databases for the area? Are they accessible to the study team?

### 2. *How does the study area operate?*

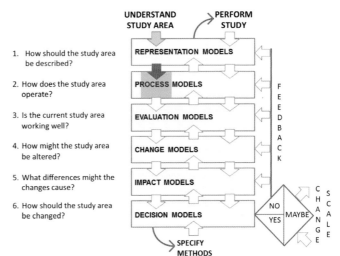

**Figure 4.4: Process.** | Source: Carl Steinitz.

The main goal in defining and understanding the processes relevant to the geodesign study is gaining a sense of scope — knowing what to include and what not to. The scope of the process models should be based on the impacts that are foreseen by and of concern to the decision makers and the people of the place. They will be important influences on decision making. We also need to identify the processes that laws and regulation will mandate for the place, such as those required for environmental impact assessments.

Process model questions might include:

- What are the area's major physical, ecological and human geographical processes?
- How are they linked to each other?

## 3. *Is the current study area working well?*

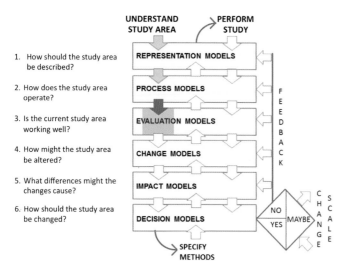

**Figure 4.5: Evaluation.** | Source: Carl Steinitz.

## 4. *How might the study area be altered?*

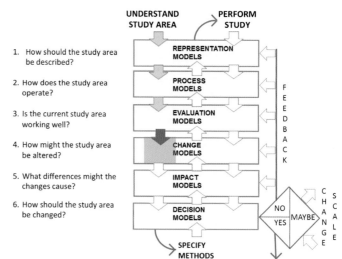

**Figure 4.6: Change.** | Source: Carl Steinitz.

It is the people of the place who most directly know and perceive the conditions of the study area, and which aspects are working well or not. Their evaluations and priorities are based on cultural knowledge, and the evaluation models must be aligned with their perspectives. In my experience, many geodesign studies are generated by a sense of fear of real and potential decline, loss, and danger, and fear of change itself. Sometimes the need for growth, jobs, houses, transportation, or perhaps resource management is the motivation for change. The politics of evaluation greatly influence the decisions to make changes.

There are social and spatial aspects to evaluation, and the geodesign team should not assume homogeneity in attitudes towards the present state of the area. There may be conflicts in public opinion towards projected change. For example, the automobile dealers and the bird-watching club probably see urban development from very different perspectives. The geodesign team should be prepared to address socially and spatially localized concerns within the study area in the design of the methodology of the study.

Evaluation model questions might include the following:
- Is the area seen as attractive? Why? Why not?
- Is the area seen as vulnerable? Why? Why not?
- Are there current environmental and other "problems" in the area?
- Are there groups with differing views on these questions?

Understanding how the people of the place regard future change will substantially influence the change models that will be applied. Change could be perceived to be a projection of the past that presents problems and/or benefits for the area, or change could be seen as a situation requiring radical intervention. Alternative perceptions will lead to differing attitudes about the reliability of the process models and the data on which they are based. Sometimes an area is facing a totally new issue which models based on the past cannot address. These may imply different ways of designing. If making a change is seen as unquestionably better than keeping things as they are in the present, then there is less reason to fear a geodesign study and more reason to become engaged in the process. However, even change that is regarded positively still requires design, and this too impacts the later choice of change models for the study.

Change model questions might include the following:
- What major changes are foreseen for the region?
- Are they related to growth or decline?
- Are they related to development or conservation (or both)?
- Are the pressures for change coming from the inside or outside?

## 5. *What difference might the changes cause?*

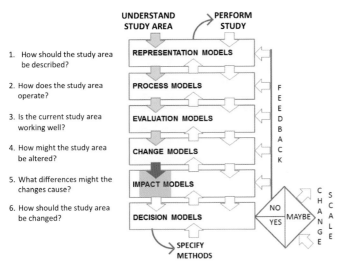

**Figure 4.7: Impact.** | Source: Carl Steinitz.

## 6. *How should the study area be changed?*

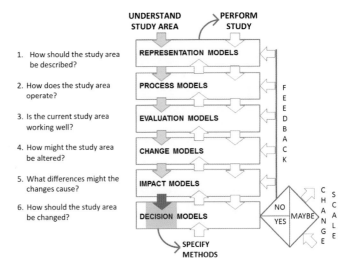

**Figure 4.8: Decision.** | Source: Carl Steinitz.

Impact assessments of the comparative consequences, benefits, and costs of alternative choices for the future will greatly influence decisions to make changes, especially when they are compared with the present situation. Some relevant consequences of change will be recognized by the people of the place, some by the decision makers, some are required by law and regulation, and others may be introduced by the geodesign team. The geodesign team must understand the needed characteristics of these assessments and how they will be used, whether informally in discussion, as bases for legislation, or in future legal proceedings. This understanding will greatly influence the scope of the geodesign study as well as the composition of the geodesign team, the selection of methods during the second framework iteration, and the manner in which the study is eventually carried out.

Impact model questions might include the following:

- In which ways are foreseen changes seen as beneficial or harmful?
- Are these impacts seen as serious? As irreversible?

It is impossible to predict whether the decision-making people will be in agreement, or represent groups that are already in conflict of kind or degree. Especially in larger geographic study areas, important decisions are likely to pass through several levels of private and governmental assessment that may have their own different objectives and decision making models. These then must also be investigated and understood. The geodesign team will need to link general statements of assumptions and objectives with specific requirements of the study and put these in some kind of ranked order. This is important, because if one gets the first and most important things wrong, or if they are ignored, the likelihood is high that the final outcome of the study will be unsatisfactory.

It will be important to the stakeholders and the people of the place to understand how the geodesign team understands *them.* If there is conflict among or within the decision-making groups, the geodesign team must be very clear from the beginning as to whether it has a position on behalf of one of the groups as an advocate, or whether it can and will maintain a neutral position. Only if the geodesign team takes a neutral position—and this is understood from the start by all participants—can it fairly present the implications of various decision models with differing objectives. This ideal is not simple to accomplish, but I think it is the right way to proceed.

Decision model questions might include the following:
- Who are the major stakeholders? Are they from the public or private sector?
- Are peoples' "positions" known? Are they in conflict?
- Which consequences of change are considered most important?

- Are there other major concerns that would influence decisions about change?

The first iteration scoping of the study is likely to result in a long and diverse preliminary list of desirable models and data. If for reasons of time, effort, or budget this study must be reduced, the most significant decision criteria must be identified and included in the scope of the study. Establishing the decision-making priorities and requirements is the most important result of the first iteration.

## Scenarios of assumptions, objectives, and requirements[1]

The activity of scoping a geodesign study involves the preliminary development of a scenario or scenarios. These are the assumptions, objectives, and requirements that will guide the design of the geodesign study methods, especially the change model(s). The word "scenario" is usually understood to mean an outline of events, typically the plot of a story, play, or film. Similarly, a scenario in geodesign is an outline for a hypothetical future of the geographical context of the study.

If the geodesign problem were a totally repetitive one, the future would be easily knowable. There would be only one scenario, and designing for it or organizing a computer model to produce it would be a relatively simple task. It likely would be done algorithmically, and geodesign as I see it would not be needed. However, planning for the future of a large area or region is a complicated and inherently uncertain process. No one can know what the actual future of such a context will be, and since no single vision of the future is likely to be accurate, it is often helpful for decision makers to consider a set of alternatives that encompasses a spectrum of possibilities before choosing the path on which to embark.

Preliminary scenarios should be developed from conversations during the first framework iteration to reflect areas of uncertainty and/or disagreement. They should be concentrated as much as possible in the realm of reasonable combinations of policy and program assumptions (figure 4.9), with the hope that they will later develop into feasible designs for the future.

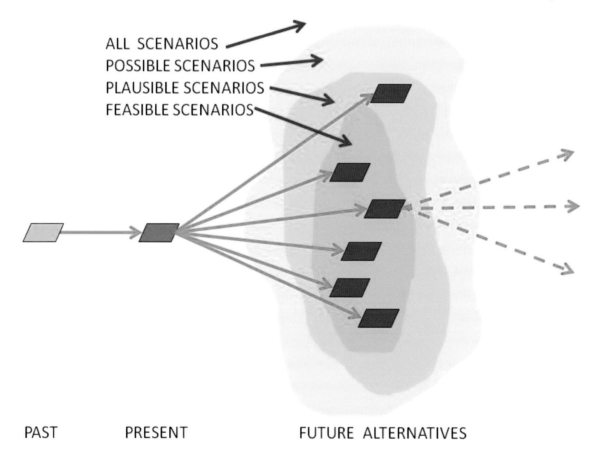

ALL SCENARIOS
POSSIBLE SCENARIOS
PLAUSIBLE SCENARIOS
FEASIBLE SCENARIOS

PAST            PRESENT                    FUTURE ALTERNATIVES

**Figure 4.9:** Scenarios should be potentially feasible (or at least plausible). | Source: Carl Steinitz.

A study with multiple scenarios has important advantages. The geodesign process can investigate several futures, and accommodate a diversity of opinion within the same study. The use of several scenarios allows the investigation of differing points of view. Scenarios allow a range of choices to vary within selected areas of concern, and different sets of assumptions or priorities can be represented by specific groups of choices. Because each scenario describes the future in similar terms there is an opportunity for sensitivity analysis, in which outcomes of individual policy or design choices can be compared.

The most important reason to use a scenario-based approach is its relevance to decision making processes. For elected officials and public administrators, scenarios can be used to test current planning ideas and explore the implications of public concerns. For landowners, scenarios can help anticipate the range of potential impacts to their lands that may result from regional changes. Scenarios can help assess how the multiple actions of property owners, or the policies of local, regional, and national governments, can affect the regional environment. For all the members of a community, scenarios illustrate and explain how today's decisions, or the failure to make important decisions, may interact to change the future.

## Is geodesign the best way forward?

During the first iteration of the framework, the geodesign team gains a general sense of the scope of the study and the issues it faces. It is appropriate to then ask whether geodesign is the best way forward. You need a strategy that clarifies what you're aiming for before thinking about how to do it and what to do. What should the outcome of the geodesign study be? What products should result? This discussion must precede the selection and definition of the methods and models which constitutes the main task of the second iteration of the framework.

In my experience, the broadest and most useful classification of problem solving strategies is in "Escape of Tigers: An Ecologic Note," a paper by William Haddon Jr. (1970).[2]

When he wrote it, Haddon was president of the Insurance Institute for Highway Safety (USA). Using a range of ecological disasters as a metaphor, he proposed ten ways of thinking about potential mitigating solutions. These are highly adaptable to the issues and problems presented in geodesign. If geodesign is seen *only* as seeking solutions defined in spatial terms, it will ignore a broad range of other approaches. As noted in Haddon's classification, spatial allocation solutions are only two of the ten alternatives.

Haddon's ten alternative solutions are
1. Prevent the marshaling of the energy
2. Reduce the amount of energy marshaled
3. Prevent the release of the energy
4. Modify the rate or spatial distribution of the release of energy
5. Separate in space or time the energy being released
6. Separation by interposition of a material barrier
7. Modify appropriately the contact surface
8. Strengthen the structure
9. Detection and evaluation by generating a signal that a response is required
10. Return to pre-event conditions

I have used Haddon's ideas for many years in the Theory and Methods course that I have taught at the Graduate School of Design at Harvard. Before students in the class read the Haddon paper, I ask them to consider two common design problems:

Problem A (figure 4.10A) is a difficult site problem, where a house has been proposed for a steep and erosion-prone site, below which is a stream that is habitat for a rare fish.

Problem B (figure 4.10B) is a cross-of-circulation problem. A group of apartment houses in which many children live is separated from the waterfront park by a major road, and at the crossing there are often accidents.

I then ask the students to solve each of these two problems in ten different ways. They do this on paper, silently and on their own. They are free to use whatever manner of representation they want, but usually they choose diagrams and words. I then go through each of Haddon's ten strategies and ask the students for examples of each. If there are no relevant solutions for a particular strategy among the students' responses, I show some from my collection (see figure sets 4.11A and B below).

We then make a frequency distribution of the students' solutions based on Haddon's ten classes. Most designers, including my students, consider very few of the ten alternative strategies. Their most common solutions are 2- and 3-dimensional spatial versions of Haddon's types 4 and 5. Once I offer examples of the others and we have a wide-ranging discussion, it is usually very clear that the students know all of these solution strategies but simply had not thought of them at the time. Their memory retrieval mechanisms required stretching. "Escape of Tigers" becomes a very useful mnemonic (an aid to memory) and a very effective heuristic (an aid to learning), to remind them to think more broadly.

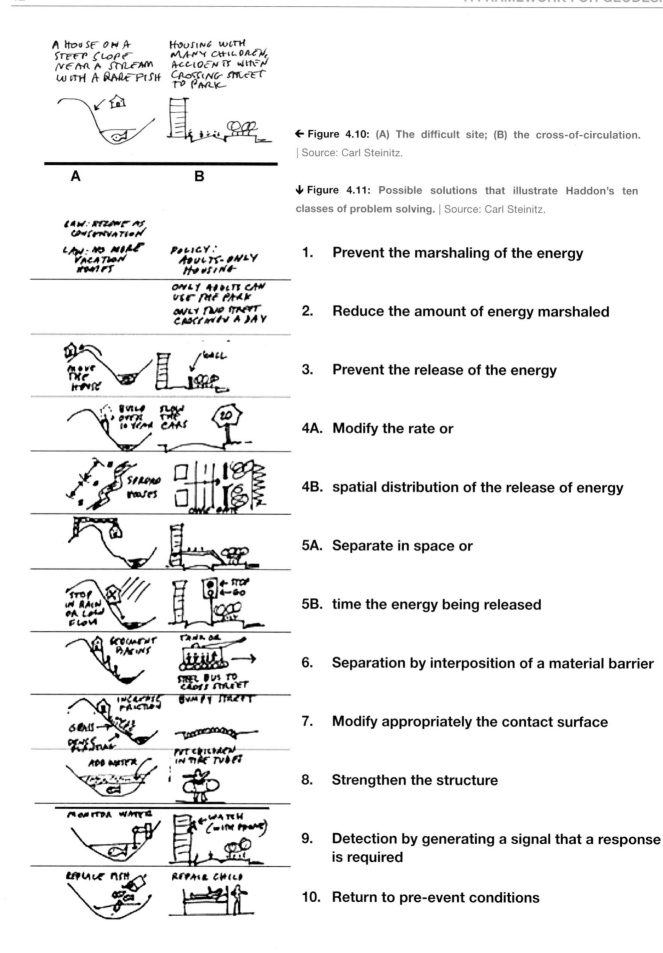

← **Figure 4.10:** (A) The difficult site; (B) the cross-of-circulation. | Source: Carl Steinitz.

↓ **Figure 4.11:** Possible solutions that illustrate Haddon's ten classes of problem solving. | Source: Carl Steinitz.

1.   Prevent the marshaling of the energy

2.   Reduce the amount of energy marshaled

3.   Prevent the release of the energy

4A.  Modify the rate or

4B.  spatial distribution of the release of energy

5A.  Separate in space or

5B.  time the energy being released

6.   Separation by interposition of a material barrier

7.   Modify appropriately the contact surface

8.   Strengthen the structure

9.   Detection by generating a signal that a response is required

10.  Return to pre-event conditions

One example of the applicability of Haddon's ten approaches to geodesign shows the many ways that problems related to water pollution can be addressed at different scales (figure 4.12).[3]

The ten different strategies found in the Haddon paper are not likely to be equally or uniformly effective for geodesign studies. When feasible, I favor the first three: prevent the marshaling of the energy, reduce the amount of energy marshaled,

| Pollution | |
|---|---|
| **Region** | **Site** |
| **1. Prevent the marshaling of the energy - Deep Reform** | |
| I   Remove polluting activities from aquifer recharge areas | I   Collect/treat runoff<br>II   Don't build on aquifer recharge areas<br>III   No agriculture, cars, polluting activities |
| **2. Reducing the amount of energy marshaled - Deep Reform** | |
| I   Reduce the number of polluting activities<br>II   Treat pollution | I   Reduce the amount of polluting activities<br>II   Small scale development in high density<br>III   Treat pollution |
| **3. Prevent the release of the energy - Deep Reform** | |
| I   Remove pollution activities on aquifer recharge areas | I   On site wastewater treatment and discharge<br>II   Allow only none-polluting activities |
| **4. Modify the rate of energy or spatial distribution of energy release - Partial Reform** | |
| I   Build off of aquifer recharge areas<br>II   Build in a dispersed pattern | I   Small buildings<br>II   Fewer cows, goats, sheep<br>III   Less industry<br>IV   Large open spaces |
| **5. Separate in space or time - Partial Reform** | |
| I   Phase construction along with mitigation measures<br>II   Alternate between grazing sites | I   Locate polluting activities off of recharge areas |
| **6. Separate by interposition of a material barrier - Incremental Advances** | |
| I   Fence off aquifer recharge areas | I   treat runoff before recharge |
| **7. Modify Appropriately the contact surface - Incremental Advances** | |
| I   Eliminate grazing areas<br>II   Eliminate roads (viaducts)<br>III   Pollution-neutralizing surface | I   Cover site with impervious material to prevent infiltration of pollutants<br>II   Pollution-neutralizing surfaces (i.e,, wetlands) |
| **8. Strengthen the structure - Holding the Line** | |
| I   Combined regional sewage storm water treatment | I   On-site sewage/storm water treatment<br>II   Full containment of pollution<br>III   Closed systems |
| **9. Detection and evaluation by generating a signal that a response is required - Slowing the Rate** | |
| I   Monitor streams and wells<br>II   Stop Modify activity | I   Monitor drains and wells<br>II   Add clean water from alternate source<br>III   Recharge with desalinized reclaimed water |
| **10. Return to pre-event conditions - Slowing the Rate of Retreat** | |
| I   Develop alternative water source<br>II   Desalinization<br>III   Water reclamation<br>IV   Abandon aquifer<br>V   Adequete water pricing | I   Pay for clean-up<br>II   Evaluate cost-benefit of aquifer protection |

**Figure 4.12: Ten strategies for reducing water pollution (based on Haddon).** | Source: A. Mueller, R. France, and C. Steinitz. "Aquifer Recharge Model: Evaluating the Impacts of Urban Development on Groundwater Resources (Galilee, Israel)." In *Integrative Studies in Water Management and Land Development Series. Handbook of Water Sensitive Planning and Design,* edited by R. L. France, 615–33. London: CRC Press, 2002.

or prevent the release of the energy. These are defensive and seek to prevent problems from arising. They are likely to be more sustainable, but they are usually more difficult to implement. These three approaches require laws and policies which can be thought of as the geodesign activities of lawyers and political representatives. These people are also geodesigners in social scientist Herbert Simon's definition of design: "Everyone designs who devises courses of action aimed at changing existing situations into preferred ones."[4]

I also recognize the short-term advantages of the last three mitigation-oriented strategies.

In any case, geodesign can and should broadly encompass *all* of Haddon's strategies when appropriate. We shouldn't limit ourselves only to the strategies of spatial allocation and organization, though these dominate the thinking of designers and geographically oriented scientists. Not all geodesign problems require solutions framed as 2-, 3- or 4-dimensional spatial allocations or physical designs. I have found "Escape of Tigers" to be a useful exercise before beginning the second pass through the framework, when methods are specified. It is a very useful way of expanding one's thinking about options for the many specific parts of the study which must be defined.

At the end of the first iteration, the geodesign team should meet with the people of the place and those involved in making decisions, and share with them their understanding of the situation up to that point. Mutual trust between the team and the decision makers needs to be developed and evolving perceptions need to be shared. This meeting will surely result in more questions and more answers. Everyone needs a common understanding of the intended scope of the study and a sense that the geodesign team can and will propose a competent and feasible methodological plan once they reach the end of the second iteration.

## Notes

1. Adapted from chapter 3 in C. Steinitz, H. Arias, S. Bassett, M. Flaxman, T. Goode, T. Maddock, D. Mouat, R. Peiser, and A. Shearer, *Alternative Futures for Changing Landscapes: The San Pedro River Basin in Arizona and Sonora* (Washington, D.C.: Island Press, 2003.

2. Adapted from W. Haddon Jr.. "Escape of Tigers: An Ecologic Note," *Technology Review* 72 (1970): 44–53.

3. A. Mueller, R. France, and C. Steinitz, "Aquifer Recharge Model: Evaluating the Impacts of Urban Development on Groundwater Resources (Galilee, Israel)," in *Integrative Studies in Water Management and Land Development Series. Handbook of Water Sensitive Planning and Design,* ed. R. L. France. (London: CRC Press, 2002), 615–33.

4. H. A. Simon, *The Sciences of the Artificial,* (Cambridge, MA: MIT Press, 1969).

# CHAPTER 5

# The second iteration through the framework: Designing the study methodology

HAVING IDENTIFIED THE SCOPE OF THE STUDY (the *WHY* questions) in the first iteration of the framework, the geodesign team then collaborates in a second iteration to design and specify the methodology for the study (the *HOW* questions). The six framework questions are asked again, but in reverse order, from 6 to 1 (figure 5.1). The decision models require the impact models in order to assess the consequences of proposed changes. The several types of impact models and their needs for analytic complexity lead to the ways in which the change models and their resulting alternatives will be created and expressed. The change models require the evaluation models and their

assessments of current and past conditions. These in turn need the process models for their understanding of the underlying functioning of the geographical context of the study. The process models require data, the ways that the study area is represented. This sequence will also influence the study's methods and technologies for information management and visualization. When all of these models are defined and made operational, they become the methodology for the geodesign study, and their outcomes will help determine the future of the particular geographical study area.

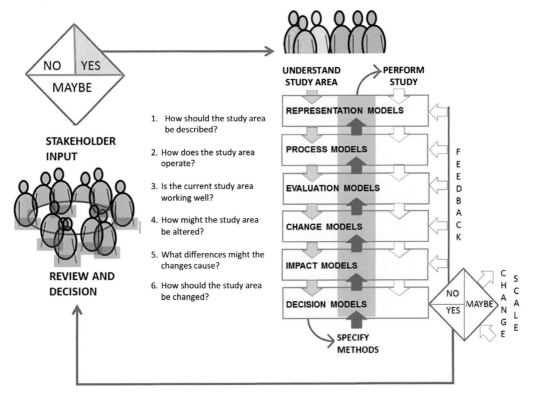

**Figure 5.1: The second iteration: the *HOW* questions.** | Source: Carl Steinitz.

There are paired relationships among the six types of models and these must be considered while specifying the methods for the geodesign study. The decision models and the evaluation models are both based on the cultural knowledge of the people of the place. For the decision makers to choose to make changes to their geography, they must believe that the potential impacts of change are predominantly positive when compared with current conditions. This means that the assessments produced by evaluation models must be in a graphic and verbal "language" that is directly related to the criteria of the decision makers and their ways of deciding.

The impact models must be the same as the process models. They produce information but the impact models are organized to assess the assumed future conditions generated by the change models. The future-oriented products of change models must be in the same categories as the representation models that describe existing conditions. Both are data. They must be in the same descriptive language and dimensions: qualitative, quantitative, graphic, spatial, and temporal. Without visualizing and understanding the differences between "before" and "after," it seems unlikely that a decision to make a change to the context geography will be made.

For the sake of organization and clarity, this chapter on the second iteration of the framework is divided into separate sections for each of the model types that the geodesign team must discuss and define during this stage. More attention will be given to the change models than the others because they are at the core of geodesign and there is less technical literature available on this subject that could otherwise guide you. I will offer examples throughout this long chapter, but will still not be able to encompass all possible circumstances that geodesign teams might face.

## Decision models

Decision models are based upon the personal, cultural, and institutional knowledge of the decision makers, and these people are highly influential in any project. There are obvious differences among decision models as a function of size, scale, and level of decision making. During any project decisions will be made by diverse groups, at multiple levels, and with different approaches to decision making (figure 5.2). Their variability makes them difficult to classify a priori. Furthermore, the geodesign team should assume that internal conflicts among the stakeholders and people of the place are likely to exist with regards to decision making and the requirements and options

for the changes to be considered. If otherwise, the study might not have been necessary in the first place.

**Question 6.** Questions related to decision models could include the following:
- What are the objectives and requirements of the decision makers and thus of the geodesign study?
- What do the decision makers need to know in order to implement changes?
- What are the relative levels of importance of their requirements?
- What are their evaluations based on? Are they scientific evaluations, cultural norms, and/or legal standards?
- Are there any binding constraints on possible outcomes of the geodesign study
- Are there issues of public communication or of visualization?

One of the principal influences of a study's size and scale, and the level of decision making that will be taking place, will be on the need for complexity in the impact models, and thus also the process models that provide such information. As a generalization, a private client or a small committee or company may be satisfied with simpler models that produce qualitative judgments. Private clients may have highly idiosyncratic ways of deciding, and even significant decisions have been made on the basis of a single picture and a few adjectives ("OK, that looks good...let's go ahead.").

This would clearly not be the case when working with regional and national governments, or toward international treaties, such as a conservation or water management strategy that crosses national borders. Here, we expect to use highly reliable process and impact models derived from geographically

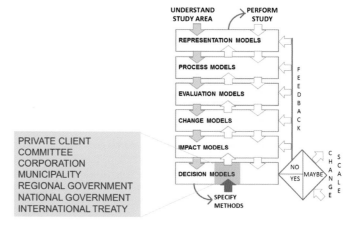

**Figure 5.2: There are varied levels of decision making and a great variability of decision makers in every project. The geodesign team must be prepared to work with all of them.** | Source: Carl Steinitz.

precise, quantitative outputs forecast over longer time periods. The subsequent design of impact and process models must therefore reflect the information requirements of these distinctive decision models.

We must recognize that situations may occur in which the decision makers cannot explain their decision model and requirements in an abstract discussion. They may need examples to compare in order to themselves understand the best way to decide what to do. In such a circumstance, the geodesign study must be designed as a preliminary exercise that produces several alternatives reflecting a wide but reasonable range of assumptions derived during the scoping investigation of the first iteration. Examples are shown in the Bermuda case study in chapter 7 and the Padova-ZIP case study in chapter 8. Ideally, in the case of a preliminary study we would follow up with a second pass through the entire framework, this time more precisely defined and leading to proposed changes to the study area geography.

Many important geodesign decisions involve values that are not necessarily measured spatially or quantitatively. Nor can they necessarily be easily combined, especially not in a formulaic algorithmic model. American psychologist Lawrence Kohlberg (1927–1987) distinguished five kinds of values:

1. Cultural values such as religious imperatives to do or not do something. Many religions have clear policies that directly relate to geodesign, and these are frequently related to the conservation of landscape features such as trees and water. For example, Judaism and Islam, viewing humans as temporary custodians of God's world, forbid cutting down the trees of an enemy;

2. Values associated with authority, such as the personal values or considerations of a property owner, a chairman of a corporation, a mayor or president, or a king;

3. Logical values presented in a compelling argument about the benefits or costs of a particular geodesign solution and probably based on a study of comparative impacts among alternatives;

4. Rational values in which an attempt is made to combine "apples and oranges" in a single metric, most frequently an economic measure such as rate of return on an investment or the economic value of ecosystem services, and

5. Emotional values based on personal feelings toward a particular geodesign solution. For example, and in my experience, people's fear of the future is a powerful component of decision making in geodesign.[1]

Regardless of the scale, size, and culture of its geographic study area, the ways of making a geodesign decision are ultimately judgments made by people. Consider the wise words of Pericles when describing Athenian democracy:

*"We Athenians, in our own persons, take our decisions on policy or submit them to proper discussions: for we do not think that there is an incompatibility between words and deeds; the worst thing is to rush into action before the consequences have been properly debated. And this is another point where we differ from other people. We are capable at the same time of taking risks and of estimating them beforehand. Others are brave out of ignorance; and, when they stop to think, they begin to fear. But the man who can most truly be accounted brave is he who best knows the meaning of what is sweet in life and of what is terrible, and then goes out undeterred to meet what is to come."*

"Pericles' Funeral Oration," Thucydides[2]

Understanding the decision model involves also determining the study's objectives and requirements, of which there may be around ten to twenty important ones in a typical study. However, these requirements will not all be of equal importance. Instead, they typically fall into one of two distributions. They can be ranked in a distribution that approximates Zipf's law,[3] in which each is about half of the importance of the preceding one, or alternatively there may be a few requirements with relatively similar and high importance and these dominate over the remaining ones (figure 5.3).

The geodesign team must be specific regarding its understanding of the decision makers' requirements for the study

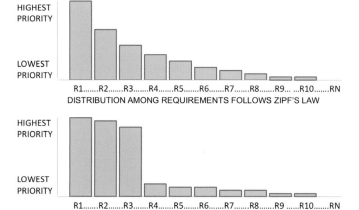

Figure 5.3: Rank order of the importance of requirements in two possible distributions. In the first, each requirement may be only half as important as the preceding one. Or, just a few requirements may be about equal in importance and much more important than all others. | Source: Carl Steinitz.

and the relative importance of each. How the requirements are distributed influences the change models, which are the ways of designing. When there are numerous requirements or objectives, and some of the more significant ones and their options are in conflict, the study will need to generate and communicate alternative futures for the geographical study area which reflect these varied positions.

As the decision models are being developed, it may be tempting to draw ideas from the large and well-developed field of "decision theory." That would make the process of decision making more automatic and reliant on externally defined models and values. However, in my experience, the development of local and personal knowledge, and trust between the geodesign team and the decision makers, are the most essential components of an effective geodesign study. There is no substitute for gaining direct personal knowledge of the people with whom you are working and who will be making decisions about the geodesign study.

## Impact models

In order to make geodesign decisions, the impact models and their established metrics are used to assess the benefits and costs of potential changes. In the second iteration of the framework we define the content and complexity of the required impact models. These will also become the bases for the process models and their evaluations of existing conditions. The impacts of potential changes are the results obtained from the process models when applied to a proposed change in the geographical context. The content of impact models varies broadly (figure 5.4). Some are particular to the geodesign problem and others are required by laws or regulations.

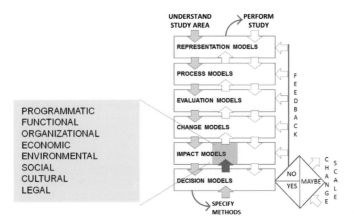

**Figure 5.4:** The content of impact models varies broadly. This reflects the different categories whose positive and negative impacts must be considered for a geodesign decision. | Source: Carl Steinitz.

The impacts of any changes that are proposed during a geodesign study will have to be assessed in multiple ways. Exactly which assessments are required will vary by project type and political jurisdiction, but typically a broad set of potential consequences will have to be considered. These will include economic and demographic impacts, functional aspects, and others related to such parameters as water pollution, air pollution, traffic, energy use, impacts on biodiversity and visual quality, employment and public safety concerns.

**Question 5.** Impact model-related questions include the following:

- Which impact models are needed by the decision model to assess and compare potential changes?
- Which impacts are not part of the decision models but should be considered nevertheless?
- What, how much, where, when, and to whom are the impacts seen as "good" vs. "bad"?
- How precise must the impact assessments be?

Most geodesign studies will be required by law to complete an environmental impact statement and review process in an early stage toward implementation. An environmental impact statement (EIS) identifies the environmental consequences of proposed major changes and developments to the geographic context. It compares these with existing conditions, as well as with projected change *without* the proposed actions. The requirements of this process will also add models and their specifications to a geodesign study. National, regional, and local governments are likely to have laws and regulations that require specific impact-related studies to accompany any major proposed action. For example, the EIS mandated by the US Department of Energy for a large solar energy project[4] may have more than a dozen impact model categories to consider (figure 5.5).

Specifying the impact models is likely to be the most complicated phase of the second iteration of the framework. This will especially be the case if the impact models require a study methodology in which their related process models are to be linked to each other in "chains" or "networks." The interactions require that each component model be designed to interact directly with those models that contribute to it and those to which it, in turn, must send information. In addition, the entire set of impact models must be designed to receive information from the change models and deliver information in the appropriate language and precision to the decision models. Clearly, this requires the attention of all the collaborating members of the geodesign team.

PROGRAMMATIC
FUNCTIONAL
ORGANIZATIONAL
ECONOMIC
ENVIRONMENTAL
SOCIAL
CULTURAL
LEGAL

1.Air Quality
2.Biological Resources
3.Cultural resources
4.Geology and Minerals
5.Hazardous Materials
6.Safety
7.Land Use
8.Recreation
9.Transportation
10.Noise
11.Socioeconomic
12.Visual Resources
13.Water Resources

**Figure 5.5: The scope and precision needs of the impact models will directly influence the requirements for complexity of the process models.** | Source: Carl Steinitz, based on US Department of Energy, Western Area Power Administration."Quartzite Solar Energy Project EIS." Scoping Summary Report, Western Area Power Administration, Phoenix, Arizona, 2010.

It is important to consider which aspects of a type of change might trigger impacts on particular aspects of the geographic context. Richard Toth[5] makes the very useful distinction between construction, maintenance, and use aspects as causes of impacts. Construction (for example, for new highway) would involve such things as blasting, grading, de-watering, and so on. Maintenance aspects might include oiling or salting, depending on the type of road and the local climate. Use aspects might involve traffic accidents, air pollution, noise, and so on. Each of these may have very different consequences on any of the diverse systems for which impact assessment is required.

The typical product of an impact assessment is a map showing the difference between a prior state of the study area and a future state for the phenomenon being investigated. It is usually assumed that that difference has been caused by the changes attributed to the design. This assumption should always be questioned. While the study can be organized so that all aspects of the geographic study area are held stable and only the attributes of the design are altered (thus making the assumption more likely to be valid), long-term stability is unlikely to be the case, especially for a large geodesign study. The context itself may be changing in ways that overwhelm the impacts generated by the subject matter of the geodesign study in the first place. We are increasingly seeing geodesign studies with this situation, for example, the design of biological

reserves or new cities under conditions of climate change or regional water depletion.

Assuming that a series of impact models has been identified and specified for the geodesign study, consideration must be given to how a diverse set of assessments expressed as maps, each on a different theme and potentially each in a different spatial, quantitative, or qualitative language, can be summarized and combined in a decision-making process. Again, Toth provides a very useful set of qualitative distinctions:

- Beneficial: the proposed changes cause improvement to the system being assessed;
- Compatible: the proposed changes coexist with the system being assessed and do not create perceivable impacts;
- Moderate: the proposed changes create impacts that can be overcome by natural processes acting over a reasonably short time period;
- Severe: the proposed changes create impacts that can be mitigated with major engineering investments;
- Terminal: the proposed changes create impacts which are sufficient to destroy the values of the system being assessed and which cannot be mitigated with major engineering investments.

I have used Toth's categories (and occasional variations) many times. In several of the case studies in this book, very complex quantitative and spatial impact models have been judgmentally summarized by Toth's qualitative categories. My colleagues and I have found them to be especially effective in public communication regarding the impacts of proposed changes.

## Change models

The basic problem of geodesign can be stated as, "How do we get from the present state of this geographical study area to the best possible future?" In the framework we answer the question: "How might the study area be altered?" with change models, the ways of designing and achieving the products of the geodesign study. The relative influences of the methodological choices made in the second iteration of the framework will *not* be equal, and change models are a particularly important element within the geodesign framework.

There are differences in how we make smaller size designs versus increasingly larger ones. One does *not* approach geodesign in the same way for projects of different sizes and this is especially the case for change models. I believe that as the crises of our environments become more significant and perceived by more people, the design of our future environments will become more important. The more significant geographic changes through geodesign for larger areas will increasingly influence the design of smaller projects.

There are multiple strategies for approaching change models, and in this section I will elaborate on a number of their aspects including the role of visualization, ways of thinking about change models, specific aspects and phases of change models, and offensive and defensive strategies for change models. I will briefly describe eight different ways of designing for change and a ninth mixed way, all of which can provide important insights to geodesign processes. In part III (chapters 7, 8, and 9) of this book, each of these change models will be described in greater detail within the context of a case study that applies it within the geodesign framework.

## Change model phases

Every change model goes through four common and hierarchically organized phases, all of which are essential for a successful decision and implementation: vision, strategy, tactics, and actions (figure 5.6). Sharp distinctions between these are difficult because the questions to which they respond overlap. Sometimes these are explicitly described, and sometimes they are implicitly understood.

Vision responds to the questions *why* and *what*? Strategy responds to *what* and *where*? Tactics refers to *where* and *how*? And actions to *how* and *when*? These should be understood as being on two important continua. Vision and strategy come from the experience of the designer or the members of the geodesign team. They may also derive from the people of the place and decision makers. They are likely to be generalizable for many geodesign applications, while actions and tactics can be taught but are unique to the case in hand.

**Figure 5.6: Four phases of a change model.** | Source: Carl Steinitz.

The reality of this continuum is one of the limiting factors of seeing geodesign as only or primarily algorithmic. Neither of the extremes—vision or actions—are easily amenable to algorithmic approaches to geodesign.

There are two main ways of thinking about change models in terms of vision and strategy. The most common "anticipatory" approach embodies the idea that the designer is expected to make a leap forward in time, first conceiving of the design as a whole "concept" and then selecting the correct choices among the many requirements and options to reproduce that original vision. The anticipatory methods require the use of deductive logic to figure out how to get from the desired future state back to the present and then ahead in time to the future.

In this type of approach, the designer or the geodesign team quickly develops alternative physical designs for future land use and/or land cover, through sketching, diagramming, and other more informal design methods. These are then comparatively assessed for their potential consequences, often through discussion with experts and stakeholders, and sometimes via formal impact models. This process can cycle many times as it develops the design for change.

The initial designed alternatives are often based on geometrical patterns (compact, diffuse, linear, and so on.) or on political interest groups (the conservationists' plan, the developers' plan, and so on.). Many early twentieth century city and regional planning studies used this approach, as have several spatially oriented land-use modeling studies carried out beginning in the 1960s. The advantage of this approach is its rapidity and its reliance on traditionally taught and experienced methods. It can be especially effective on smaller projects, as misleading oversimplifications can result on studies of larger geographic areas. Its principal disadvantage is that while it might create a sense of what the future might be, it may be impossible to identify the set of policies needed to achieve that future.

The "exploratory" approach more closely resembles the typical decision-making process underlying the many governmental, organizational, and individual choices that shape a region's future. The exploratory approach requires a scenario based on requirements and a sequence of assumptions that aim us from the present state to the future. The geodesign team then asks, "In what future state might this scenario result?" Thus exploratory strategies most frequently require the use of inductive logic. They are frequently amenable to algorithmically produced solutions. This approach identifies the most important objectives and requirements that are potentially responsive to policy and design decisions, along with the widest range of options pertaining to each issue. Each policy option alters either a spatially varied characteristic that can attract or repel future change, or it alters a parameter in one of the several process models that assess the impacts of future change. Choices are made, and the selected scenarios are used to direct the allocation of future land uses using a model of the developmental process. The alternatives are then assessed for their consequences.

This approach provides for the creation of various alternative futures for a region, and gives guidance on how to achieve them because the alternatives themselves are based on a set of policy and/or design decisions. An additional benefit is the ability to test the effects of individual policy choices by using sensitivity analyses. The principal liability of such approaches is that they require more initial specification before seeing any results.

As was the case with anticipatory strategies, the exploratory approach is relatively easy if the problem is a simple one. But if it is large and complex, and if each single requirement has several options to be considered, the exploratory approaches may fail because there are too many combinations to consider. The models cannot achieve a sufficient level of precision and detail, and taking the wrong path may be too risky. In these situations, the best solution may be to carefully assess the essential initial steps or their combinations with sensitivity analyses and agree not to worry too much about the details until later in the process.

An individual designer might skip back and forth between anticipatory and exploratory strategies. But how should the geodesign team begin? Here, the issues of "size," "scale," and "risk" must be considered. Scale matters. In my view, smaller projects, such as a residential site plan, present fewer real risks of being wrong than do larger design projects and regional landscape planning studies that involve enormous cost, large numbers of people, many unknowns, and a longer time horizon. Decision and implementation are easier for smaller projects while the larger ones frequently require fundamental institutional change. Smaller projects conclude with working drawings and constructed physical change, while it is rare for a larger regional studies to be directly built. Rather, their more frequent aim is to influence the way society values and changes its geography, including by changing land and water use policy. At the extremes these varied scales require different initial strategies. For larger and more complex projects, exploratory methods are likely to be a more appropriate starting strategy.

## Offensive and defensive strategies

Geodesign change models will frequently combine "offensive" development-oriented allocation strategies and "defensive" conservation strategies. *Offensive* strategies are those in which the design solution attempts to identify characteristics that are considered highly attractive and seen as opportunities for change, such as finding locations with low costs and high profitability,

good transportation access, beautiful views, and so on. *Defensive* strategies focus on the constraints at locations considered vulnerable to change, avoiding design decisions that entail substantial risk of negative impacts. An example would be the avoidance of locations at risk of erosion, earthquakes, flooding, and so on. For different objectives or requirements, risk is present when attractive and vulnerable locations overlap.

One can fairly ask which should come first, the offensive or the defensive strategies? After all, in sports, which is better, to save a goal defensively or to make a goal offensively? There is a yin-yang relationship between offensive and defensive strategies. The offensive criterion "seek a flat location" is not so different from the defensive criterion "avoid a steep location." The way that the decision model defines the issues that are reflected in the requirement priorities for the change model will influence the balance between offensive and defensive strategies. If one sees the situation as presenting high risk and low control, defensive strategies will prevail. However if the situation is seen as having high control at low risk, offensive strategies will dominate.

The scales within which the geodesign problem is conceived and carried out will also influence geodesign strategy and the balance between *offensive* considerations of attractiveness and desirability and *defensive* considerations of vulnerability, risk, and protection (figure 5.7). If the sizes and scales change within the design of the study, this will further affect the balance of strategies. If the change model is modified from a larger region to a smaller site, and from coarser- to finer-scaled data, it will typically begin with broad defensive strategies and then continue offensively with decisions related to allocation, and at each stage assessing impacts before revising the design. However, when a geodesign problem is carried out from smaller areas with finer scaled data it frequently begins offensively

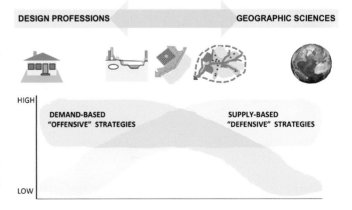

**Figure 5.7:** Size and scale considerations influence the relative balance between "defensive" and "offensive" change strategies.
| Source: Carl Steinitz.

with concepts for the allocation of change before considering defensive issues.

I believe that the geodesign team should *always* consider the defensive strategies prior to the offensive ones. This is analogous to the primary medical ethic *Primum non nocere*, Latin for "First, do no harm." There is also a more pragmatic reason. Defensive strategies generally are more rapidly effective in reducing the number of possible future change options that must be generated and considered, thus reducing the workload and allowing the team to focus more quickly on potentially feasible solutions.

## Allocation, organization, expression, and visualization

All change models combine decisions related to allocation, organization, and expression, and all require visualization and communication. *Allocation* refers to where changes are located, such as the placement of new housing in the landscape, the conversion of forest to agriculture, or the protection of a rare animal's habitat, and so on. *Organization* refers to the interrelationships among the elements of the design, such as how the school, the shopping area, the park, the bus system, and both low- and high-density housing all fit together in

the design of the new community. *Expression* refers to the way in which the design is perceived. For example, is it seen as a residential community, or as a friendly place, or an expensive one, etc.

These three characteristics of allocation, organization, and expression are rarely applied with equal emphasis in change models. As a general rule, the larger the size of the design study, the more emphasis is placed on allocation. By contrast, the smaller the project, the more emphasis can be placed on expression. This change of emphasis is characteristic of the differences between landscape planning and garden design, or regional planning and architectural design. In terms of the change models to which they apply, these are different in degree of emphasis and they share the same overarching template for design, but they are likely to require different change models.

Designers have long appreciated the power of visualizing and communicating change. Humphry Repton (1752–1818) was perhaps the most famous English landscape designer. In order to illustrate the benefits of his designs he showed them using two visualizations, a "before" and an "after." Repton's Red Books[6] included watercolor illustrations of his designs with flaps that fold over the areas where changes are planned.

**Figure 5.8: Water at Wentworth, South Yorkshire, before proposed landscape change designed by Humphry Repton.** | Source: H. Repton, *Observations on the Theory and Practice of Landscape Gardening* (London: Printed by T. Bensley for J. Taylor, 1805).

When you lift the flap, the new design is revealed and can be distinguished from the existing conditions (figures 5.8 and 5.9).

As geodesign develops in the future, change models will be affected by computer technologies becoming more powerful, decentralized, inexpensive, ubiquitous, and user friendly. We (and I mean "we" in the broadest sense, including the people of the place) will have a much more complex perspective on what constitutes a design process, how change is designed, and by whom, and how it is visualized.

## A template for specifying the change model

Any type of change model has four fundamental components that are essential to keep in mind: history, facts, constants, and requirements. The first is *history*. Knowing the history of the geographical context within which the geodesign study will occur is essential, particularly the history of any previous designs for that area. In my long experience, I have never worked in a region that didn't already have past designs, and the people who made them were not fools.

Next are *facts*. Facts are aspects of the geography that are assumed not to change over the life of your design. These can be aspects or results of the study's representation, process or evaluation models. We might be working toward a point in time 20 or 30 years in the future, and such things as subsurface geology or a major river pattern or the evaluation of an historic palace are not likely to change within that time frame.

Then there are *constants,* things that are certain to occur in the time-frame of your geodesign study. You must find out about them, because if you don't, none of your alternatives will be implemented. An example of a constant could be a highway or sewage treatment system in the study area which has already been proposed, approved, designed, funded, and though not yet constructed, is contracted to begin within the next year or two.

Lastly, there are the *requirements and their options,* the things that should and could happen. Capturing the major, strategic, and generating requirements and their alternative choices is key here. The most important assumptions must be part of the beginning of the sequence of change-decisions, since if you make the first steps wrongly, you will certainly end up wrong. Then again, if you make the right first steps you still may end up wrong, but you have a better chance of success. Spatial analysis frequently plays its most critical role in the assessment of these initial and strategic alternative choices. You have to be able to say: "either here, here, or here," or "in one of these several ways."

**Figure 5.9: Water at Wentworth, South Yorkshire, after proposed landscape change by Humphry Repton.** | Source: H. Repton, *Observations on the Theory and Practice of Landscape Gardening* (London: Printed by T. Bensley for J. Taylor, 1805).

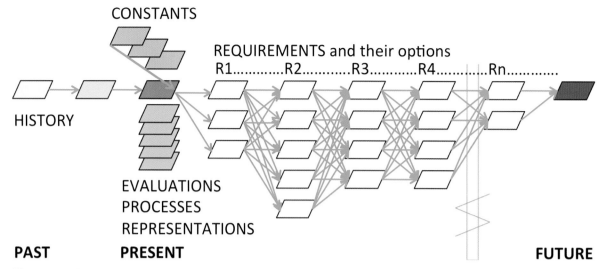

CONSTANTS

REQUIREMENTS and their options
R1............R2............R3............R4............Rn............

HISTORY

EVALUATIONS
PROCESSES
REPRESENTATIONS

PAST          PRESENT                                                    FUTURE

**Figure 5.10:** The template for change models. The parallelograms can best be understood as map layers of spatial representations needed for the geodesign study, such as data layers within a GIS. The arrows are the links in the cumulative process of making the design. | Source: Carl Steinitz.

Multiple strategies exist for change models, and many of these have common elements. To help understand these strategies, I have created a general template that can be adapted by a geodesign team, all the while acknowledging that this template must be seen as a graphic simplification of a far more complex reality (figure 5.10). Later in this book, in chapters 7, 8, and 9, I will also use this template to review case studies. Every change model for geography at the sizes that we typically consider in geodesign can include the template's elements. This template is adaptable to changes in time and/or scale. Since it is complicated to illustrate in a single static diagram, we shall describe the template systematically.

Every design is set in time, with a past, a present, and an eye toward the future.

The historical conditions and context are indicated by parallelograms in light peach colors.

The present context is symbolized in brown.

The future state of the study area, the geodesign target, is represented by the dark brown parallelogram.

Evaluations are shown in gray. During the second iteration of the framework, are these required by the decision model. Evaluations of the current state of the study area establish the base for assessing future impacts.

The constants, in light blue are those design-related decisions that have already been made or committed to. We must assume that these things *will* happen, and their results must be accommodated in *any* design for the future.

R1... The requirements (R1, R2,...Rn) are issues or elements that must be resolved and integrated in the design. These are numbered to indicate a sequence of decreasing importance within a change model.

The options from which the geodesign team chooses are located below the symbol of their related requirement.

The parallel lines with zigzags represent a foreshortening of the requirements and options. In reality a geodesign project could entail several dozen different requirements and options, but their representation in this template has been simplified for graphical clarity.

Thin, light green arrows indicate sets of optional decisions that must be considered in the change model.

The sequence of decision making within the change model is represented by green arrows.

In order to make the design for change, one can "move" around this template in several ways, reflecting the kinds of decisions that can be made within a change model (figure 5.11).

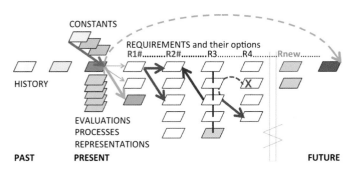

**Figure 5.11: The "moves": decisions within the template for change models.** | Source: Carl Steinitz.

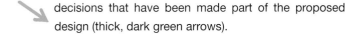 We can add, remove, or change the evaluations (in orange)

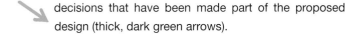 and/or the constants (in yellow)

The process of decision making is represented by green arrows.

→ This diagram indicates both optional choices that must be considered (thin, light green arrows) and

↘ decisions that have been made part of the proposed design (thick, dark green arrows).

Lines of other colors represent specific variations that will be described within a particular change model.

◢ One can move forward in a straightforward manner (in green)

↙ or back to a prior step (in indigo).

↘ Two or more options can be chosen for purposes of sensitivity analyses (in violet) and contribute to different future designs.

| A set of options can be compared, (dark blue line),

◢ and a new option created (light green).

↘ Mistakes can be made and corrected (in red).

The geodesign team can go *beyond the information given.*

**Rnew** New requirements (in olive) and

◢ new options can be added (in olive green).

 And final designs can always be altered (in dark brown).

When there is uncertainty or disagreement on important assumptions, the template can be adapted to a study based on sensitivity analyses. This might also be necessary when the assumptions of a requirement are unclear or have more than one possible outcome, or when the multiple options for the resolution of a set of important requirements need careful assessment or follow through to envision their design implications (figure 5.12).

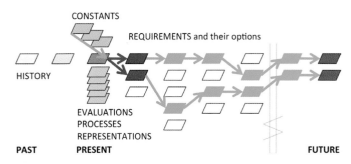

**Figure 5.12: Sensitivity analysis leading to different designs.** | Source: Carl Steinitz.

The template can also be adapted for change models that require study via time stages or at different time periods (figure 5.13).

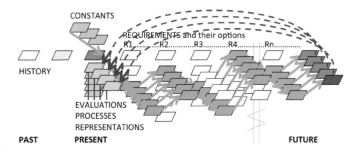

**Figure 5.13: The template in a study over several time-stages.** | Source: Carl Steinitz.

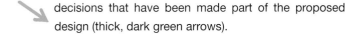 At any time stage (light brown),

- - - - feedback from its design (in red dashed line)

| can be combined with an updating of data, process models, and evaluations (in red line)

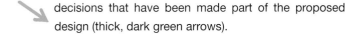 to reflect that new time-state of the study area (in orange).

The change model would then be applied as before, or altered with all the possibilities for adaptation described above, in as many time periods as the study requires, to achieve its final design.

For changes in scale during a study, the same template of procedures as described above would apply, but the resulting change model would likely be modified to reflect scale-related requirements.

## Eight ways of designing, plus one mixed example

Just as there are multiple strategies for using the geodesign template, there are multiple strategies for approaching change models altogether. In this section, I will briefly describe eight different ways of designing for change and one additional way that mixes methods, all of which can provide important insights to geodesign processes (figure 5.14). In part III (chapters 7, 8, and 9) of this book, each of these will be described in greater detail and within the context of a case study that applies it within the geodesign framework.

The names of each of these change model strategies reflect their primary approach or characteristic: anticipatory, participatory, sequential, constraining, combinatorial, rule-based, optimized, and agent-based. All eight support the use of scenarios, recognizing that there are an infinite number of future options. At the same time, all of them eventually reduce the possible number of alternatives from the infinite to a manageable

number. In the end, the change models must include the most important issues and produce an appropriate range of policy and design choices. Although nearly all designs are the result of combinations of these eight ways, during a given geodesign project one of these eight is likely to dominate. *The way that the change model is organized and started is crucial and should be preplanned in this second iteration of the framework.*

**Question 4.** Change model-related questions include the following:

- What are the assumptions for change?
- What are the requirements?
- Who defines the scenarios for change? How?
- Which scenarios are selected? Toward which time horizon(s)? At what scale(s)?
- How shall change be visualized and communicated?
- Which change models, or way(s) of designing, are most appropriate for this geodesign study?

### Anticipatory

The anticipatory approach is based on the premise that the designer's confidence and experience can provide the "great leap forward" to a concept of what might be the basis for a good design (figure 5.15). This necessarily assumes that the designer has a sufficient and adequate amount of experience from which to draw upon. He or she will then need to go back to existing conditions, and through deductive logic move forward through the many requirements and their options to try to achieve the preconceived design. In chapter 7 we will see how the anticipatory approach was used to create six alternative designs for the future of the Camp Pendleton region, between Los Angeles and San Diego, California, USA.[7]

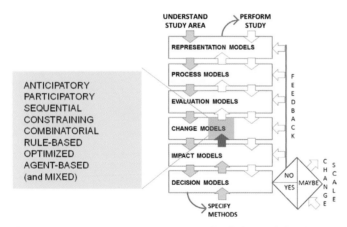

**Figure 5.14: Nine change models.** Each of these eight change models, plus one mixed example, represents a different strategy for approaching and organizing the design and/or simulation of change. Each will be described and discussed below, as well as in part III of the book with a case study that applies it within the framework for geodesign. | Source: Carl Steinitz.

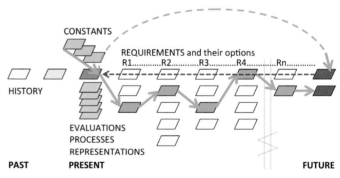

**Figure 5.15: The anticipatory change model.** | Source: Carl Steinitz.

## Participatory

The participatory design approach assumes that there is more than one participating designer, and that each has a concept about what the future design should be (figure 5.16). This premise expects the designers to have a sufficient sense of place and time to provide a future-oriented design, while still recognizing that their designs are different and must be aggregated into one consensus design. In chapter 7 we will review a case study of the Osa Peninsula in Costa Rica,[8] where over 40 people contributed their designs for the future of the region. These were tested for agreement leading toward a consensus design.

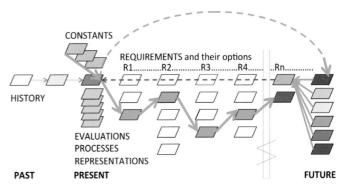

**Figure 5.16:** The participatory change model. | Source: Carl Steinitz.

## Sequential

Under the sequential approach, the designer makes a series of confident choices that systematically develop into the future design (figure 5.17). This approach begins with present conditions and uses abductive logic as it moves with certainty directly through a single set of choices for each requirement. The sequential approach will be illustrated in chapter 7 by a study for the future design of the Bermuda garbage dump,[9] in which each of 14 designs were generated by a purposely selected sequence of choices. In the end, one was eventually chosen as "best."

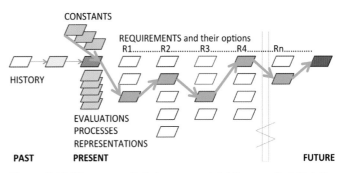

**Figure 5.17:** The sequential change model. | Source: Carl Steinitz.

## Constraining

The constraining method (figure 5.18) is useful when the client and/or the geodesign team are not sure of the decision models, or when the relative importance of the study's objectives or requirements approximate Zipf's Law (figure 5.3) but where there are also many options for each requirement. In many ways it is similar to the sequential and the combinatorial approach (which I will describe next). In chapter 8, the constraining approach will be illustrated by a study of the Zona Industriale and the Parco Roncajette in Padova, Italy.[10] The purpose of this study was to clarify the true objectives and requirements of the city for the Roncajette park and the largest industrial zone in Italy with regards to their future plans.

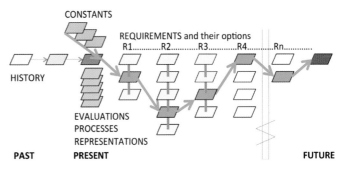

**Figure 5.18:** The constraining change model. | Source: Carl Steinitz.

## Combinatorial

When the designer or the client is not sure of the appropriate choices in the sequence of decisions to create the design, the combinatorial approach is useful (figure 5.19). This strategy is commonly applied to investigate alternative scenarios for the future. It is especially appropriate when the few main objectives are of similar importance (figure 5.3) and a combination of the key requirements must be resolved before continuing with less important ones. Its case study in chapter 8 will describe a study of the future options for the expansion of Cagliari, the capital city of Sardinia, Italy.[11]

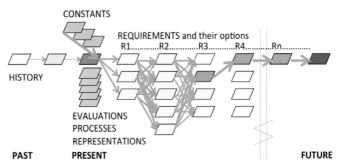

**Figure 5.19:** The combinatorial change model. | Source: Carl Steinitz.

## Rule-based

The rule-based approach assumes that the geodesign team is knowledgable and confident enough to specify a set of formal rules for developing the design (figure 5.20). Such approaches are normally organized as a set of computer algorithms, but they can also be expressed as mental steps which can be followed manually. The rules can be constraining and related to vulnerability, such as, "Do not build on easily erodable soils on slopes greater than 20 percent." Or they can be related to attractiveness, "Build on flat dry land between 20 and 100 meters from a two-lane paved road." The rules for each requirement are combined in a sequence of design decisions comparable to that in a sequential approach (figure 5.17). In chapter 9, this approach will be exemplified in a study of the growth of La Paz, the capital city of Baja California Sur, Mexico.[12] In the study, economic and environmental assessments were used to identify the range of "best choices" for a policy that combines the two.

## Optimized

The optimized approach is perhaps the most difficult of the eight different design methods to implement (figure 5.21). It requires that the client and the geodesign team understand beforehand the relative importance of each of the desired requirements and also its decision criteria. The optimizing decision model is based on the cultural knowledge of the decision makers and reflects their goals, the values by which they make judgments about the design, and the relative importance they attach to these goals and values. This approach needs these criteria to be identified and comparable in a single metric, such as a financial rate-of-return or potential votes, etc., in order to be able to declare a design "optimal" in the end. The optimized approach will be illustrated in a chapter 9 example of the future of the Telluride region of Colorado, USA.[13] In this study, locations for new development were based on hedonically modeled economic measures and priorities based on willingness to pay.

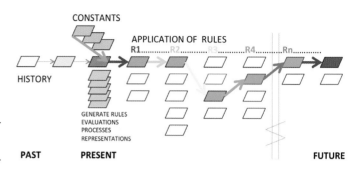

**Figure 5.20:** The rule-based change model, with each colored arrow in the diagram representing a different requirement, frequently a sub-model for a different land use. | Source: Carl Steinitz.

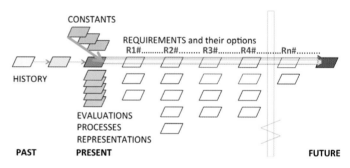

**Figure 5.21:** The optimized change model, with each colored line in the diagram representing a different requirement, frequently for a different land use. | Source: Carl Steinitz.

### Agent-based

In the agent-based approach, the future state of the study area is the result of interactions among policy and design decisions that direct, attract, or constrain the independent but rule-based actions of independent "agents" (figure 5.22). Agents can be stakeholders, or decision makers, or people of the place, or be defined as home seekers or developers or conservationists, for example. For each type of agent, there are different "rules" for where they can be in the study area "landscape" and how they will interact with others in their own group and among other groups. These rules are embedded into a computer model, and the changes occur simultaneously and adjust in reaction to the sequence of requirements for the design. Agent-based models are necessarily computer-intensive and require substantial technical expertise to execute. In chapter 9, this approach will be shown in a case study of the interactions between fire management and fire modeling in the area of Idyllwild, California, USA.[14]

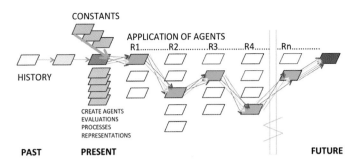

**Figure 5.22: The agent-based model, with each colored arrow in the diagram representing a different sub-model for a land use, all acting simultaneously.** | Source: Carl Steinitz.

### Mixed

In a mixed approach, several different ways of designing are combined, in whole or in part. The number of possible combinations of change models is almost infinite. An example of a mixed change model might involve a design for increasing camping capacity in a national park. The geodesign team might propose the conceptual design for a new road that transforms the location attractiveness and constraints within the park, and then allow the independent actions by campers (as represented by the computer agents in an agent-based model) to locate where they want to camp.

The mixed case study in chapter 9 is a research study of the history of West London,[15] where a mix of sequential and agent-based models was used (figure 5.23). During the nineteenth and twentieth centuries, the geodesign teams of their times designed the transportation infrastructure using what possibly was a sequential change model. Their solutions were then transformed into the evaluation-inputs for changes brought about by many independent development actions, as simulated in the research by an agent-based change model. This change model then continues through several time stages and updated evaluation models to model the growth of West London.

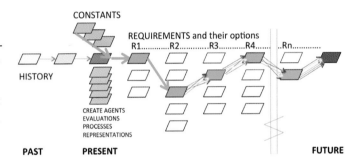

**Figure 5.23: Mixed ways, e.g., sequential and agent-based.** | Source: Carl Steinitz.

## Selecting among change models approaches

The most important consideration in selecting an approach to design is how certain or uncertain the collaborators in geodesign are about the decision model and its related assumptions and requirements. Anticipatory, participatory, sequential, and optimized change methods all assume (relative) certainty on the part of the geodesign team. In contrast, the combinatorial and constraining approaches assume uncertainty and therefore include the need to systematically explore component options of the assumptions and requirements before integration and commitment. The rule-based, optimized, and agent-based methods presume uncertainty in the assumptions and the final design outcome, but certainty with regards to the rules-of-the-game and how changes occur "in the real world." Thus these change models are frequently used for testing the sensitivity of the outcome to the parameters of that uncertainty, or when there are several scenarios for change.

At this point in this chapter, we have focused on decision models, impact models, and change models (questions 6, 5, and 4). These models all look to the future, the principal outlook for geodesign. Understanding how public and private decisions to change a geographic study area are made is critical knowledge for a geodesign team developing its methodology. Teams must be familiar with the issues and the criteria defining acceptable impacts that decision makers and their constituents apply, and be able to identify planning and policy choices that may influence future change.

We next will focus on evaluation models, process models, and representation models (questions 3, 2, and 1). Evaluation models help us understand and assess past and existing geographic conditions so we can specify particular geographic process models. Once the processes are understood, and data needs identified, we can move to the requirements for data acquisition and appropriate means of information management and visualization.

# Evaluation models

The contents of the evaluation models are derived from the decision models (figure 5.24). They are based on the decision makers' needs to assess the comparative impacts of the present state of the context geography together with its likely future state that may develop following any proposed design changes. The evaluation models will directly influence the change models by focusing the design on areas which need change as well as those which should be protected and conserved.

**Question 3.** Questions for the evaluation models as they relate to the decision model include:

- What are the measures of evaluation across distinct but relevant fields (ecology, development economics, visual preferences, politics, etc.)?
- What are their spatial, temporal, qualitative and quantitative metrics?
- Are they scientifically or judgmentally based?
- Are they related to legal standards?

## Criteria for evaluation

Geodesign relies heavily on evaluative criteria related to the geographical context of the study area. These can be conveniently grouped into three categories: site, location, and administration. Site derived criteria relate to the specific place being studied: its physical characteristics such as terrain, geology and ecology, and social characteristics such as the demographics of its people. Location derived criteria move beyond the exact location to the surrounding geography and include such spatial effects as whether it is influenced by upstream hydrology, upwind fire risks, ugly outward views, etc. Administrative criteria include such things as zoning and planning laws and regulations, and various property rights.

Evaluation criteria should be expressed as the answers to three questions:

- What is important?
- How is it important?
- How important is it?

Simply describing a criterion by a single data category is inadequate. "Steep slope" is not a statement of a criterion by itself, since it does not inform us whether a steep slope is good or bad, significant or insignificant. It may make good summer habitat for a herd of elk, but it could be very bad for the construction of a shopping center. A more appropriate statement would

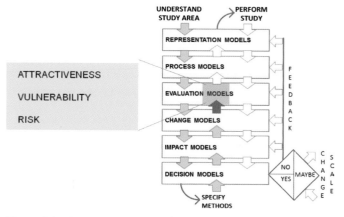

**Figure 5.24: Evaluation models.** | Source: Carl Steinitz.

be "steep slope is an important and positive attractiveness criterion for summer habitat of elk."

Evaluation criteria can come from various sources: a client, a committee, the "best professional judgment" of the designer, an expert consultant, a panel of users or experts using Delphi methods, or an empirical analysis of similar data via statistical regression methods such as hedonic pricing, for example. They can also come from a law, a religious imperative, or a tradition. Size and scale once again become considerations. For smaller projects or ones where risk perception is likely to be lower and less regulated, evaluation criteria can be more idiosyncratic. However, criteria for larger geodesign problems with greater potential risk will be more robust when based on more reliable and statistically derived sources.

The criteria and values that underlie evaluation models can be characterized on a continuum between facts and opinions. The continuum is related to the slowness with which values change (and they do change over time). "Facts" that are derived through scientific investigation tend to be stable. An example would be knowing the classification of a site's subsurface geology, or the bearing capacity of a soil type. Next in variability might be local collective experience and consensus, the cultural and traditional conventions that have caused geographic changes to be carried out in certain ways in the past. Next along the continuum might be the expertise of people who have studied a situation but who may have a narrower spatial and temporal perspective, for example, a specialist-scientist. Then might come judgment based upon personal experience. And finally one has idiosyncratic opinion. A typical geodesign study is likely to encounter several of these sources of values. However, because they are not equally reliable, larger geodesign studies with higher associated risks are best served by sources that have demonstrated greater reliability and stability over time.

## Attractiveness, vulnerability, and risk

Evaluation criteria are typically expressed in relation to their positive characteristics, such as their attractiveness for a particular purpose, or for their negative characteristics, including their contribution to the vulnerability of a particular resource, location, or action. These positive and negative criteria have a yin-yang relationship, for example one can "seek a flat slope" or "avoid a steep slope." They are sometimes combined in a more complex evaluation model, but in my experience it is best to select only one of these two forms of expressing criteria. Risk occurs when a highly attractive assessment for a potentially harmful activity coincides spatially with an evaluation of high vulnerability for a valuable site resource.

As an example, consider the simple risk assessment that was one part of a complex case study in La Paz, Mexico[16] (figure 5.25; also discussed in more detail in chapter 9 of this book). The maps reproduced here illustrate the relative attractiveness for development based on an aggregate index of economic criteria for commerce, industry, and housing.

We evaluated the environment of the region by generating an index that combined its ecological, visual, and recreational vulnerabilities (figure 5.26).

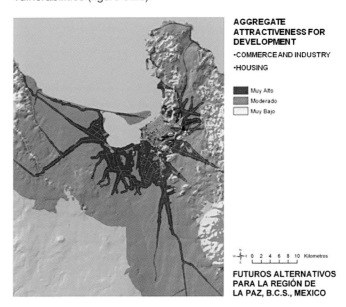

**Figure 5.25: Attractiveness for development, the region of La Paz, Mexico. Areas in darker red are more likely to be developed than those in lighter red.** | Source: La Paz geodesign team.

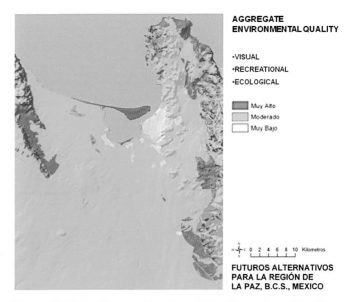

**Figure 5.26: Environmental vulnerability, the region of La Paz, Mexico. Areas in darker green have greater priority for protection.** | Source: La Paz geodesign team.

We then combined the two prior evaluations of high development pressure and high environmental value, and the result indicates the areas of greatest relative risk to the environment from development (figure 5.27). It is these areas that require the immediate attention of policy makers.

The Bay of Balandra and its hilly hinterland are located in the northwestern-most corner of the Balandra peninsula, near La Paz. One outcome of the La Paz study has been the public protection of this ecologically and recreationally important landscape (figure 5.28).

Evaluation models ultimately depend upon the cultural knowledge of the people who are establishing the decision

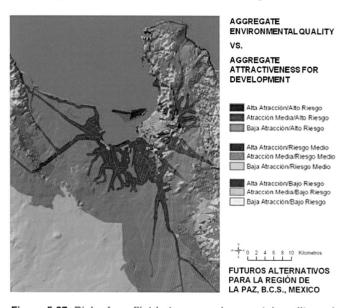

Figure 5.27: **Risk of conflict between environmental quality and development, the region of La Paz, Mexico. Areas in red are likely to be developed at a low-to-moderate environmental cost. Areas in green are under less or no pressure for development and are therefore likely to be protected, even if passively. Areas in dark brown are at greatest environmental risk.** | Source: La Paz geodesign team.

models and their purposes. Evaluative criteria and their relative importance are not universal, but vary substantially depending upon the geography and culture within which they are derived. As an obvious example, the words "tall building" and "crowded" have very different meanings in Hong Kong than in Phoenix, Arizona. They also depend upon the size and scale of the geography being evaluated.

I will share here two examples, both from similar geographic contexts, that illustrate the influence of purpose, size and scale. The architect Frank Lloyd Wright (1867–1959), when discussing the design of his famous house Fallingwater, built in the late 1930s in western Pennsylvania, (figure 5.29), said "There in a beautiful forest was a solid, high rock ledge rising beside a waterfall, and the natural thing seemed to be to cantilever the house from that rock bank over the falling water."[17]

In contrast, the landscape architect/planner Philip H. Lewis Jr., when assessing the entire state of Wisconsin for potential state parks, identified the landscape corridors of water and

Figure 5.29: **Fallingwater, a house built during 1936–1939 in western Pennsylvania, by Frank Lloyd Wright, architect.** | Photo by Tess Canfield.

Figures 5.28: **Balandra Bay.** | Photo by Tess Canfield.

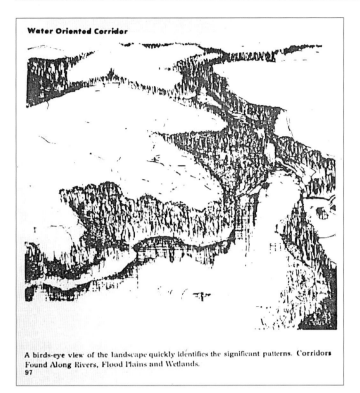

**Water Oriented Corridor**

A birds-eye view of the landscape quickly identifies the significant patterns. Corridors Found Along Rivers, Flood Plains and Wetlands.
97

**Figure 5.30: Philip H. Lewis Jr. identified steep, rocky, riparian areas as significant landscape patterns in Wisconsin most valuable for conservation.** | Source: Philip H. Lewis Jr., *Tomorrow by Design: A Regional Design Process for Sustainability* (New York: Wiley, 1996).

steep, rocky, and forested riparian areas as having the highest priority for statewide conservation (figure 5.30).[18]

Each of these distinguished design professionals was looking at similar landscape features in similar regional landscapes, but at different sizes and scales, for different purposes and in a contrasting way. Wright assessed attractiveness for building while Philip Lewis evaluated environmental vulnerabilities for conservation. Each drew an opposite conclusion, and each may have been right.

# Process models

Process models are required by the decision models to assess the impacts of proposed changes (figure 5.31). The information needs of different decision models and their consequent impact, change, and evaluation models require an understanding of the processes involved in geographic change. Understanding these processes leads directly to the identification of the characteristics of the data *needed* for a geodesign study and the appropriate mode(s) of representation.

**Question 2.** Questions for process models as they relate to and are linked with impact models include the following:
- Which models should be included?
- How complex should the models be?
- How shall the impacts be summarized and visualized?
- Which processes models are beyond the modeling capabilities of the geodesign team?

## Process model requirements

Every process model shares certain characteristics, whether expressed implicitly or explicitly. According to the urban systems modeler Ira S. Lowry, these include a philosophy, a theory, a general form, specifics, and data.[19] All of these have a place on a continuum of transferability to other geographic study areas. The philosophy and theory are the most generalizable, and the specifics and data are the least. Lowry also distinguishes between the theorist and the modeler (a distinction that to some extent also distinguishes geographic scientists and the design professionals). The theorist seeks logical coherence, generality, and cause-effect relationships. The modeler seeks an empirically relevant model that can be applied to the case under consideration. The modeler seeks descriptive generalizations that frequently lack explicit causal structure and are often achieved under constraints of data, cost, timeliness and the need for answers.

Process models for geodesign are most frequently derived from the geographic sciences. Since these are often associated with specialized and distinct academic and professional institutions and fields, it is not surprising that when a geodesign study requires assessments from a diverse set of process models, they are seen as separate and nonoverlapping. Yet we have been aware for a very long time that processes are inexorably linked to each other and that a change in one causes

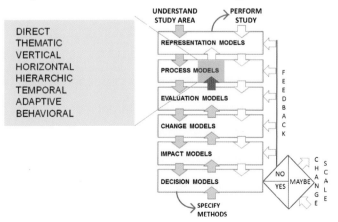

**Figure 5.31: Process models. These are based on the need for impact models.** | Source: Carl Steinitz.

consequent changes in many others. In 1930, the geologist-geographers C. C. Fagg (1883–1965) and G. E. Hutchings (1900–1964) published *An Introduction to Regional Surveying*, one of the first textbooks on how to make regional landscape plans.[20] Their central idea was the recognition that landscapes are interrelated systems, with complex elements that are connected to each other, as shown in figure 5.32.

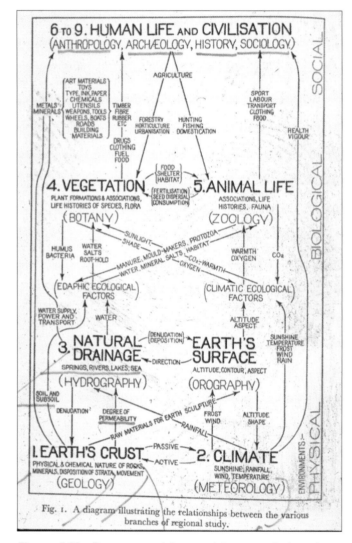

Fig. i. A diagram illustrating the relationships between the various branches of regional study.

**Figure 5.32: Process models are interconnected systems.** | Source: C. C. Fagg and G. E. Hutchings, *An Introduction to Regional Surveying* (Cambridge, UK: The University Press, 1930).

The need to incorporate interacting process models presents an opportunity and also a challenge for the geodesign team. If several processes are included in a geodesign study (and this is usually the case), and a sequence of computer programs representing the processes must be linked, we create a "chicken and egg" problem. Which process models come first? Resolution of this sequence becomes more important as the time-frame of the study becomes longer. In my experience, there are at least three solutions:

1. Keep them separate, which is a common solution when the geodesign team is functioning as a group of independent specialists. It is the easiest, but likely the least accurate response. For an example, see the Camp Pendleton study in chapter 7.

2. Link them into "chains" so that one model's output becomes the input into one or more other models. The sequence requires both a theoretically valid basis and a close collaboration for the design of models that I encourage in the framework. See the La Paz study in chapter 9.

3. Link them via immediate feedback loops in behavioral models based on cellular automaton and other agent-based modeling types. This also requires a theoretically valid basis, but also intensive computing capacity. See the Idyllwild study in chapter 9.

## Process model complexity[21]

The need for reliably predictable impact models leads to the need for appropriate levels of spatial-analytic complexity of the process models. I believe that there are eight levels of increasing spatial complexity associated with impact and process models (figure 5.33). Each of the eight levels *cumulates*, which means it also answers the questions at prior levels, resulting in a cumulatively more complex process model. The answers are the analytic capabilities of the model type. I think that the larger the size of the geodesign study, and the likely larger resulting risk, the more the analytic methods should aim to achieve more complex levels of understanding and predictability. By contrast, simpler analytic levels may suffice when projects are smaller and the corresponding risks may be fewer and slighter in magnitude. In the section below, I will review each of these eight different levels of complexity in turn.

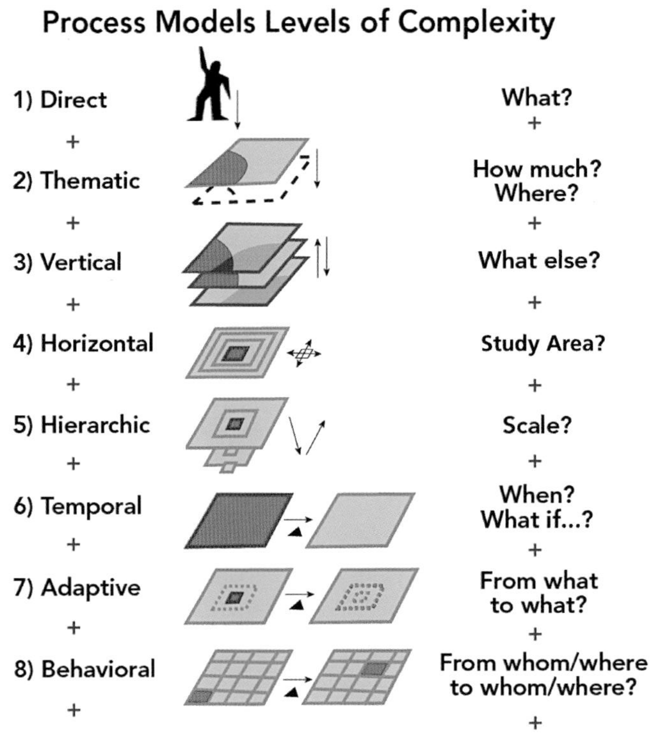

## Process Models Levels of Complexity

1) Direct                                  What?
   +                                          +
2) Thematic                              How much?
                                            Where?
   +                                          +
3) Vertical                              What else?
   +                                          +
4) Horizontal                           Study Area?
   +                                          +
5) Hierarchic                             Scale?
   +                                          +
6) Temporal                               When?
                                          What if...?
   +                                          +
7) Adaptive                             From what
                                          to what?
   +                                          +
8) Behavioral                         From whom/where
                                       to whom/where?
   +                                          +

**Figure 5.33:** Eight levels of process model complexity. | Source: Carl Steinitz.

To summarize the numbered points from figure 5.33 above:

1. **Direct process models** are based on direct personal experience and ask "What is going on here?" For example, if you are standing below an avalanche zone in the Telluride region of Colorado, the lesson is clear: Don't build here! (figure 5.34).

   Direct models become more reliable as they encompass the wisdom gained from a longer history of personal experiences. Patrick Geddes (1854–1932) was a biologist, sociologist, philosopher, educator, and city planner. He traveled and practiced city planning in a number of different countries, notably in India, the former Palestine, and in his native Scotland. As an evolutionist and a global thinker, he was interested in the interrelationships among people, their activities, and their environment. Geddes' Valley Section diagram,[22] a redrawn version of which is shown in figure 5.35 below, expresses his direct experience in observing timeless relationships that are visible everywhere. It begins in

Direct: What?

**Figure 5.34:** Avalanche zone, Telluride region, Colorado, a bad building site. | Photo by Tess Canfield.

Direct: What?

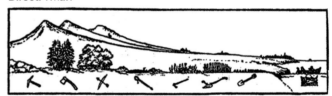

Valley section, with typical vegetation and characteristic regional occupations.

MINER   WOODMAN   HUNTER   SHEPHERD        PEASANT      GARDENER        FISHER
                                         (VILLAGE     TOWN      CITY)

**Figure 5.35:** The Valley Section of Patrick Geddes. | Source: V. Brandford and P. Geddes. *The Coming Polity: A Study in Reconstruction.* London: Williams and Norgate, 1917.

the mountains and extends to the coast. At the highest elevations in the mountains, it is natural and usual to find miners; in less high areas to find forests and woodsmen; lower to find hunters and shepherds; still lower, peasant farmers and gardeners; and finally, along the shore, cities, and in the waters, fishermen. Failure to respect these long-standing human-landscape interrelationships either doesn't work or requires too much energy and too high a risk, and ultimately will not be sustainable. The Geddes Valley Section can be seen as a model of good practice for geodesign.

2. **Thematic process models** are shown in the most common form of thematic map, very often by implication. Such maps identify "what" and "where," and if there is a histogram, "how much." Data such as shown on traditional topographic maps are useful for interpreting several process models such as water flows, microclimate, and the history of the development pattern. Thematic maps produced by the US Geological Survey (and their equivalent in other countries) are probably the most easily acquired land map, and they are especially useful in the scoping iteration of the framework , and for smaller geodesign projects. Figure 5.36 shows a portion of a thematic 1:24,000 scale USGS map of Petersham, Massachusetts, USA. While two-dimensional planimetric maps like the USGS topographic maps are very helpful for identifying thematic regions in the study area, the addition of additional quantitative thematic information can be very helpful as well. Sometimes this kind of information is displayed in three dimensions, allowing map readers to more readily evaluate and compare the data across the geodesign study space.

Direct: What?                                    Thematic: How much? Where?

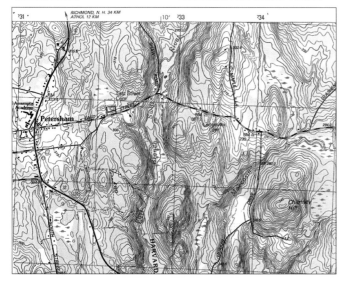

**Figure 5.36: A section of a 1:24,000 USGS topographic map of Petersham, Massachusetts, USA. Maps similar to these are available for most regions in the world.** | Source: United States Geological Survey.

3. **Vertical process models** add or infer overlain data and ask "What else is below or above and how do they combine?" They are, accordingly, frequently represented vertically. In the 1920s and 1930s, when modern regional planning began as a profession, courses were designed and delivered to train the people who were responsible for the bureaucracy of planning. A classic book from around that time is *Regional Planning: An outline of the scientific data related to planning in Great Britain* by L. B. Escritt (1902–1973), first published in 1943 and only about one centimeter thick.[23] In 1947, after electing a socialist government, Great Britain nationalized planning control of all its land. They quickly implemented a very good planning system because they used relatively simple and effective methods, together with textbooks, to teach the new planners (the organizers of the

Direct: What?

Thematic: How much? Where?              Vertical: What else?

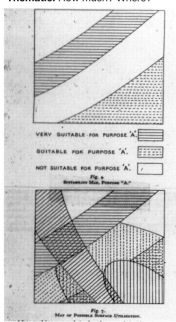 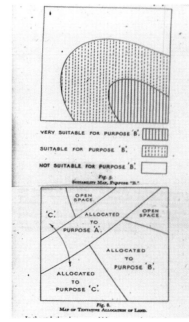

**Figure 5.37: Graphic overlay method, from Escritt.** | Source: L. B. Escritt, *Regional Planning: An Outline of the Scientific Data Relating to Planning in the United Kingdom* (London: George Allen & Unwin, 1943).

geodesign teams of their time). It included a section on how to make graphic vertical models by overlaying maps related to evaluation criteria in Boolean logic, and how to use them to analyze areas for particular purposes (figure 5.37).

4. **Horizontal process models** add spatial analyses and ask such questions as "What distance, size, shape or pattern, etc., do we seek/want/need here?" As an example, Sullivan and Schaeffer (1975) were studying faunal preserves and established priority rules for the shape of conservation areas (figure 5.38).[24] They prescribed that it would be better for a faunal preserve to be large, or have one single one that is medium sized instead of many that are smaller, and be compact rather than spread out, etc.

The horizontal process models of Kevin Lynch (1918–1984) and Richard Forman and Michel Godron are two of the most influential ones for geodesign. Lynch, an urban planner and theorist who was also my teacher and mentor, believed that designers should understand and consider the way ordinary people perceive their environment before proposing changes. He wrote many books on many topics, but his most significant work is *The Image of the City.*[25] For the first time, verbal and mapping interviews were analyzed to learn how ordinary people perceive and understand a city. These were described and explained in a horizontal process model. Lynch believed that design could make the city more understandable. He assumed that a good city form should have an imageable form which is not imposed by designers and planners, but derives from the perceptions of the people who use the place.

In 1986, ecologists Richard Forman and Michael Godron wrote a very influential book titled *Landscape Ecology,* which is also organized around an horizontal process model.[26] Today, landscape ecology is a growing academic and professional field that helps us understand the effects of past and potential change by looking at the spatial structure of landscapes in ecological terms. Lynch, and Forman and Godron suggested horizontally spatial, structuring models with many similarities, though they used different terms (figure 5.39).

**Direct:** What?                                 **Vertical:** What else?
**Thematic:** How much? Where?      **Horizontal:** What context?

## PRINCIPLES FOR THE DESIGN OF FAUNAL PRESERVES

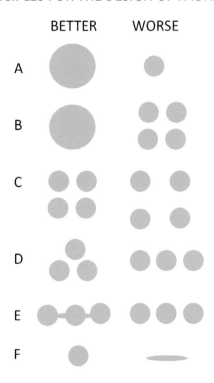

**Figure 5.38: Principles for the design of faunal preserves.** | Source: Carl Steinitz after A. L. Sullivan, and M. L. Shaffer, "Biogeography of the Megazoo," *Science* 189 (1975):13–17. Copyright ©1975, American Association for the Advancement of Science.

**Direct:** What?                                 **Vertical:** What else?
**Thematic:** How much? Where?      **Horizontal:** What context?

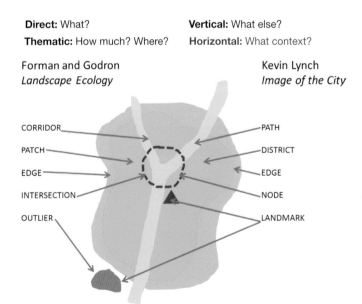

**Figure 5.39: The horizontally spatial models of Lynch, and Forman and Godron.** | Source: Carl Steinitz, based upon original ideas of Lynch, and Forman and Godron.

5. **Hierarchic process models** ask: "What happens at different 'nested' scales?" As an example, Virginia Dale and H. Michael Rauscher, ecological scientists at Oak Ridge National Laboratory, noted how different modeled processes interact across spatial and time scales ranging from a regional landscape to 1/10 hectare, and from centuries to a week (figure 5.40). Using these hierarchical relationships, they investigated different phenomena related to aphid infestation in the southeastern USA pine forests (figure 5.41). [27] They modeled and linked the relevant ecological processes at their appropriate spatial scales and time frames.

**Direct:** What?                          **Vertical:** What else?

**Thematic:** How much? Where?    **Horizontal:** What context?        **Hierarchic:** What scale(s)?

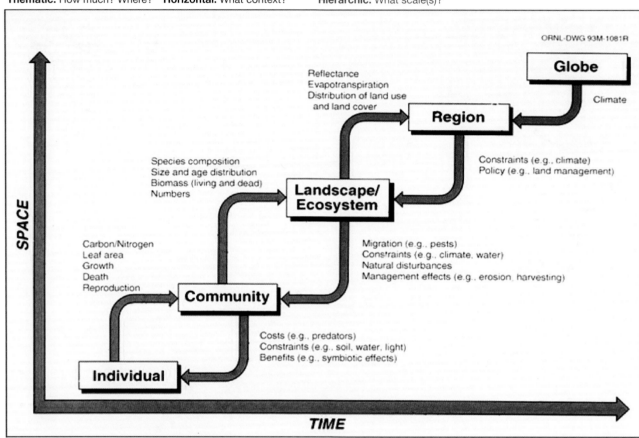

**Figure 5.40: Process models at different space and time scales related to aphid infestations.** | Source: V. H. Dale and H. M. Rauscher, "Assessing Impacts of Climate Change on Forests: The State of Biological Modeling," *Climatic Change* 28 (1994):65–90.

Direct: What?          Vertical: What else?
Thematic: How much? Where?    Horizontal: What context?    Hierarchic: What scale(s)?

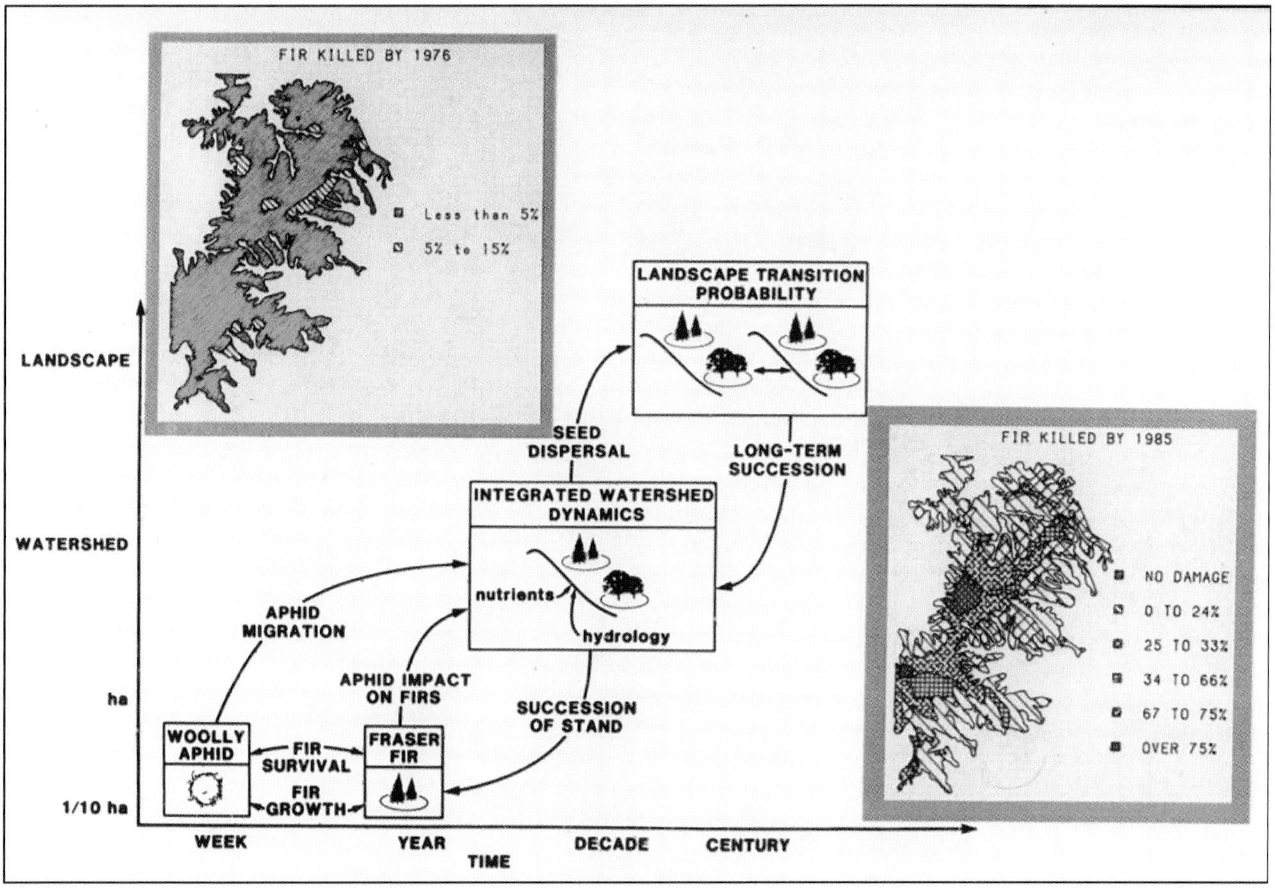

**Figure 5.41: Process models at different space and time scales related to aphid infestations.** | Source: V. H. Dale and H. M. Rauscher, "Assessing Impacts of Climate Change on Forests: The State of Biological Modeling," *Climatic Change* 28 (1994):65–90.

6. **Temporal process models** add the question "At what time are we considering the landscape?" They introduce the dynamics of landscape change into the processes of assessment and design. In one of the case studies profiled in chapter 9, we compared potential habitat for the Gunnison Sage Grouse in 2008 and that which is projected for 2030 under conditions of high growth, current regulations, and a fully developed extractive mineral industry in the Telluride region of Colorado, USA (figure 5.42). [28]

**Direct:** What?              **Vertical:** What else?        **Hierarchic:** What scale(s)?
**Thematic:** How much? Where?   **Horizontal:** What context?   **Temporal:** When? What if...?

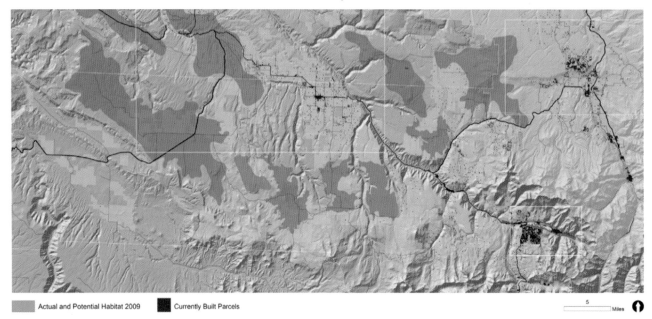

Actual and Potential Habitat 2009     Currently Built Parcels                    5 Miles

## Potential Habitat, Gunnison Sage Grouse, 2008

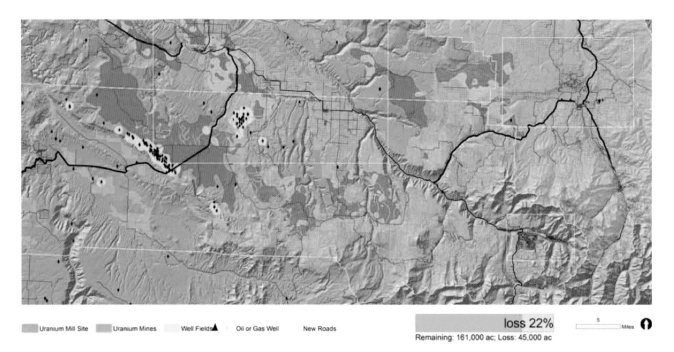

Uranium Mill Site     Uranium Mines     Well Fields     Oil or Gas Well     New Roads        loss 22%     5 Miles
                                                                                    Remaining: 161,000 ac; Loss: 45,000 ac

## Potential Habitat, Gunnison Sage Grouse, Scenario #9. Telluride Region, CO

**Figure 5.42:** Change in potential habitat, Gunnison Sage Grouse, 2008 to 2030. The temporal process models used in this study are described in chapter 9. | Source: Telluride geodesign team.

7. **Adaptive process models** take a more complex but also a more predictable attitude toward the dynamics of landscape change. They ask: "From what and where to what and where?" They are typically based upon long-observed stages of transformation, and are common in the ecological and geographic sciences. Models of plant succession are an example.

Adaptive models have also been developed for cities and other human activities. Architect and planner Russell A. Smith designed an eight-stage model of the transformation of tropical beach resorts in Southeast Asia (figure 5.43). [29] His model shows the sequence of stages as they adapt from free camping on an open beach to a fully developed resort city that has significant problems.

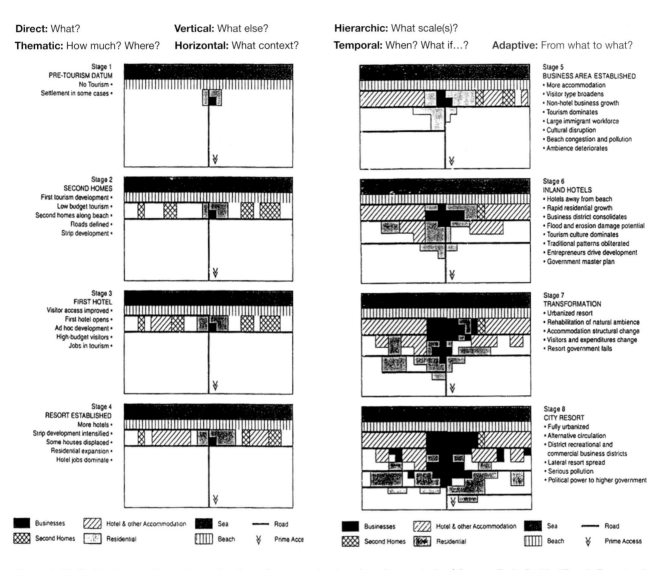

**Figure 5.43: Eight stages of transformation from free camping to a beach resort city.** | Source: R. A. Smith, "Beach Resorts: A Model of Development Evolution." *Landscape and Urban Planning* 21, no. 3 (1991): 189-210.

8. **Behavioral process models** add the complexity of understanding "From whom doing what, where, and when, to whom doing what, where and when?" Behavioral models have been applied to study the growth of several phenomena, including fire and cities. Figure 5.44 shows the progression of a single fire from landscape planner Michael Flaxman's agent-based fire model, which accounts for the behavior of fire and fire management strategies of homeowners in the region of Idyllwild, California. It is a case study in chapter 9.

Behavioral models have also been applied to study the growth of cities. In 2008, geographer and planner Michael Batty conducted a research study titled *Generating Cities from the Bottom-Up: Using Complexity Theory for Effective Design* [30] in which he used agent-based models to study urban growth patterns (figure 5.45).

**Direct:** What?    **Hierarchic:** What scale(s)?
**Thematic:** How much? Where?    **Temporal:** When? What if…?
**Vertical:** What else?    **Adaptive:** From what to what?
**Horizontal:** What context?    **Behavioral:** From what and where to what and where?

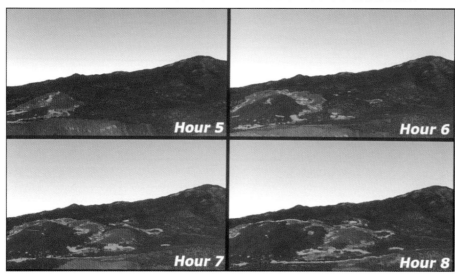

**Figure 5.44: Fire moving over the landscape.** | Source: M. Flaxman, "Multi-scale Fire Hazard Assessment for Wildland Urban Interface Areas: An Alternative Futures Approach" (D. Des. diss., Graduate School of Design, Harvard University, 2001).

**Direct:** What?    **Hierarchic:** What scale(s)?
**Thematic:** How much? Where?    **Temporal:** When? What if…?
**Vertical:** What else?    **Adaptive:** From what to what?
**Horizontal:** What context?    **Behavioral:** From what and where to what and where?

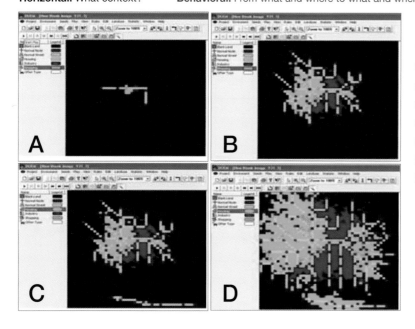

**Figure 5.45: Urban growth moving toward a new road. This begins with a small village on a small road (A). The village continues to grow (B), a new bypass road is constructed nearby (C), and continued growth moves toward the road (D).** | Source: M. Batty. "Generating Cities from the Bottom-Up: Using Complexity Theory for Effective Design." *Cluster* 7 (2008): 150–61.

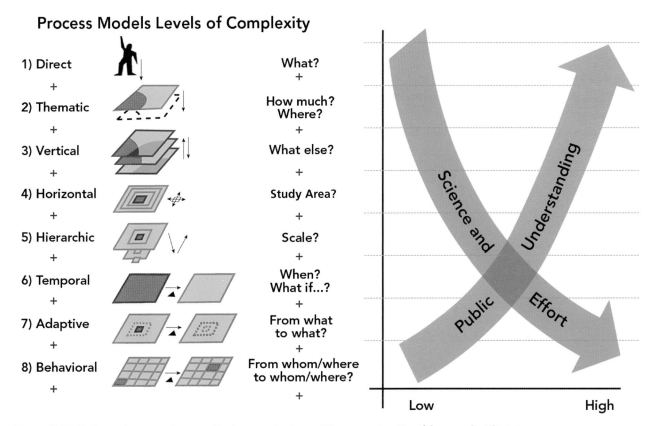

**Process Models Levels of Complexity**

1) Direct
+
2) Thematic
+
3) Vertical
+
4) Horizontal
+
5) Hierarchic
+
6) Temporal
+
7) Adaptive
+
8) Behavioral
+

What?
+
How much?
Where?
+
What else?
+
Study Area?
+
Scale?
+
When?
What if...?
+
From what
to what?
+
From whom/where
to whom/where?
+

Low                                    High

**Figure 5.46: Better science and more effort versus better public understanding.** | Source: Carl Steinitz.

As process models increase in their levels of complexity, we experience a corresponding communication challenge. Models of greater complexity require more (and presumably better) science and more effort, but the simpler levels are easier to describe and explain, and easier for the general public and decision makers to understand (figure 5.46). One must either compromise the analytic complexity or (preferably) simplify communication to an audience increasingly interested in "transparency." As Albert Einstein said, "Everything should be as simple as it is, but not simpler."[31]

## Representation models

During this second iteration through the framework, the geodesign study should be organized and specified to identify the *minimum* amount of data actually needed for the study. The aim then is to acquire, organize, and use *only those data*, avoiding the expense and effort of gathering and preparing any data unnecessary for the study. For this to occur, specifying the preceding decision, impact, change, evaluation and process models must happen first. In addition, the representation model and

its visualization methods must also consider how change will be visualized.

There is no such thing as an all-purpose, all scales, all sizes, all geographies data base. The geodesign team should expect that some data will be shared by multiple models and some may be unique to one. Some data will be easily available and some will not. This inevitably will require choices and prioritized decisions that may have potential consequences for certain models.

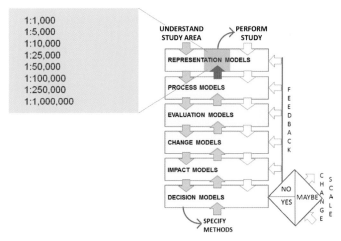

**Figure 5.47: Representation models.** | Source: Carl Steinitz.

**Question 1.** Questions related to representation models include the following:

- Which data are needed? For which geography? At what spatial scale? At which classification? For which times? From which sources? At which cost? In which mode of representation?
- What are the appropriate data management technologies?
- What are the appropriate visualization technologies?

The spatial scale of a representation model is especially important. It implies the lens through which the geodesign team is thinking about the problem and geography at hand. As a general rule, a closer lens requires and allows for more complex classification and spatial visualization of data from any category. Figure 5.48 shows air photos of Beijing and Phoenix originally at 1:200,000, 1:25,000 and 1:5,000 scales.

## Identifying data needs

Herbert Simon was correct when he wrote,

> *"… in an information-rich world, the wealth of information means a dearth of something else: a scarcity of whatever it is that information consumes. What information consumes is rather obvious: it consumes the attention of its recipients. Hence a wealth of information creates a poverty of attention and a need to allocate that attention efficiently among the overabundance of information sources that might consume it."* [32]

If we begin with the assumption that the representation models (the data) will in fact be shared among the collaborating members of the geodesign team, then all members of the team must participate in defining the data needs. For each

**Beijing, China**

**Phoenix, Arizona**

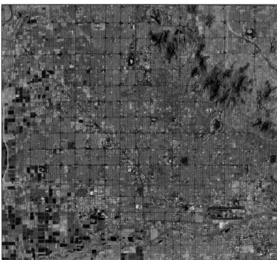

**Figure 5.48: Size and scale matter, as can be seen in these air photos of Beijing, China (above) and Phoenix, Arizona, USA (below), at three different scales.** | Source: Pho: 1:5000, Pho: 1:200000, Bei: 1:200000 courtesy of i-cubed, information integration & imagine, LLC - distributed through i-cubed's DataDoors Archive Management www.datadoors.net; Bei: 1:5000, Bei: 1:25000, Pho: 1:25000 courtesy of GeoEye Satellite Imagery.

component model in the entire framework, someone must take the responsibility to produce a "needs list," calibrated to the level of model complexity previously decided upon. Scale will again be a central concern, as different scales provide different lenses to look at the geographic study area. Scale will imply content, and it should not be assumed that data, and especially its internal classification, will scale up and down easily.

As a starting point, I have found that the simple technique of first listing each data type needed for each model on a separate, small (and old-fashioned) paper card works very well as a starting point. The card should contain the model and team identification, the role of the data in the relevant criterion and how it may be used, the required scale(s) and classification(s) of

the data for the criterion, and the relative importance of having the data. As a second step, we transfer the hand-written card information to a large spreadsheet that describes each model in a row and its data requirements in a series of columns coordinated by data type (figure 5.49). This way, common interest in data to be shared across models can also be identified.

Each model and the reason(s) for its data needs are then presented at a meeting of the entire geodesign team as an argument for data acquisition and inclusion. When prioritized, the spreadsheet format can be organized for data and metadata acquisition and management throughout the course of the geodesign study.

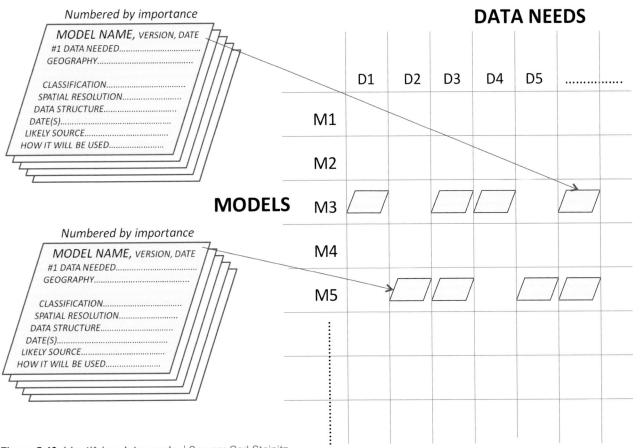

**Figure 5.49: Identifying data needs.** | Source: Carl Steinitz.

# Choices must be made

The scope of the geodesign study had been determined during the first iteration of the framework, and in the second iteration, each component model is defined and operationally specified. The geodesign team must choose the geodesign methods and tools "tightly" to fit the circumstances. This requires six major sets of choices, and in the order of questions 6 to 1 as shown by the green arrows in the example in figure 5.50. In the imagined example in figure 5.50, a large automobile company intends to build a major assembly factory and has asked the geodesign team to conduct a study that identifies a building site and generates a 20-year-plan for its development. Part of the plan must be to consider the impacts of the new factory and its associated projected employment and secondary industry on the municipality and region within which the factory will be located.

With all of these possible options, making wise choices about the models during the second iteration is crucial for the geodesign study to be efficient, and these choices, summarized lower, take place in the ordered sequence of decision models through representation models.

6. Decision models establish their needs for information from impact models and their implications for evaluation models,

5. *therefore* the content and complexity of impact models establish specifications for process models,

4. *therefore* the several ways of designing from which we must chose have implications on how the geographic study area should be represented,

3. *therefore* the evaluation models are specified,

2. *therefore* the process models are specified, and

1. *therefore* the representation models, the data needs, and the ways of information management and visualization can be identified.

These choices organize the specific geodesign strategies. When taken all together, these are the methodology for the particular geodesign application that will help to decide the future of the geographical study area in which we are working.

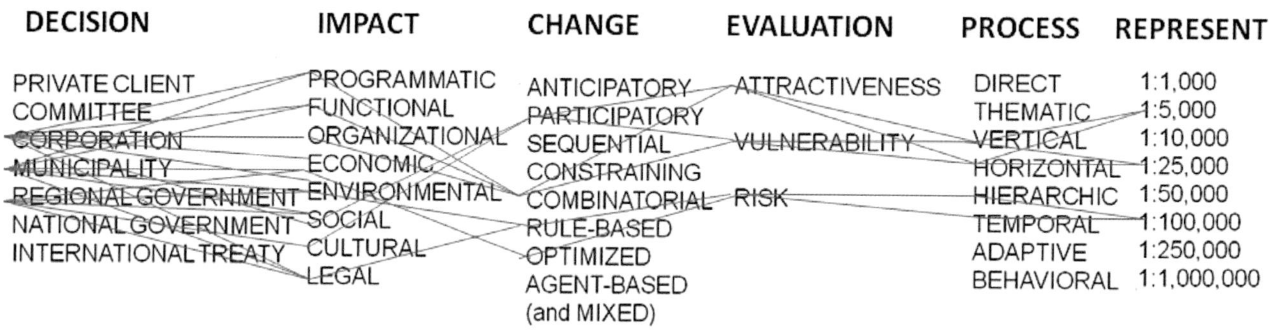

| DECISION | IMPACT | CHANGE | EVALUATION | PROCESS | REPRESENT |
|---|---|---|---|---|---|
| PRIVATE CLIENT | PROGRAMMATIC | ANTICIPATORY | ATTRACTIVENESS | DIRECT | 1:1,000 |
| COMMITTEE | FUNCTIONAL | PARTICIPATORY | | THEMATIC | 1:5,000 |
| CORPORATION | ORGANIZATIONAL | SEQUENTIAL | VULNERABILITY | VERTICAL | 1:10,000 |
| MUNICIPALITY | ECONOMIC | CONSTRAINING | | HORIZONTAL | 1:25,000 |
| REGIONAL GOVERNMENT | ENVIRONMENTAL | COMBINATORIAL | RISK | HIERARCHIC | 1:50,000 |
| NATIONAL GOVERNMENT | SOCIAL | RULE-BASED | | TEMPORAL | 1:100,000 |
| INTERNATIONAL TREATY | CULTURAL | OPTIMIZED | | ADAPTIVE | 1:250,000 |
| | LEGAL | AGENT-BASED | | BEHAVIORAL | 1:1,000,000 |
| | | (and MIXED) | | | |

**Figure 5.50:** Choices made in the second iteration will shape the study methods. Note that even with the simplified set of choices and options in figure 5.50 which we have already listed in discussing each of the framework's models, there are potentially more than *two trillion* combinations. No two geodesign studies will ever be identical. | Source: Carl Steinitz.

There is a politic to the choices and specifications of models that cannot be avoided and which must be managed within the social contract among the collaborators and the requirements of each study. It may seem simple and out-dated in this age of distributed computing and videoconferencing, but for many of the second iteration meetings in which I have participated and in which geodesign studies have been designed and specified, I have found no better way than when all participants meet in one large room, "face to face," and no one leaves until there is general agreement on how to carry out the geodesign study. During this phase, all members of the geodesign team must collaborate in designing the geodesign methodology in order to ensure that all information is efficiently linked and transferred among the project's many participants.

I typically conduct such meetings in a large room with considerable display and writing space. Every participant will need an overview of the whole approach, and even more important, knowledge of his or her role, expectations, tasks, and personal and technical relationships within the study and to other members of the geodesign team. I have found it very useful to make one large master chart which can accommodate the diagrams and specifications for each of the elements of the study. An example is shown in figure 5.51. Once the methods have been decided, a chart such as this can be reorganized as a spreadsheet, and each box can be made a hyperlink to the further implementation of the study design in the third iteration of the framework.

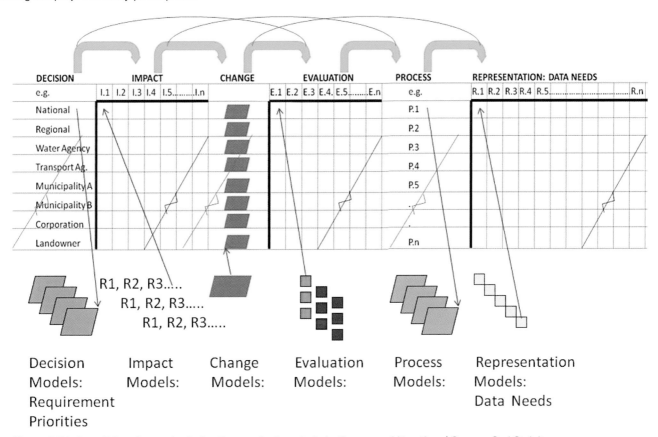

**Figure 5.51: Specifying the methods for the geodesign study in the second iteration.** | Source: Carl Steinitz.

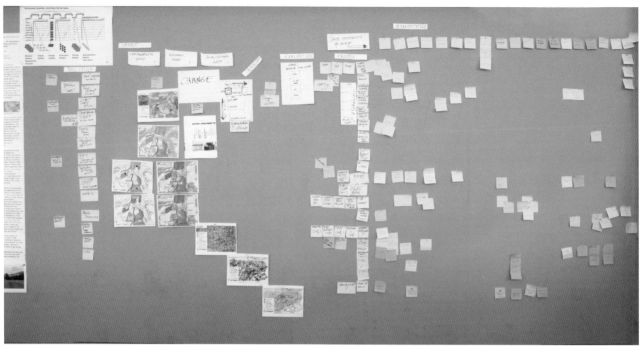

| Decision | Impact | Change | Evaluation | Process | Representation |
|----------|--------|--------|------------|---------|----------------|
| Models: | Models: | Models: | Models: | Models: | Models: |
| | Requirement | | | | Data Needs |
| | Priorities | | | | |

**Figure 5.52:** In practice, an informal and flexible chart used for recording the discussion in the second iteration of the framework can be very useful. | Photo by Brian Orland.

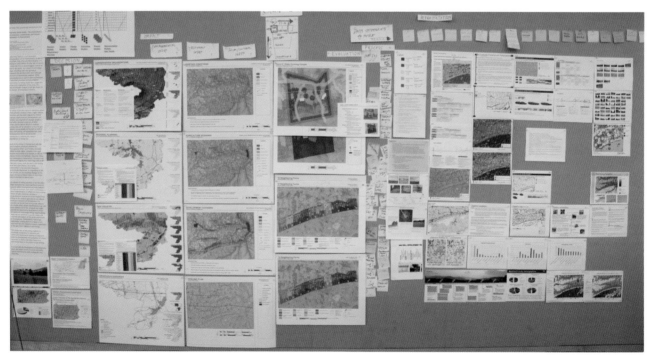

| Decision | Impact | Change | Evaluation | Process | Representation |
|----------|--------|--------|------------|---------|----------------|
| Models: | Models: | Models: | Models: | Models: | Models: |
| | Requirement | | | | Data Needs |
| | Priorities | | | | |

**Figure 5.53:** Some initial experiments and tests. | Photo by Brian Orland.

This meeting frequently results in a document-of-understanding, information that may also generate a time schedule and financial budget if the study is part of a professional or research contract funding proposal. Such a document aids the management of the subsequent geodesign activities.

In practice, and when meeting face-to-face with a group, a more informal and flexibly organized and managed chart can also work very well. Figure 5.52 is an example from a recent study that I helped organize at the Pennsylvania State University.[33] A team of faculty and students were beginning a study of the impacts of shale gas exploration and exploitation in the Marcellus Shale area of Bradford County, Pennsylvania. The large tack board shown in this figure reflects the status of the project's methodology after a scoping-orientation at the end of the first week. It is the product of several long and intense discussions among the many study participants.

In the subsequent three weeks, the specifications reflected in figure were altered several times. The tack board itself became a management tool, as initial products of experiments and tests of the methods replace the specifications (figure 5.53).

Soon after this point in the framework, the geodesign team should meet with the stakeholders and present its proposed approach, in the style of, "This is how we understand your situation and this is what we propose to do…."

## Notes

1. S. K. Williams, "Process and Meaning in Design Decision-making," in *Design + Values,* (1992 Council of Educators in Landscape Architecture Conference Proceedings, edited by Elissa Rosenberg, Landscape Architecture Foundation/Council of Educators in Landscape Architecture. 1993), 199–204.; Williams summary from Lawrence Kohlberg, *The Philosophy of Moral Development* (New York: Harper & Row, 1981).

2. Thucydides, "Pericles' Funeral Oration," in *History of the Peloponnesian War* (New York: Penguin Books, 1954), 147.

3. Zipf's law is named after the Harvard linguistics professor George Kingsley Zipf (1902—1950), who first proposed it in *The Psychobiology of Language* (Houghton-Mifflin, 1935). Zipf's law occurs when a power law relationship exists in which the frequency or size of a phenomenon is inversely proportional to its rank in a frequency table. The same power law relationship occurs in many other rankings, unrelated to language word frequency, such as the population ranks of cities in various countries, corporation sizes, income rankings, earthquake magnitudes, etc. A power-law implies that large instances are extremely rare while small occurrences are extremely common. From L. A. Adamic, *Zipf, Power-laws, and Pareto—A Ranking Tutorial* (Palo Alto, CA: Information Dynamics Lab, Hewlett Packard Labs, date unknown), original citation G. K. Zipf, *The Psychobiology of Language* (Boston: Houghton-Mifflin, 1935).

4. US Department of Energy, Western Area Power Administration, "Quartzite Solar Energy Project EIS," (Scoping Summary Report, Western Area Power Administration, Phoenix, Arizona, 2010.)

5. Richard Toth first shared these very useful ideas (and others) with me in the late 1960s. They are in two of his unpublished teaching papers, "An Approach to Principles of Landscape Planning and Design" (1972) and "A Planning and Design Methodology" (1974), and they are summarized in R. Toth, "Theory and Language in Landscape Analysis, Planning and Evaluation," *Landscape Ecology,* 1 no. 4 (1988): 193–201.

6. Repton, H., (1752-1818) *Observations on the Theory and Practice of Landscape Gardening : including some remarks on Grecian and Gothic architecture, collected from various manuscripts, in the possession of the different noblemen and gentlemen, for whose use they were originally written; the whole tending to establish fixed principles in the respective arts* : London : Printed by T. Bensley for J. Taylor, 1805. Cite properly?

7. C. Steinitz, M. Binford, P. Cote, T. Edwards, Jr. ,S. Ervin, R. T. T. Forman, C. Johnson, R. Kiester, D. Mouat, D. Olson, A. Shearer, R. Toth, and R. Wills, *Landscape Planning for Biodiversity; Alternative Futures for the Region of Camp Pendleton, CA.* (Cambridge, MA: Graduate School of Design, Harvard University, 1996), and C. W. Adams and C. Steinitz, "An Alternative Future for the Region of Camp Pendleton, CA," in *Landscape Perspectives of Land Use Changes,* eds. U. Mander and R. H. G. Jongman, Advances in Ecological Sciences 6. (Southampton, UK:WIT Press, 2000), 18–83.

8. J. C. Vargas-Moreno, "Participatory Landscape Planning Using Portable Geospatial Information Systems and Technologies: The Case of the Osa Region of Costa Rica" (D. Des. diss., Graduate School of Design, Harvard University, 2008.)

9.  C. Steinitz, ed. 1986. *Alternative Futures for The Bermuda Dump*. (Cambridge, MA: Graduate School of Design, Harvard University, 1986), and Bermuda, Department of Planning, *The Pembroke Marsh Plan 1987* (Bermuda: Department of Planning, Government of Bermuda, 1987).

10. C. Steinitz, L. Cipriani, J. C. Vargas-Moreno, T. Canfield. *Padova e il Paesaggio-Scenarui Futuri peri I Parco Roncajette e la Zona Industriale / Padova and the Landscape - Alternative Futures for the Roncajette Park and the Industrial Zone* (Cambridge, MA: Graduate School of Design, Harvard University, Commune de Padova and Zona Industriale Padova, 2005.

11. C. Steinitz, C. "Teaching in a Multidisciplinary Collaborative Workshop Format: The Cagliari Workshop," in *FutureMAC09: Alternative Futures for the Metropolitan Area of Cagliari, The Cagliari Workshop: An Experiment in Interdisciplinary Education/FutureMAC09 : Scenari Alternativi per l'area Metropolitana di Cagliari, Workshop di Sperimentazione Didattica Interdisciplinare,* by C. Steinitz, E. Abis, V. von Haaren, C. Albert, D. Kempa, C. Palmas, S. Pili, and J. C. Vargas-Moreno (Roma: Gangemi, 2010).

12. C. Steinitz, R. Faris, M. Flaxman, J. C. Vargas-Moreno, G, Huang, S.-Y. Lu, T., Canfield, O. Arizpe, M. Angeles, M. Cariño, F. Santiago, T. Maddock III, C. Lambert, K. Baird, L. Godínez, *Futuros Alternativos para la Region de La Paz, Baja California Sur, Mexico/Alternative Futures for La Paz, BCS, Mexico.* (Mexico D. F., Mexico: Fundacion Mexicana para la Educación Ambiental, and International Community Foundation, 2006), and C. Steinitz, R. Faris, M. Flaxman, J. C. Vargas-Moreno, T. Canfield, O. Arizpe, M. Angeles, M. Carino, F. Santiago, and T. Maddock. "A Sustainable Path? Deciding the Future of La Paz," *Environment: Science and Policy for Sustainable Development* 47 (2005): 24–38.

13. M. Flaxman, C. Steinitz, R. Faris, T. Canfield, J. C. Vargas-Moreno, *Alternative Futures for the Telluride Region, Colorado*. Telluride, CO: Telluride Foundation, 2010).

14. M. Flaxman, M., "Multi-scale Fire Hazard Assessment for Wildland Urban Interface Areas: An Alternative Futures Approach" (D. Des. diss., Graduate School of Design, Harvard University, 2001.)

15. K. Stanilov. and M. Batty, "Exploring the Historical Determinants of Urban Growth Through Cellular Automata," *Transactions in GIS* 15, no. 3 (2011): 253–271.

16. C. Steinitz, R. Faris, M. Flaxman, J. C. Vargas-Moreno, T. Canfield, O. Arizpe, M. Angeles, M. Carino, F. Santiago, and T. Maddock, "A Sustainable Path? Deciding the Future of La Paz," *Environment: Science and Policy for Sustainable Development* 47 (2005): 24–38.

17. F. L. Wright "A Conversation with Frank Lloyd Wright," interview by Hugh Downs, "Wisdom", NBC News, recorded May 8, 1953.

18. Philip H. Lewis, Jr., *Tomorrow by Design: A Regional Design Process for Sustainability* (New York: Wiley, 1996).

19. Ira S. Lowry, "A Short Course in Model Design," *Journal of the American Institute of Planners* 31 (May 1965): 158–65.

20. C. C. Fagg and G. E. Hutchings, *An Introduction to Regional Surveying* (Cambridge, UK: The University Press, 1930).

21. Adapted from C. Steinitz, "On Scale and Complexity and the Need for Spatial Analysis," (Specialist Meeting on Spatial Concepts in GIS and Design, Santa, Barbara, California, December 15–16, 2008).

22. P. Geddes, *Cities in Evolution: An Introduction to the Town Planning Movement and to the Study of Civics* (London: Williams & Norgate, 1915).

23. L. B. Escritt, *Regional Planning: An Outline of the Scientific Data Relating to Planning in the United Kingdom* (London: George Allen & Unwin, 1943).

24. A. L. Sullivan, and M. L. Shaffer, "Biogeography of the Megazoo," *Science* 189 (1975):13–17.

25. K. Lynch, *The Image of the City* (Cambridge, MA: MIT Press, 1960).

26. R. T. T. Forman and M. Godron. *Landscape Ecology* (New York: Wiley, 1986).

27. V. H. Dale and H. M. Rauscher, "Assessing Impacts of Climate Change on Forests: The State of Biological Modeling," *Climatic Change* 28 (1994):65–90.

28. M. Flaxman, C. Steinitz, R. Faris, T. Canfield, and J. C. Vargas-Moreno, *Alternative Futures for the Telluride Region, Colorado* (Telluride, CO: Telluride Foundation, 2010).

29. R. A. Smith, "Beach Resorts: A Model of Development Evolution," *Landscape and Urban Planning* 21, no. 3 (1991): 189–210.

30. M. Batty, "Generating Cities from the Bottom-Up: Using Complexity Theory for Effective Design," *Cluster* 7 (2008): 150–61.

31. Quote attributed to Albert Einstein.

32. H. A. Simon, "Designing Organizations for an Information-Rich World," in *Computers, Communication, and the Public Interest,* by M. Greenburger. (Baltimore, MD: The Johns Hopkins Press, 1971).

33. The Pennsylvania State University, College of Arts and Architecture, Landscape Architecture 414, Depth Studio. Professors Brian Orland and C. Andrew Cole.

# CHAPTER 6

# The third iteration through the framework: Carrying out the study

FOR THE THIRD ITERATION of the geodesign framework, we return to the questions and models in numerical order, from 1 through 6. In this iteration these become the *WHAT, WHERE,* and *WHEN* questions, and their answers from the workflow of the geodesign methodology which was specified in the previous iteration are the products of geodesign.

The brevity of this chapter is disproportional to the amount of time the geodesign team would actually spend on carrying out the study in the framework's third iteration. There are two reasons for this. First, I reiterate that this is not a textbook on how to "do" geodesign. The process of implementing the methodology of a geodesign study is inevitably unique, specific to the members of the team in its situation and geographical study area. However, while methods and products cannot be copied, they can sometimes be adapted to fit other similar circumstances. For those seeking direction on this, I suggest consulting the large and always-expanding collection of technical literature that provides guidance and instruction for these many steps of a geodesign study. Second, when one is gaining experience, I believe that case studies and examples are more helpful and powerful than a prescription of technical rules, as these will always be changing. Therefore, the next section of this book, part III, will show how the geodesign framework has been applied in diverse case studies. Each of these will illustrate an application of the framework, but vary in their change models, which are the ways of designing.

## Questions 1 through 6 and implementing the models

In practice, it is during this third iteration of the framework when much of the project is carried out, and this phase can be a lengthy process. It is now that the data are gathered, organized, and represented in formats useful for the particular study's models and their purposes. We implement the process models so their output can be used by the evaluation models to assess the existing landscape. This creates a baseline from which to compare the predicted impacts of change. We prepare at least one or more designs to simulate future states. The effects of these can be assessed by impact models, and the geodesign team can then better understand the possible future consequences of the choices that they will later present to the stakeholders for review and decision (figure 6.1).

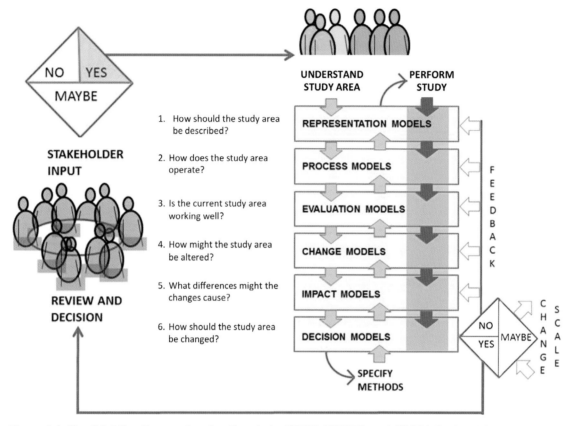

**Figure 6.1:** The third iteration, performing the study: *WHAT*, *WHERE*, and *WHEN*. During this iteration the framework questions are asked and the models are implemented and used in numerical order, preliminary decisions are made on whether to use feedback to revisit any of the models specified earlier, or to decide to change the scale or size of the project, or to proceed further to review and final decision making. | Source: Carl Steinitz.

The several models are implemented in the third iteration from 1 through 6 as follows:

### 1. Representation models

- Obtain the needed data.
- Organize them in an appropriate technology.
- Visualize the data over space and time.
- Organize them to be shared among the members geodesign team.

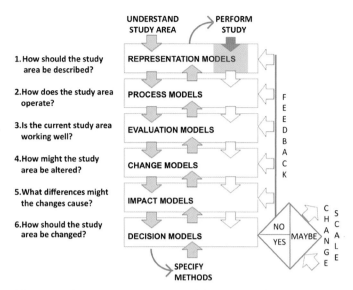

**Figure 6.2: Representation models.** | Source: Carl Steinitz.

### 2. Process models

- Implement, calibrate, and test the process models.
- Link them to each other as appropriate.
- Link them to the expected change models.

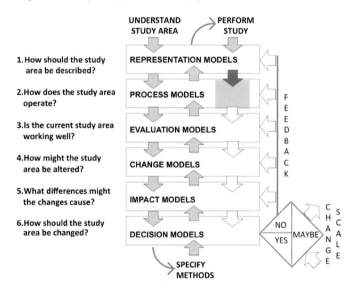

**Figure 6.3: Process models.** | Source: Carl Steinitz.

### 3. Evaluation models

- Evaluate past and present conditions.
- Visualize and communicate the results.

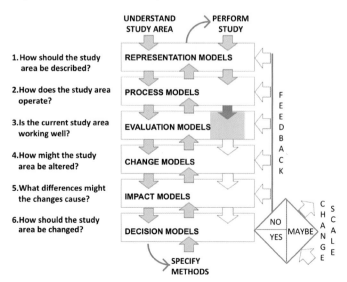

**Figure 6.4: Evaluation models.** | Source: Carl Steinitz.

## 4. Change models

- Propose and /or simulate future changes.
- Represent them (as data).
- Visualize and communicate them.

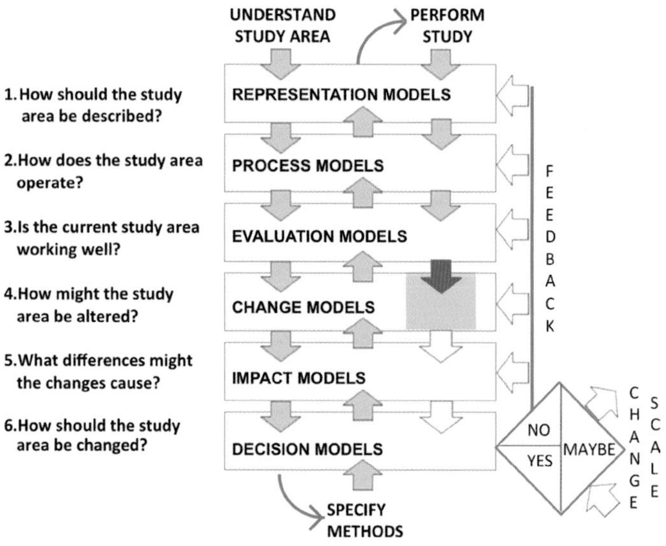

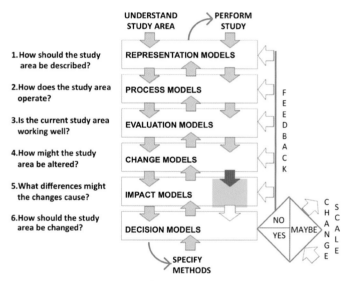

Figure 6.5: **Change models.** | Source: Carl Steinitz.

## 5. Impact models

- Assess and compare the impacts of each change model via the process models.
- Visualize and communicate the results.

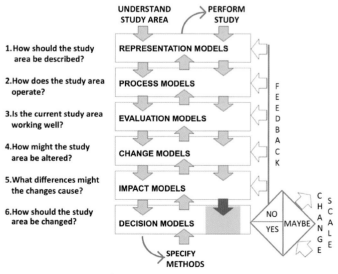

Figure 6.6: **Impact models.** | Source: Carl Steinitz.

## 6. Decision models

- Compare the impacts of the change models and decide:
  "No," which requires feedback, OR
  "Maybe," which may require further study at a different size or scale, OR
  "Yes," which leads to presentation to the stakeholders for their decision and possible implementation.

Figure 6.7: **Decision models.** | Source: Carl Steinitz.

# Reaching the first decision stage: *No, Maybe,* or *Yes*

When the geodesign team considers the preliminary products of a geodesign study, possibly in conjunction with stakeholder representatives, they have three basic choices on how to proceed toward review by the stakeholders and their decision on whether or not to implement the results of the study: *No, Maybe,* and *Yes* (figure 6.8). A *No* generates a feedback loop in the framework and the geodesign team may be prompted to return to any of the previous questions, models, or products for revision. A *Maybe* may mean changing the scale, size, or time of the study. If the team reaches a *Yes* conclusion, the project is ready to present to the stakeholders for their final review and decision.

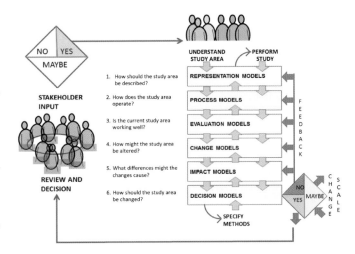

**Figure 6.8:** The first decision point for the geodesign team. | Source: Carl Steinitz.

# Feedback strategies

During the course of any geodesign study, it is highly likely that something will need to be modified or adjusted. Any of the six framework questions can be the focus of feedback that indicates what else or what different may be needed. There could be recommendations for more or better data, a revised and possibly more complex process model, re-evaluation by revising criteria for attractiveness or vulnerability, redesign of the proposed changes by revision of the change models (the most frequently applied feedback strategy), mitigation of a problematic impact, or a different approach to communication with the decision makers (figure 6.9).

Rapid feedback, especially in the assessment of impacts for changing designs, is one of the central advantages of using digital geodesign technologies. For decision models with clearly defined objectives, rapid feedback may provide a hedge against having made an inefficient choice in the way of designing by producing equivalent results regardless of method. It enables fast "hill-climbing" as a method of improving designs generated from any of the change models previously described.

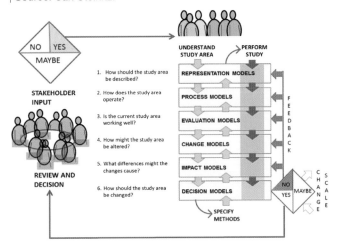

**Figure 6.9:** Feedback options. When a *No* decision results, the resulting feedback will bring the geodesign team back to one or more of the six framework questions. | Source: Carl Steinitz.

# Changing scale and/or size

A *Maybe* decision (which still functions as a contingent *No*) may trigger the need to shift scale and/or size of the geographic context of the study (figure 6.10). Shifts in size or scale may also have been part of the original scope, design and specification of the geodesign study during the first and second iterations of the framework. Following a scale or size shift, the geodesign team will again need to proceed through the three framework

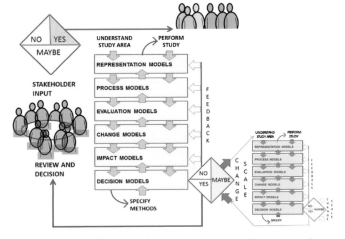

**Figure 6.10:** A shift in scale or size can be either up or down. Once this occurs, the whole framework is used again, but at that different scale or size, and probably with different models. | Source: Carl Steinitz.

iterations. The six questions themselves won't change, but they will be adapted to the new scale or size. The models, on the other hand, are likely to require revision or fundamental change, and therefore will be different.

Shifts in scale or size can be to a larger or smaller size and/or scale for the problem under study. Examples might be the regional impact of a local development decision, or the local contribution to a regional conservation strategy, both of which were part of the La Paz case study in chapter 9 and the resulting conservation of Balandra (figures 5.25 through 5.28).

## Yes, and to review by the decision makers

After incorporating feedback and possible changes to size or scale as needed, a study continues until the geodesign team completes the carrying out of the third iteration and achieves what it considers a positive *Yes* decision. Designs and alternatives are then presented to the stakeholders for their review and final decisions (figure 6.11). In practice, presentation may involve several events and require several different formats of communication.

At this point in the process, the stakeholders can return the same three possible answers that the geodesign team had made earlier: *No, Maybe,* and *Yes* (figure 6.6). A final *No* may mean the end of the study and the relationship with the geodesign team (and I have seen this happen). *Maybe* likely means a reconsideration of some aspect(s) of the study and subsequent feedback as needed. A *Yes* decision means that the geodesign study has been completed, and implies that implementation will follow. When implemented, the changed aspects of the geographic study area will need to be updated in representation models that reflect the new reality (figure 6.12).

Finally, I must reiterate that geodesign is neither a routine nor a linear process. Though I have laid out structured ways that questions and models can be followed in an orderly manner within a framework, the reality will never be a smoothly linear process (figure 6.13). Experienced professionals know that surprises will occur within even the clearest of frameworks, the most appropriate methods, and the best made plans. An advantage of having a clear, succinct, and robust framework is that the geodesign team always knows where it is in the overall process and can more efficiently regroup and restart, if needed—and in an efficient and collaborative manner.

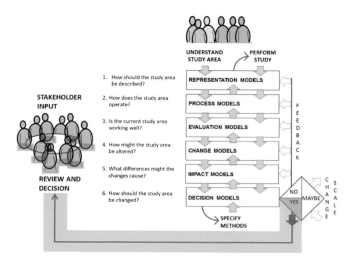

Figure 6.11: A *Yes* decision by the geodesign team means that the study is ready to be presented to the stakeholders for their decisions. | Source: Carl Steinitz.

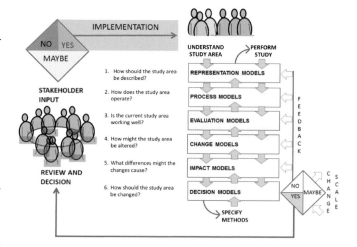

Figure 6.12: A final *Yes* decision by the stakeholders means the designs are ready for implementation. | Source: Carl Steinitz.

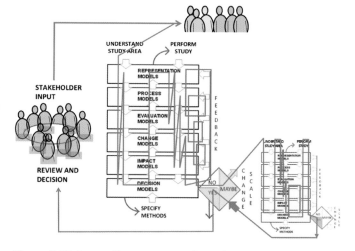

Figure 6.13: In practice, progress through a geodesign study is unlikely to be neatly ordered and linear, as in this imagined flow through the framework. | Source: Carl Steinitz.

# A caution: adaptability *(or, the trouble with "a strong concept, fully worked out")* [1]

Stakeholders and professional designers often wonder how to pick the best design from among the presented alternatives and reach that final *Yes* decision. A common viewpoint, often heard in design schools and during design juries and competitions, is that the best design is "a strong concept, fully worked out." This view is so popular it has essentially become part of the folklore of the design professions. But under what conditions is this ideal a valid one, and under what conditions is it not only invalid, but even harmful?

Let's break this idea into its two parts: one, "a strong concept," and two, "fully worked out," and consider them in turn. To begin, a design critic or a decision maker is often delighted when he or she is presented with a thoroughly developed "strong" geometric or prototypical design, complete with an easy-to-comprehend formal structure. However, strength and clarity of the design do not necessarily make it a better one. Sometimes it is necessary and helpful to draw from fields other than design. For example, political dictatorship is a very strong concept, but its strength and clarity do not make it either right or good. The analogy to the tyranny of design is purposeful. Time has shown us that many "strong" concepts of physical form carry with them harmful social connotations which people may ultimately reject. We can draw from projects that in their time were both highly regarded and significant in the design professions. For example, Pruitt-Igoe Homes was a large public housing complex in Saint Louis (Missouri, USA), consisting of 33 large and similar buildings. The project was designed by the influential architect Minoru Yamasaki (1912–1986), and completed in 1956. Yamasaki was indirectly influenced by the 1922 La Ville Radieuse proposal from the famous French architect le Corbusier (1887–1965). Yet only 16 years later, the entire Pruitt-Igoe complex was ordered demolished by the federal government and its destruction was started in 1972 (figure 6.14).

From many perspectives, the Pruitt-Igoe design would have been evaluated as "a strong design, fully worked out." I believe that the people of the place would have favored physical forms and ways of living that are far more diverse, decentralized, and adaptable, instead of being based on the "strong" values and methods of a single dominant bureaucracy and its designer.

**Figure 6.14: The destruction of Pruitt-Igoe Homes. This strong design concept was poorly aligned with its inhabitants' needs and desires, and demolition became the only change option.** | Source: Courtesy of U.S. Department of Housing and Urban Development.

The second and perhaps more important part of the phrase is "fully worked out." Again, size and scale matter. I have come to believe that virtually every commonly-held design goal for a very small project will be an error if it is applied to a very large project of regional impact. For example, the goal of "completeness" is perfectly reasonable for a design of a small temporary pavilion, but it becomes impossible, and even ridiculous, when the design is for the settlement of a large region. The freedom of the designer to fully implement his or her own ideas, which is perfectly reasonable when working for one's own private use and enjoyment, becomes not only impossible but dangerous when a geodesign team is making a design that involves large areas, huge sums of someone else's money, and the lives of tens of thousands of people.

Geodesign must necessarily involve adaptability. I believe that large geodesign projects naturally fall beyond the scale of a single, complete, whole, fully organized or fully developed design. Large projects, such as an extensive waterfront project or a design for regional development, will always be filled with unknowns. In the first 20 years after implementation of such a project, imagine the evolving and emerging effects of all of the different decisions made by the myriad of government, corporate and private participants. It does not seem reasonable for a large design to ever be considered fully worked out, if only because we almost never have had an implemented design that lasted well over 20 or more years without some major changes. *It is the fragility of the assumptions when projected over a long period of time that requires a design to be NOT fully worked out.*

The only way to possibly ensure that a proposed design will serve for a longer time is to build in the ability for others to make future changes directly into the design itself. Thus the paradox: the larger the geodesign study's area and the longer the design's planned life expectancy or use phase, the more flexibility and adaptability must be built into the design as opposed to having all the components "fully worked out."

This argument was made many years ago by my mentor, urban planner Kevin Lynch (1918–1984) in a 1958 paper titled "Environmental Adaptability,"[2] a paper that I would strongly urge anyone interested in geodesign to read. As an analogy, Lynch posed the following problem: There are 100 people and they each need a cup. He then described three fundamental design strategies, each of which has a basic problem. The first strategy is to design and make the average cup 100 times. This should satisfy everyone to some extent, but not really satisfy anyone perfectly except for the very few "average" users. The second strategy is to design and make 100 unique cups, and let individuals chose among them. This should satisfy the people who choose early, but is unlikely to serve those who come last. The problem of equity arises—who gets to choose first and why? The third and final strategy is to give everyone clay and let each person make his or her own cup. This has the problem that it requires everyone to learn how to make a cup that meets his or her needs. Some people won't know how and won't be able to make a cup. But if the individual's learning process is the real objective, then only the third strategy works, especially for the long term.

As the design professions move toward a more decentralized, collaborative and even participatory view of what geodesign is about, I believe they will increasingly be influenced by Lynch's third strategy, and also by the broader perspectives of the geographical sciences. Then the designers' values that favor "a strong concept, fully worked out" will lose some of their appeal. At the same time, this perspective is an argument against seeking fully deterministic or standardized algorithmic outcomes from the activities of geodesign. This is especially important for larger studies and ones that are more poorly defined, with higher risk of changes to baseline assumptions and to future unknowns. As Publilius Syrus, a slave in Rome and writer of maxims, said around two thousand years ago, "It is a bad plan that admits no modification."[3]

## The choices matter

Each choice that is made and carried out during the three iterations of the framework matters. The *WHY* questions of the first iteration provide a sense of the scope and objectives of the geodesign application: the problem, the geographical study area, and the relevant scale(s). They also imply the decision model(s) of the people of the place. The *HOW* questions of the second iteration matter as they define the methods of the geodesign application that contribute to the future of the place. The *WHAT*, *WHERE,* and *WHEN* questions of the third iteration, together with feedback, scale and time changes, matter in that they are part of the project's realization and implementation. Meanwhile, we are continuously aware that while we design at our selected scale, someone else is probably looking at the same area from a design perspective at a larger scale, or looking at a more detailed scale, or that someone has done this before us and that someone surely will do this again after we are finished. *Geodesign is an ongoing process of changing geography by design.*

## Notes

1. Adapted from C. Steinitz, "The Trouble With 'A Strong Concept, Fully Worked Out,'" *Landscape Architecture* (November 1979): 565–67.

2. K. Lynch, K. "Environmental Adaptability," *Journal of the American Institute of Planners* 14, no.2 (1958): 16–24

3. D. Lyman Jr., *The Moral Sayings of Publius Syrus, a Roman Slave* (Cleveland, OH: L. E. Barnard & Company, 1856), maxim 469.

# PART III

# Case studies in geodesign

In this part of the book, I have selected a series of case studies to illustrate how the framework has previously been applied. Each demonstrates a different change model as the principal way of designing. I include nine case studies in all, eight for the different change models previously described in chapter 5, and a ninth mixed case that combines two others. I chose them for their diversity and have included both older and more recent geodesign studies. The studies themselves lasted from four days to two years in duration, ranged from no budget to a large budget, had digital and non-digital and mixed methods, and involved two to 15 principal participants. Some were sponsored by government, foundation, or private stakeholders. They took place in various countries, within geographic study areas of differing sizes and scales. Their main subject-themes varied and they were associated with teaching, research, or consulting activities.

I have organized the case studies in three different groups. The three ways of designing that I cover in chapter 7 (anticipatory, participatory, and sequential) all assume that the designer or the geodesign team is confident in the ability to directly develop the design for the future state of the study area. In chapter 8, the constraining and combinatorial case studies assume that the geodesign team is not certain of the crucial initial decisions and must first assess the major requirement-variables before developing the rest of the design. In the case studies of chapter 9, the geodesign team is assumed to understand the rules that guide the processes of change, but also is obligated to test the variability of the main requirements in order to develop the most beneficial design solution. Here we explore the rule-based, optimized, and agent-based approaches, along with a mixed model that in this case happens to involve sequential and agent-based ways of designing.

# CHAPTER 7

# Geodesign with certainty

THE ANTICIPATORY, PARTICIPATORY, AND SEQUENTIAL change models all assume that the designer or the geodesign team is confident in their ability to directly develop the design for the future state of the study area. This confidence normally derives from personal experience, either as a designer or scientist, or as a direct participant in the context and issues under study. It can also originate from very clear instructions from the people of the place and the stakeholders regarding how they want the design developed.

## The anticipatory change model

While using an **anticipatory** change model, the designer "sees the whole solution" from the outset (figure 7.1). For experienced designers, this is not a rare occurrence. They may frequently have a clear and often diagrammatic "concept" envisioned from the very beginning. The difficulty is almost always in trying to apply deductive logic to figure out how to get from the imagined future *back* to the present conditions, and then to specify the number of assumptions that are needed to potentially implement the design. As a generalization, this approach is frequently successful for smaller design projects. It is also a useful approach when one needs to work rapidly, and in initial phases of large studies when general patterns of change are to be rapidly assessed and compared. Because anticipatory designs are most frequently based on clear but simple diagrams, they are less likely to succeed when the design problem is large, complicated, less well defined, and of longer duration in time.

Where does the conceptual insight come from? Experiences. Perhaps the best explanation is the model presented by Kristian Hammond, the co-director of the Intelligent

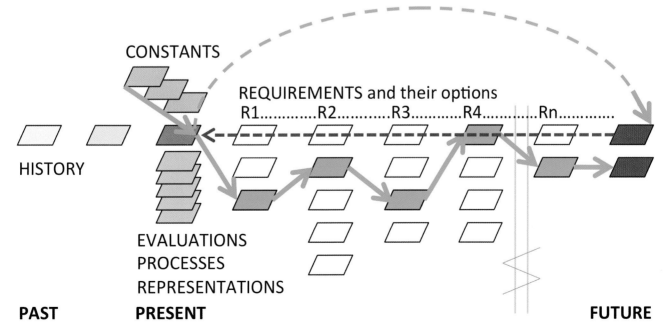

**Figure 7.1: The anticipatory change model.** | Source: Carl Steinitz.

Information Laboratory at Northwestern University (figure 7.2). Clearly, this design approach places a premium on having a

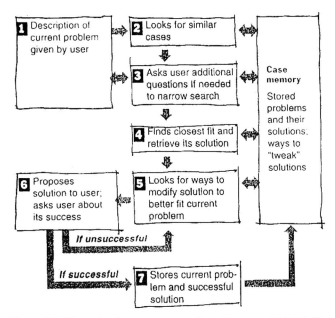

Figure 7.2: The role of case memory, from Hammond (1990). The "case memory" is a powerful collection of experiences from which one can draw as new design problems are encountered. | Source: Kristian Hammond.

large and sophisticated case memory, either already part of one's mental collection or somehow otherwise accessible, possibly via the Internet.

The case memory consists of three things: successful design solutions, unsuccessful design solutions, and the rules by which both of these classes have been and are judged. Most often the case memory is derived from the designer's personal experiences, including travel, reading, education, media, and one's own design activities. Enlarging one's case memory can be achieved in many ways, now including easy access to sources on the Internet. However, a disconnect is likely to exist between reading about and indirectly seeing past solutions, and truly understanding how they might be relevant to the current problem under study. Familiarity with the relevant history of the particular field of design in question is a major advantage. In a sense, the case memory functions as a repository for design as a *noun,* and perhaps most important, stores the principles that allow the designer to select and evaluate designs. This will aid in deciding what *not* to do and to focus instead on potentially successful "concepts."

A change model derived from case memory is frequently a caricature, a simplified solution often expressed as a diagram (figure 7.3). These may have been based on a dominant

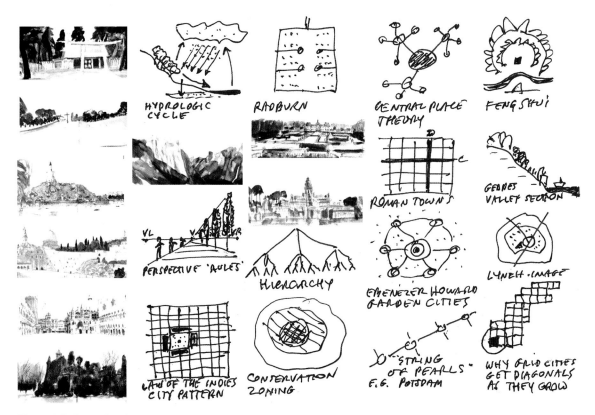

Figure 7.3: Examples from my own case memory: places I have seen and drawn and concepts I have studied. The Ebenezer Howard diagram (figure 7.13) within this collection was particularly influential in the Camp Pendleton case study that will be discussed in this chapter. | Source: Carl Steinitz.

objective or a famous historical example, a simple geometry, or a personal view. While very useful as initial concepts, most geodesign problems will eventually require more spatially complex solutions.

For some people, geodesign is seen as combination of algorithmic strategies for allocating points, lines, areas, networks, etc. However, when I work from my case memory, I prefer to think in terms of objects, of more geometrically complex and integrated content-types: neighborhoods and parks, streets and cities, rivers and watersheds, drainage patterns and utility networks, for example. Most people who were trained in design and who are involved in geodesign come from that perspective. These content types and their component elements influence the choice of the change model (the design strategy). This in turn influences the choice among appropriate computer algorithms. Except for simple and repetitive design problems one cannot a priori define the whole set of element-geometries or algorithms, and most geodesign problems are neither simple nor repetitive. An applicable concept from case memory is very unlikely to be algorithmic.

When working in an anticipatory design mode, the designer will make the first pass of questions 1–6 through the framework, or use a clear problem-statement that the client has provided. The designer then relies on experience and confidence to directly derive a (or the) potential solution. The decision (on the part of the designer) that the design will be successful is most frequently based on the designer's internalized impact models rather than from formal process models. The anticipatory approach certainly favors the experienced designer with an agreeable client.

## The region of Camp Pendleton, California [1]

The Camp Pendleton case study was a two-year research program (1994–1997) that explored how urban growth and change in the rapidly developing area located between San Diego and Los Angeles might influence the region's future biodiversity (figure 7.4). The six alternative designs compared in this study were initially conceived via the anticipatory change model. Our large geodesign team had members from the Harvard University Graduate School of Design, Utah State University, the National Biological Service, the USDA Forest Service, The Nature Conservancy and the Biodiversity Research Consortium. We also relied on the cooperation of two relevant regional agencies, the San Diego Association of Governments (SANDAG) and the Southern California Association of Governments (SCAG), along with Marine Corps Base (MCB) Camp Pendleton.

The geodesign team hypothesized that the major stressors on biodiversity impacts in the study region were related to

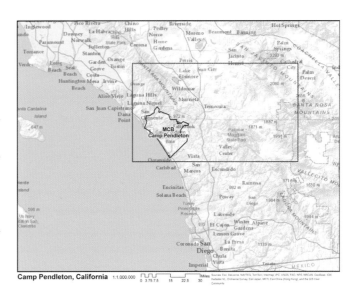

Camp Pendleton, California   1:1,000,000

**Figure 7.4:** The region of Camp Pendleton, California, USA.

urbanization, and this formed the basis of their research strategy. The effects on biodiversity would depend on several factors including where and how people built homes, where new industry would be located, where new infrastructure would be built to support urbanization, and whether and where land was conserved. There were also indirect, secondary, and cumulative effects through hydrologic and fire influences which affected habitat and, ultimately, biodiversity.

### Representation

In the 1990s, the region surrounding Camp Pendleton, comprising portions of San Diego, Orange, and Riverside counties, was one of the country's most desirable places to live and work. The population during the 1994–1997 study period was about 1.1 million, and it has continued to grow rapidly since. The area was and is still one of the most biologically diverse environments in the continental United States. Within the region were over 200 plants and animals listed by federal or state agencies as endangered, threatened, or rare. The 49,857 hectare landscape within Marine Corps Base (MCB) Camp Pendleton, the largest unbuilt portion of land on the southern California coastline, was central to maintaining the long term biodiversity of the area. At the same time, the primary mission of Camp Pendleton was (and still is) the training of Marines, and its entire area was administered for diverse functions toward that goal. Of unique importance, Camp Pendleton was the only facility on the west coast where amphibious assault maneuvers could be practiced. Moreover, the marines at Camp Pendleton expected that training activities on the base would be expanded and intensified as units relocated there from decommissioned bases. The combination of the increasing development pressures both on the base and in the surrounding region, together with the region's rich biodiversity, created a setting where natural resource issues came into sharp focus (figure 7.5).

An extensive geographic information system (GIS) was prepared and shared among the geodesign team. While Camp Pendleton was largely unbuilt, it was not undeveloped (figure 7.6). Camp Pendleton's 27 kilometer coastline remained the only large habitat area for marine birds in southern California. Its northeast boundary abutted the San Mateo Wilderness Area of the Cleveland National Forest, and it was close to the Santa Rosa Plateau Ecological Reserve, which maintained the largest remaining native California bunchgrass grassland. Thus, Camp Pendleton has always played an increasingly key role in the connectivity of the region's ecosystems.

**Process, evaluation**

The geodesign team developed a set of process models to evaluate both the existing conditions and the impacts of change. We used soils models to evaluate the local agricultural productivity and hydrology models to predict the 25-year storm hydrographs, flooding heights, and water discharge for each of the area's rivers and their sub-watersheds. Combining these sets of models allowed us to predict the resulting soil moisture throughout the study area. Multiple fire models assessed both the need for fire to maintain vegetation habitat, as well as the risks of fire and its suppression. The visual model was designed

to allow stakeholders and decision makers to assess scenic preferences in the region's landscape. Biodiversity, and the land critical for maintaining biodiversity, was defined and modeled in three ways: a landscape ecological pattern model, ten selected single-species potential habitat models, and a species richness model. Some models required the results of other models as their inputs. For example, this "chaining" process was evident in the cougar habitat model being partly dependent

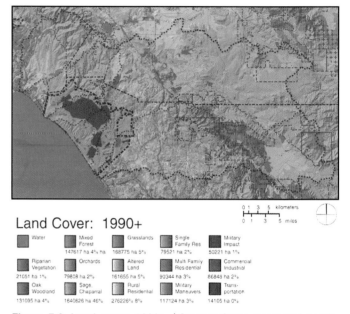

Land Cover: 1990+

| Water | Mixed Forest 147617 ha 4% ha | Grasslands 168775 ha 5% | Single Family Res 79521 ha 2% | Military Impact 50221 ha 1% |
| Riparian Vegetation 21051 ha 1% | Orchards 79808 ha 2% | Altered Land 161655 ha 5% | Multi Family Residential 90344 ha 3% | Commercial Industrial 86848 ha 2% |
| Oak Woodland 131095 ha 4% | Sage, Chaparral 1640626 ha 46% | Rural Residential 276226% 8% | Military Maneuvers 117124 ha 3% | Trans-portation 14105 ha 0% |

**Figure 7.6: Land cover, 1990+.** | Source: Camp Pendleton geodesign team (1996).

**Figure 7.5: Camp Pendleton region.** | Source: Photo by Scott Sebastian.

upon modeled mule deer habitat. Lands at risk from impacts of development were also modeled and identified, including flood plains, prime agricultural soils, riparian zones and areas of high visual quality.

## Change

We generated and drew six alternative conceptual designs that simulated regional change based on projected development, all based on the same set of demand assumptions. Each alternative was then allocated in two stages: its projected state by the year 2010, which accommodated the forecasted population increase of about 500,000 additional people, and its projected state at legal build-out based upon the current local plans. All six alternatives were designed via the anticipatory change model and drawn by me.

After further design development using the GIS-based evaluation models, each alternative regional design was represented as a land cover map with the same land-use classifications as the 1990+ baseline. Future change was also simulated via designs prepared at three other sizes and scales: a third order watershed, a large residential subdivision, and several restoration projects.

In Alternative #1, called Plans Build-Out (figure 7.7), the pattern of urban development was based upon the then-current local and regional plans as summarized by the Southern California Association of Governments, the San Diego Association of Governments, and those of Camp Pendleton. These plans generally proposed a far more concentrated development pattern than what was then developing in the region.

Alternative #2, Spread (figure 7.8), was based on the premise that development in Southern California would continue its then-current spread pattern of single family residences in medium density developments in the valleys and extensive rural residential growth with altered vegetation throughout the landscape. It assumed no new conservation land would be purchased, no new major roads or other public transportation systems would be built, and that development would occur without special regard for the environment.

Alternative #3, Spread with Conservation 2010 (figure 7.9), also followed the same spread, low density development assumptions that were the basis of Alternative #2, but it proposed a conservation strategy scheduled to begin in 2010. Development practices from 1990+ to 2010 would have altered the regional hydrology, fragmented critical areas of the landscape ecological pattern, and threatened regional extinction of some native fauna. This would increase the public's desire to protect remaining areas of natural vegetation from development. Therefore, this alternative assumed that all remaining

areas of high conservation priority and all areas of riparian vegetation, coastal sage scrub, and chaparral, would be conserved beginning in 2010 by purchase or other means. All land outside protected zones and not developed by 2010 would be developed as zoned, to build-out.

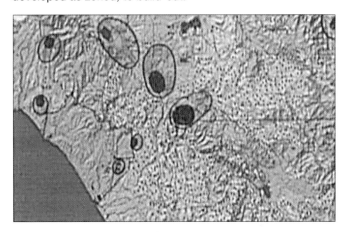

**Figure 7.7: Plans Build-Out.** | Source: Camp Pendleton geodesign team (1996).

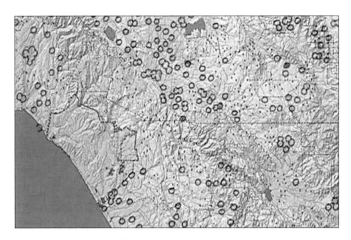

**Figure 7.8: Spread.** | Source: Camp Pendleton geodesign team (1996).

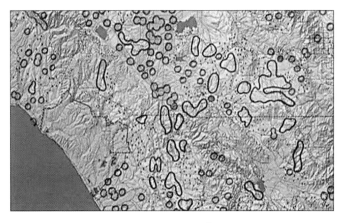

**Figure 7.9: Spread with Conservation.** | Source: Camp Pendleton geodesign team (1996).

Alternative #4, Private Conservation (figure 7.10), assumed that public resources to acquire land for conservation would be unavailable into the foreseeable future. This alternative proposed extensive conservation of biodiversity by means of private large-lot ownership and management of land adjacent

**Figure 7.10: Private Conservation.** | Source: Camp Pendleton geodesign team (1996).

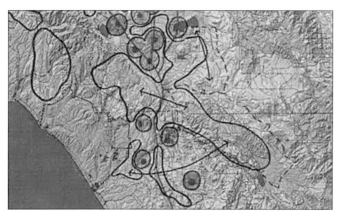

**Figure 7.11: Multi-Centers.** | Source: Camp Pendleton geodesign team (1996).

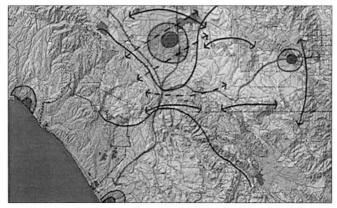

**Figure 7.12: New City.** | Source: Camp Pendleton geodesign team (1996).

to and within important habitat areas. It presumed that the benefits of thoughtful development, in accordance with existing plans, would outweigh the potential risks associated with very low density housing.

Alternative #5, a Multi-Centers strategy (figure 7.11), focused on cluster development of new communities to create the least possible impact on the ecological regimes. The geodesign team identified eleven regional locations as "centers," seven in Riverside and Orange Counties and four in San Diego County. Conservation purchases and greenbelts were added after the centers were located as a way to provide identifiable edges and connective corridors. The combined pattern of development and conservation provided a highly linked network of natural areas and greenways aimed at maintaining the region's biodiversity while accommodating population growth.

Alternative #6, a New City (figure 7.12), concentrated most regional growth in one new city, linking and expanding the Temecula Valley communities in Riverside County. Transportation, sewer, and water infrastructure were available, and conservation could be focused on protecting prime agricultural soils and species richness as well as maintaining the existing landscape ecological pattern. To encourage this potential development within areas appropriate for urban development and away from areas critical for biodiversity, the New City design focused on incorporating existing urban areas as satellite communities.

The diagrammatic concept design for the New City alternative was influenced (via my case memory) by the conceptual diagram of the Garden City as proposed by Ebenezer Howard and Raymond Unwin, and published by Howard[2] in 1902 (figure 7.13). Howard (1850–1928), a bank clerk, and Unwin (1863–1940), an architect and planner, were deeply troubled by the terrible housing conditions in nineteenth century industrial England. In that period, the poor and working classes were limited to housing that was overcrowded, dangerous, and polluted, and the Garden Cities Association was formed in 1898 by a small group of intellectuals who were distressed by this housing plight. Their most important proposed idea was the Garden City concept, aimed at lowering a city's population density by surrounding it with a band of countryside and relocating people to smaller new towns, connected by efficient public transportation. Our team transformed Howard's 1902 diagram into a conceptual diagram for locating the New City and its outlying towns in the study region (figure 7.14), and I then sketched it as an urban design idea (figure 7.15). The central New City was then located, allocated and developed in more detail via the evaluation models (figure 7.16), and then visualized (figure 7. 17).

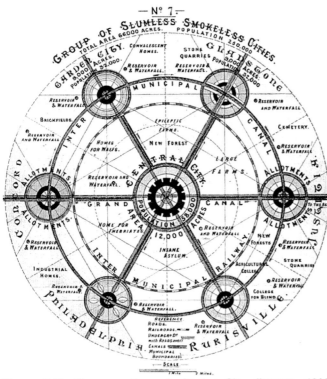

**Figure 7.13: Ebenezer Howard, Garden City diagram, 1902.** | Source: E. Howard, *Garden Cities for Tomorrow* (London: S. Sonnenschein & Co., Ltd., 1902).

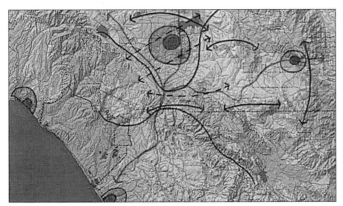

**Figure 7.14: The Garden City diagram adapted to the study region.** | Source: Camp Pendleton geodesign team (1996), Carl Steinitz.

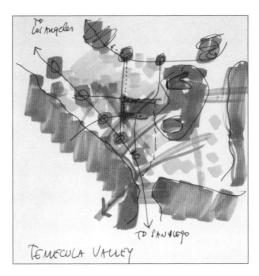

**Figure 7.15: The New City conceptual design sketch.** | Source: Camp Pendleton geodesign team (1996), Carl Steinitz.

**Figure 7.16: The New City design.** | Source: Camp Pendleton geodesign team (1997).

**Figure 7.17: The New City visualized.** | Source: Camp Pendleton geodesign team (1997).

## Impact

The six alternatives (Plans Build-Out, Spread, Spread with Conservation 2010, Private Conservation, Multi-Centers, and the New City) were all assessed for their effects by each of the spatial and quantitative impact models (the process models under changed conditions). To support communication and understanding of these effects, side-by-side graphs that reflect a relative, qualitative summary were very helpful (figure 7.18).

Neither the "Plans Build Out" nor the "Spread" alternatives had management of biodiversity as one of their primary objectives and subsequently performed poorly from that perspective. Not surprisingly, "Private Conservation" succeeded in that area, as it was intended to protect the most significant habitat areas,

but at the risk of impacts associated with very low density and clustered development in some of the region's most sensitive environments. Yet if its development process could be managed well, these private land management policies might prove the most effective in conserving the region's biodiversity. The "MultiCenters" and "New City" strategies sought to conserve biodiversity by attracting more concentrated development into appropriate locations while at the same time minimizing public cost for conservation and infrastructure. In the forecast period to 2010, these seemed to be plausible strategies for biodiversity, although no one underestimated the difficulties in implementing development patterns that diverged substantially from the lower density "Plans Build Out."

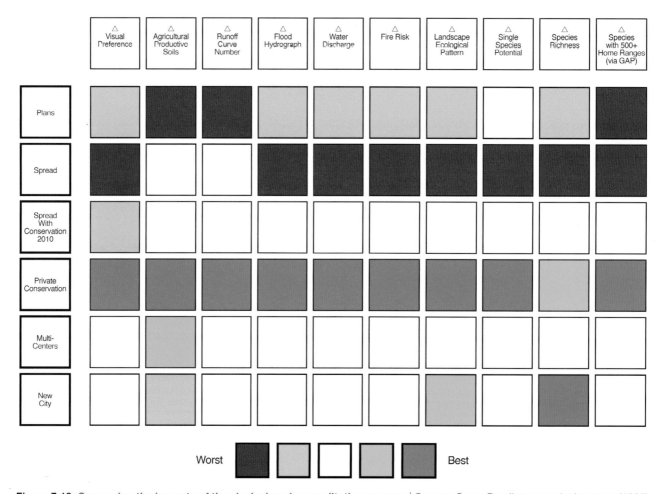

**Figure 7.18: Comparing the impacts of the six designs in a qualitative manner.** | Source: Camp Pendleton geodesign team (1996).

When considered over a longer time frame, in which the scenarios were carried forward to their build-out, all six alternative futures converged to a generally similar pattern of impacts caused by the transformation of a predominantly natural regional landscape to a predominantly urbanized pattern. All of the alternatives sacrificed agriculturally productive soils, increased erosion and sedimentation, changed soil moisture, reduced water tables in the river basins, and dramatically increased flood discharges. The net effect was a reduction of biological diversity in the Camp Pendleton region as the hydro-period of the riparian zone became shorter and floods washed out sediments and their associated native vegetation. The direct consequences on biodiversity were negative in *all* of the scenarios, to varying degrees. The landscape's ecological patterns became increasingly fragmented. Natural areas became smaller and increasingly isolated within urbanized regions. Some of the most important single species, such as the gnatcatcher and cougar, were seriously impacted, and their long-term regional survival was put in doubt. Patterns of species richness would be dramatically altered by invasive species.

On the positive side, the forecasted population for 2010, and even population numbers several times larger, could be easily accommodated within all six scenarios. If one assumes that water continued to be imported to the area, as all the regional plans and alternative scenarios did, the models indicated that the region would be able to accommodate growth into the longer-range future.

**Decision**

If biodiversity was and is to be maintained in the Camp Pendleton region, innovative decision making would be needed. In 1996, the plans and policies of Camp Pendleton and the several surrounding jurisdictions were completely separated. At the regional scale, greater coordination of planning for both development and conservation was urgently needed. This was easy to say and difficult to accomplish, particularly because some of the most significant issues crossed jurisdictional boundaries. Upstream development in the Santa Margarita watershed caused downstream flooding on Camp Pendleton and in other jurisdictions. The East Side Reservoir's conservation areas in Riverside County were not linked to proposals generated by

neighboring San Diego County. Riparian channelization in one jurisdiction disrupted a regional habitat pattern. In addition, there were obvious needs for joint water supply and fire management planning.

The relationship between the base and its regional study area was being increasingly driven by new development in the surrounding region that was affecting all environmental systems. One anticipated outcome was increased pressure for environmental management on Camp Pendleton, and therefore potentially increased tension between the base's primary mission of military training and any habitat conservation objectives. From a biodiversity perspective, even the largest public landscapes, such as the Cleveland National Forest and MCB Camp Pendleton, could no longer be seen as isolated, self-contained, and self-managed entities.

One of the most significant direct consequences of this geodesign study was the widespread recognition that the interests of MCB Camp Pendleton and its neighboring regional jurisdictions were symbiotic, and their roles in the future management of biodiversity would require active partnership. Though it has taken many years and considerable effort, this mutual recognition and considerable joint planning have been accomplished.

After our initial multi-day scoping visit, we realized how important it would be for Camp Pendleton's leadership and the military sponsors to be able to quickly visualize a set of alternatives that had been well-thought through. This was one reason that the anticipatory approach was the right fit for this project. The alternatives would need to be diagrammatic, relevant, clearly differentiated and understandable. When the entire research team initially considered possible change models for this study, we decided to select four different "nested problems," each to be studied at a different scale. We decided use the anticipatory approach as a starting point for each of the four sizes and scales of context at which geodesign was to be applied. Different members of the research team were delegated to lead these, and since I worked on the region as a whole, I produced the six diagrammatic designs presented above. In a second study that followed, the Camp Pendleton's New City design was developed further by a team of graduate students as a studio exercise applying anticipatory, sequential, and constraining change models.

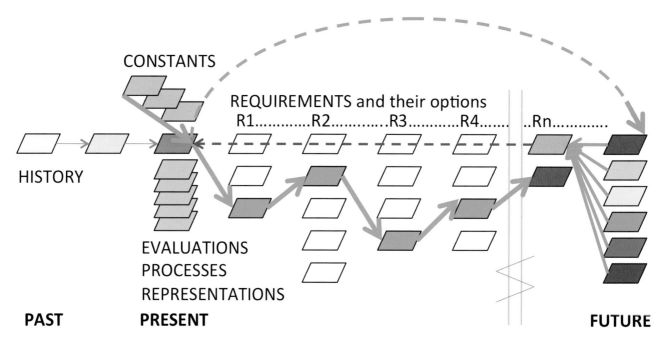

**Figure 7.19:** The participatory change model, in which the ideas of each participant are considered. Possible disagreements in the participants' initial designs are indicated by the differently colored "futures." | Source: Carl Steinitz.

## The participatory change model

If you are following a **participatory** change model, the end users of the design (the people of the place) are most often assumed to be "the participants." Thus the participatory change model has the advantage of being potentially more democratic than other methods. However, a team of collaborating designers also sometimes uses this approach, in which their individual ideas (often achieved via anticipatory methods) must be reconciled into one proposal for change. Any diverse group of participants is unlikely to be in total agreement regarding desirable futures for a study area. This is a common circumstance when a committee is formed to make the design. Thus the major liability of this model is the need to reconcile and aggregate potentially conflicting designs into one coherent and implementable plan. So even if and when agreement is achieved, participatory change models will still require a feasible design to be developed.

### The Osa region, Costa Rica [3]

This case study is adapted from "Participatory Landscape Planning Using Portable Geospatial Information Systems and Technologies: The Case of the Osa Region of Costa Rica," a 2008 doctoral dissertation study by Juan Carlos Vargas-Moreno at Harvard University, for which I was an advisor. Costa Rica, situated between Panama and Nicaragua in Central America,

has a population of about 4 million. Its central volcanic mountain range extends in a north-west direction across the country, forming an abrupt topography and a series of plains along each coast. The region of study, the Osa Peninsula, is located in the Puntarenas Province on the Pacific Ocean, approximately 370 kilometers southeast from Costa Rica's capital, San Jose (figure 7.20).

Because the study region is one of rapidly changing conditions, direct integration of local and nonlocal stakeholders into the design process was seen as essential, and this study

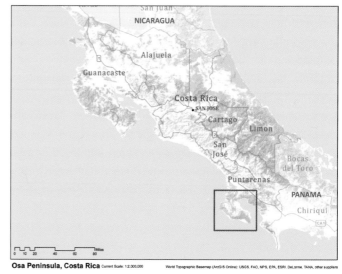

Osa Peninsula, Costa Rica Current Scale: 1:2,000,000     World Topographic Basemap (ArcGIS Online): USGS, FAO, NPS, EPA, ESRI, DeLorme, TANA, other suppliers

**Figure 7.20:** Costa Rica and the location of the Osa Peninsula.

therefore implemented a participatory method. This approach aimed at rapidly acquiring stakeholder-generated designs for change, with the potential to generate a consensus-based design. By selecting a participatory approach, the research assessed potential areas of agreement and disagreement (i.e., conflict) among stakeholders, to seek areas of possible collaboration and to better inform decision making and, ultimately, change.

While several participatory design procedures had been conducted previously by other researchers, the techniques and methods typically employed often lack direct and spatially-explicit modes of inquiry. They are compromised by involving mediators who—based on their own interpretation—represent on a base map the stakeholder' desires of change, thus implicitly transforming the information. The methods proposed in this study used GIS as well as an array of stakeholder participatory techniques to *directly* elicit and exchange stakeholder knowledge about spatial land use alternatives.

The methods were implemented during multiple individual and community participatory mapping workshops conducted in the Osa region of Costa Rica in spring 2006. During these meetings, Vargas-Moreno worked with 40 different participants, locals and nonlocals, to capture their ideas for future land-use allocations. The final results defined geographic patterns of conflict and agreement, both of land-use types and among stakeholder groups. The case study proved highly informative for national planning authorities as well as local resident and scientific groups. It improved capacity building, governance, and ultimately more informed decision making.

**Representation**

The region of study is 175,000 hectares, consisting of two counties (Osa and Sierpe) and eight districts. According to the 2000 Costa Rica National Census, the Osa region had a population of approximately 25,000 people. Osa's landscape includes small, forested mountains and flat lands with agriculture and forestry activities (figure 7.21).

Osa's urban development has been limited to a series of small towns and villages that lie along the Pan-American Highway and the peninsula's access road that parallels the coast, spreading up to the southern entrance of Corcovado National Park (figure 7.22). Puerto Jimenez, with a population of about 1,800, is the major town of the Osa region.

The majority of the GIS data for the study were provided by Departments and Ministries of the Government of Costa Rica, including their regional offices located in the study region.

Osa plays a central role in Costa Rica's conservation strategy. The region of study is part of the Conservation Area of Osa (ACOSA in Spanish), one of 11 areas that cover the whole country and together comprise the National System of Conservation Areas (SINAC). Within the Osa Conservation Area, only national parks and mangrove wetlands were state property. In the rest

**Figure 7.21: The Osa Peninsula, view towards Golfo Dulce from Mogos.** | Source: J. C. Vargas-Moreno, "Participatory Landscape Planning Using Portable Geospatial Information Systems and Technologies: The Case of the Osa Region of Costa Rica" (D. Des. diss. Graduate School of Design, Harvard University, 2008).

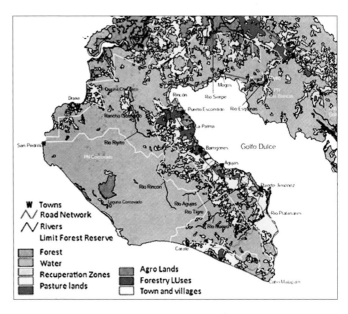

**Figure 7.22: Osa Peninsula land cover.** | Source: J. C. Vargas-Moreno, "Participatory Landscape Planning Using Portable Geospatial Information Systems and Technologies: The Case of the Osa Region of Costa Rica" (D. Des. diss. Graduate School of Design, Harvard University, 2008).

of the protected area system, land is mostly privately owned, and payment for ecosystem services (PES) is used as a financial incentive mechanism to promote forest conservation. The most important protected area in the study region is Corcovado National Park, Costa Rica's largest national park and the only remaining extent of low elevation, wet forest in Central America.

**Process, evaluation**

Osa's economic history is one of "boom or bust." From the 1930s to the 1980s, a steady flow of domestic migration to Osa occurred. Workers were attracted by companies capitalizing on the area's precious resources, and the region was made more accessible by the opening of the Inter-American Highway. Over the course of the twentieth century, the region's economy and social practices were based on resource extraction: gold mining in the 1930s, bananas through the 1950s, timber extraction in the 1960s through 1980s and agro-industrial exports in the 1980s and 1990s (primarily bananas and palm oil). However, the agro-industrial sector that served as a major engine for development elsewhere in the country was highly constrained in Osa due to unsuitable soils and a shortage of optimal agricultural areas. This has inhibited the establishment of any prosperous and sustainable agro-based society there.

Due to its natural resources and desirable environments, ecotourism had become an attractive and profitable activity in Osa by the 1990s, and continues to today. This emerging economy captivated the interest of both residents and outsiders, challenging the traditional land and natural resource management practices. Tourism related activities and forest harvesting became the biggest economic sectors, followed by subsistence agriculture, cattle ranching, and small-scale commercial fishing. The most tangible challenge continues to be the rapid land-use change from forest and agriculture to settlement and tourism-related land uses.

**Change**

Several factors made the study of participatory, stakeholder-based perspectives on future landscape change in Osa of particular interest. Osa was one of the less populated regions of Costa Rica and also one of the more ecologically fragile places in the country. It had garnered much attention because of its tourism development, active conservation disputes, strong land speculations and controversial planning processes. The composition of its social fabric has always been complex and diverse, including indigenous groups, numerous social and civil-based groups, and a strong and proactive foreigner community. The region enjoyed a national reputation for its civic involvement and engagement, and its strong interest in managing its resources and creating opportunities for sustainable livelihoods. Osa was one of the country's regions with the highest concentration of non-government agencies (NGOs) and community-based initiatives. There was a clear demand for public participation in all aspects of the decision-making process.

To best suit the social context in Osa, this study proposed a method for conducting rapid and participatory stakeholder-based design for change, with the potential for generating a consensus-based design. A total of 40 participants were selected and divided into two domains (figure 7.23). The participants represented two groups: (1) stakeholders from the region, identified as "local experts", and (2) other participants from academic, scientific and government groups, who were "nonlocal experts."

One of the distinctive characteristics of this study was the use of GIS in coordination with participatory design methods to collect, analyze, and visualize proposed landscape changes in real time. This strategy helped address some of the concerns about external consultants that local citizens in the region had raised. By using computers with interactive pen displays,[4] all

| Domain | # | Stakeholder Group | Stakeholder Group Code | Ind. Code | Participant |
|---|---|---|---|---|---|
| NONLOCALS | 1 | National Government Agents | GOV_X | GOV_X_1 | Regional policy planner |
| | 2 | | | GOV_X_2 | Dir. conservation area |
| | 3 | | | GOV_X_3 | Tourism planner |
| | 4 | Non-Government Organizations | NGO_X | NGO_X_1 | Conservation NGO |
| | 5 | | | NGO_X_2 | Sustainability NGO |
| | 6 | | | NGO_X_3 | Conservation NGO |
| | 7 | Consultants, Scientists, and Academics | CSA_X | CSA_X_1 | Planning consultant |
| | 8 | | | CSA_X_2 | Agro forestry consultant |
| | 9 | | | CSA_X_3 | Demographic expert |
| | 10 | | | CSA_X_4 | Env. management expert |
| | 11 | Developers | DEV_X | DEV_X_1 | Land development company |
| | 12 | | | DEV_X_2 | Tourist developer |
| | 13 | | | DEV_X_3 | Commercial developer |
| LOCALS | 14 | Local Government Agents (Osa) | GOV_L | GOV_L_1 | Protected areas official |
| | 15 | | | GOV_L_2 | Community coordinator |
| | 16 | | | GOV_L_3 | Agro forestry official |
| | 17 | | | GOV_L_4 | Land management official |
| | 18 | | | GOV_L_5 | Tourism coordinator |
| | 19 | | | GOV_L_6 | Wildlife official |
| | 20 | Local Consultants and Scientists | CSC_L | CSC_L_1 | Ecology expert |
| | 21 | | | CSC_L_2 | Agronomy expert |
| | 22 | | | CSC_L_3 | Forestry engineer |
| | 23 | Local Non-governmental Agents | NGO_L | NGO_L_1 | NGO agronomy expert |
| | 24 | | | NGO_L_2 | NGO environment |
| | 25 | | | NGO_L_3 | NGO forestry expert |
| | 26 | Local Business Representatives | BUS_L | BUS_L_1 | Prof. land services |
| | 27 | | | BUS_L_2 | Tourism operator |
| | 28 | | | BUS_L_3 | Tourism operator |
| | 29 | Local Agro-Forestry Sector | AFS_L | AFS_L_1 | Farmer & com. representative |
| | 30 | | | AFS_L_2 | Farmer & com. representative |
| | 31 | | | AFS_L_3 | Farmer & com. representative |
| | 32 | | | AFS_L_4 | Farmer & com. representative |
| | 33 | Community Activist | COM_L | COM_L_1 | Community leader (com. assoc.) |
| | 34 | | | COM_L_2 | Community leader (com. assoc.) |
| | 35 | | | COM_L_3 | Community leader (com. assoc.) |
| | 36 | | | COM_L_4 | Community leader (young) |
| | 37 | | | COM_L_5 | Community leader (indigenous) |
| | 38 | Foreign | FOR_L | FOR_L_1 | Foreigner and hotel owner |
| | 39 | | | FOR_L_2 | Foreigner - local volunteer |
| | 40 | | | FOR_L_3 | Foreigner - retired |

**Figure 7.23: Stakeholder composition and domains.** | Source: J. C. Vargas-Moreno, "Participatory Landscape Planning Using Portable Geospatial Information Systems and Technologies: The Case of the Osa Region of Costa Rica" (D. Des. diss. Graduate School of Design, Harvard University, 2008).

participants were able to draw directly onto the maps on the computer screens, thus enabling each person to contribute individually and easily to the design process. The devices allowed people to work intuitively, relatively quickly, and independently. This experience provided all participants with a strong sense of control, involvement, and contribution.

Using their digital input pen devices, all participants were asked to sketch their desired land use and land cover projections for a time horizon of 10 years into the future. They chose from among 13 different categories of land use and drew their new allocations directly onto the computer screen, over the representation of the existing landscape (figure 7.24). The GIS was specially designed to provide immediate impact assessments on the allocations and enable the participant to "redo" any part which had significantly negative consequences. The 10-year-long time period was chosen because it represented approximately two cycles of regional governments in Costa Rica, and sufficient time for large land use projects to be implemented and monitored.

A series of questions were asked of each participant during the participatory interview process (listed below), and the sketches and responses provided in return became new

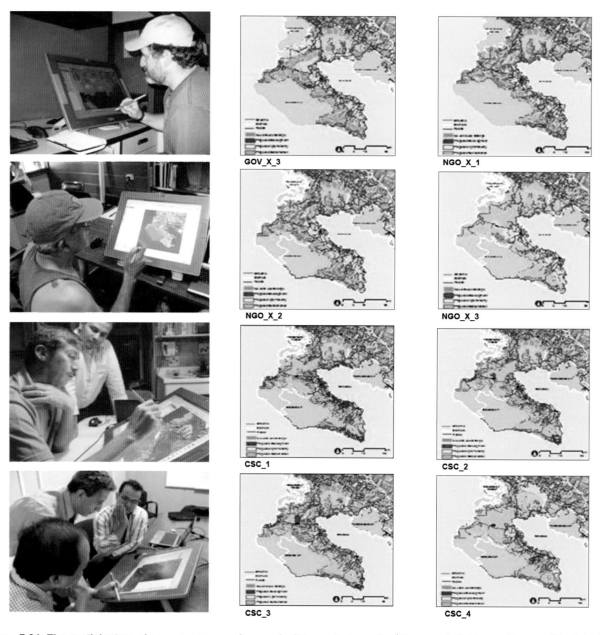

**Figure 7.24: The participatory change process and several of the varied results.** | Source: J. C. Vargas-Moreno, "Participatory Landscape Planning Using Portable Geospatial Information Systems and Technologies: The Case of the Osa Region of Costa Rica" (D. Des. diss. Graduate School of Design, Harvard University, 2008). Photos by Juan Carlos Vargas-Moreno.

GIS data sets, and qualitative, implicit criteria and feedback to use in the Osa planning process.

1. Using each of the land uses provided to you by the tool, please draw the areas that you think should change in this landscape according to your desires, knowledge and needs?
2. Why did you locate that land use in those places?
3. Why did you allocate those amounts of land to each land use category?
4. How do you think that (your design) affects the region?

**Impact**

Since the primary area of research centered on "agreement" and "conflict" among the participating stakeholders, the impacts that needed to be assessed were primarily social and political, rather than directly environmental or economic. The following questions guided the analysis:

1. What is the level of representativeness of the aggregations of the participants' allocations?
2. What are the different levels of agreement and conflict among participants?
3. How can a regional land use plan be drafted from participants' land use allocations?
4. What is the usefulness of the information generated and when could this information be used in decision making?

To simplify the analyses of spatial agreement and conflict, the land-use categories were aggregated from the original 13 down to three: conservation, development and agro-forestry. To enable the use of map algebra calculations, the hand-drawn vector features were transformed to raster-based values within a grid of 10 × 10 meters. "Agreement" was evaluated using overlay analysis to show where different participants had indicated the same land use in the same cell location. Since there were three variables, the analysis could indicate seven different types of conflict and one of agreement. The minimum aggregation that could be called "agreement" occurred when all participants' land use cell values matched. Consensus was reached when one-half plus one of the number of participants coincided in the same location with the same type of land use.

Fourteen representatives of the major stakeholder groups were then again individually surveyed as to whether aggregated land-use allocations were representative of their own original desires and insights about future landscape change. The fourteen interviewees were asked whether their views were being represented at each of four levels of aggregation, for each of the three possible land uses (figure 7.25). Mapped versions of the spatial land-use allocations representing the different cumulative levels of aggregation were prepared. The lowest level represents the individual designs of all 40 participants. Their maps

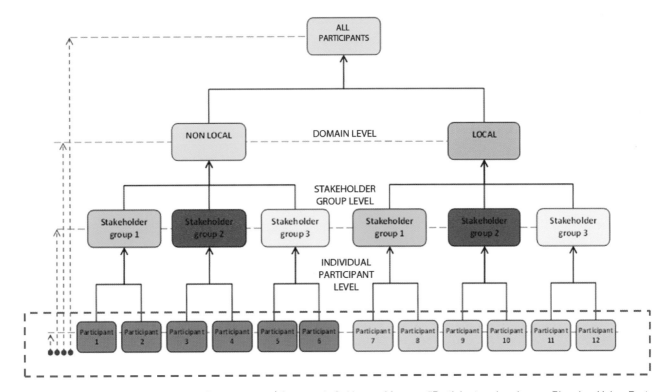

**Figure 7.25: The four-level aggregation process.** | Source: J. C. Vargas-Moreno, "Participatory Landscape Planning Using Portable Geospatial Information Systems and Technologies: The Case of the Osa Region of Costa Rica" (D. Des. diss. Graduate School of Design, Harvard University, 2008).

were then "aggregated" into stakeholder groups such as fisher-men, foreign tourists, and government planning officials. At the next level, the maps were further combined into two designs representing nonlocal and local participants. Finally, all 40 designs were aggregated into one. In addition to the maps, the analysis produced a statistical assessment of agreement.

The degree of agreement and conflict among the partici-pants' designs represented the most important indicator of the analysis. The results shown in figure 7.26 indicate that as each participant's designs were aggregated up the chain, they felt the land-use pattern was becoming less and less representa-tive of their own desires. While the drop between the individ-ual and stakeholder group levels was marginal, the change was

significant between the stakeholder and domain levels, where almost all participants indicated marginal to no degree of "rep-resentativeness." At the division between the stakeholder and domain (local, nonlocal) levels of aggregation, people were most likely to have agreed over areas selected for *conserva-tion*, followed by *agro-forestry* and lastly by *development*. The development land uses were the most controversial and, when aggregated, least recognizable as being representative of and matching with a participant's original choices. Therefore, the best potential for agreement might be found in comparing the consensus designs aggregated by "locals" versus "nonlocals," and in planning for conservation and agro-forestry.

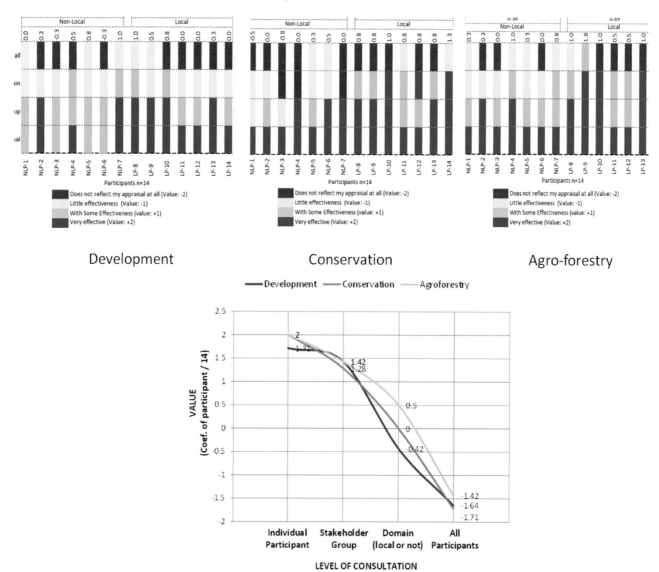

**Figure 7.26: Agreement among levels of land use aggregation by participant groups.** | Source: J. C. Vargas-Moreno, "Participa-tory Landscape Planning Using Portable Geospatial Information Systems and Technologies: The Case of the Osa Region of Costa Rica" (D. Des. diss. Graduate School of Design, Harvard University, 2008).

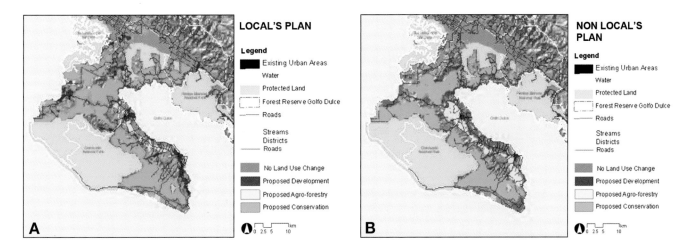

**Figure 7.27A and B: Local and nonlocal aggregated designs.** | Source: J. C. Vargas-Moreno, "Participatory Landscape Planning Using Portable Geospatial Information Systems and Technologies: The Case of the Osa Region of Costa Rica" (D. Des. diss. Graduate School of Design, Harvard University, 2008).

## Decision

The proposed, future land use patterns were predominantly similar between the aggregated designs of the local and nonlocal participants (figures 7.27A and B). Overall, the patterns of conservation focused on consolidating buffer zones and increasing landscape connectivity. At the same time, three major areas of differences were identified. Locals favored more and larger conservation areas than nonlocals, and focused on connectivity. Locals also preferred that urban development take place in smaller, serviced clusters near existing towns, with a new larger area proposed close to the tip of the peninsula, on flat areas close to the existing major town. In contrast, nonlocals tended to design a long and wide central corridor of development in the peninsula. That central corridor area was highly contested among locals. Lastly, nonlocals tended to favor allocations for new agro-forestry much more than locals did, as much as fourfold. This difference can be attributed to the central government favoring agro-industrial services for development purposes, and to a lesser degree, on tourism, while the locals' primary development goals relied on tourism and conserving natural assets.

Open-ended interviews and surveys were then conducted with the subset of 14 participants to assess the effectiveness and usefulness of this participatory design methodology. The analysis indicated that acquiring each individual person's land use designs, using GIS and the digital pen as an input device, was highly effective: 95 percent of participants approved of the process. However, the analysis also indicated that as the data from participants became more aggregated, the system became less effective at reflecting any individual participant's insights. However, in spite of the differences, there were

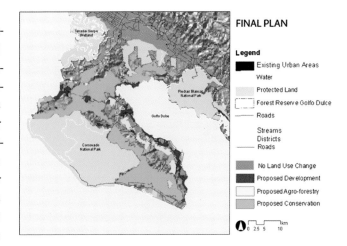

**Figure 7.28: Osa consensus. Areas in color indicate where participants agreed over proposed new land uses, while other areas were in conflict or participants thought no change should occur.** | Source: J. C. Vargas-Moreno, "Participatory Landscape Planning Using Portable Geospatial Information Systems and Technologies: The Case of the Osa Region of Costa Rica" (D. Des. diss. Graduate School of Design, Harvard University, 2008)

still many areas of strong agreement which could be moved towards implementation (figure 7.28).

Locations throughout the Osa region where participating stakeholders agreed on possible land use changes could form the basis for a final consensus plan, but any further work would require further negotiations. During our follow-up interviews, the participants acknowledged that more rounds of using participatory design negotiations, with GIS to support the process, would help all participants reach a higher level of consensus.

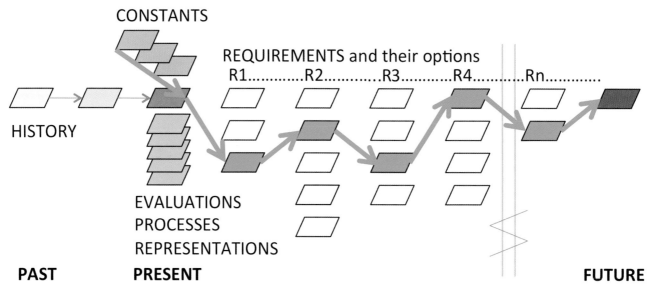

**Figure 7.29: The sequential change model.** | Source: Carl Steinitz.

## The sequential change model

The **sequential** approach makes the assumption that the designer or design team is confident in making the series of choices that become the design for future change (figure 7.29). While the designer may be aware that each of the requirements that he or she encounters is likely to have alternatives, these are not formally considered or compared. Instead, sequential decisions about the future design are based principally on the preferences and experience of the designer, though possibly influenced by the wishes of the client. The sequential way of designing favors experienced designers because their case memories are more likely to provide efficacious guidance.

There are two special cases of the sequential change model. In one, the requirements *and* their choices are given a priori, for example by the client, and they are to be integrated by the change model. In another, multiple designers sequentially follow purposely different choices among the requirements' options to develop a wide range of preliminary ideas for the future. It is this latter situation that I will describe here.

## The Bermuda dump[5]

The small island nation of Bermuda is located about 600 miles off the coast of the eastern United States (figure 7.30). In 1986, shortly after Bermuda achieved independence from Great Britain, its first Prime Minister, John Swan, requested a study of the future of its garbage dump, intending to convert the site into a new central park and other facilities. There was already a plan in place to build a new waste incinerator, but knowing it might take many years for that project to become operational, I offered to teach a studio course that would illustrate different development ideas. The Prime Minister accepted my offer, and students volunteered for the studio, knowing it would be organized similar to a design competition and that they would follow different sequential change models in preparing their initial designs. My description of this project has here been adapted from C. Steinitz, ed., *Alternative Futures for The Bermuda Dump* (Cambridge, MA: Graduate School of Design, Harvard University, 1986); and Bermuda, Department of Planning, *The Pembroke Marsh Plan 1987* (Bermuda: Department of Planning, Government of Bermuda, 1987).

## Representation

The existing garbage dump was surrounded by civic institutions, a large wetland, popular sports fields, the well fields that supplied drinking water to most of Bermuda, and the British Governor-General's home. All of this was adjacent to a residential area inhabited by the poorest people in the country, as well as Prime Minister Swan (figure 7.31).

## Process, evaluation

As I described in earlier chapters, having the geodesign team make site visits is essential for acquiring as much local knowledge and context as possible. The students visited the study area and heard several presentations about how the dump and its surrounding area function. We attended open meetings and kept careful track of the issues that were raised and the ideas for program elements, physical designs, and policies that were presented by residents and officials to the students. Each evening during my meetings with students, I had them list and

**Figure 7.31: The Bermuda dump and its surrounding study area.**
| Source: C. Steinitz, ed., Alternative Futures for The Bermuda Dump (Cambridge, MA: Graduate School of Design, Harvard University, 1986).

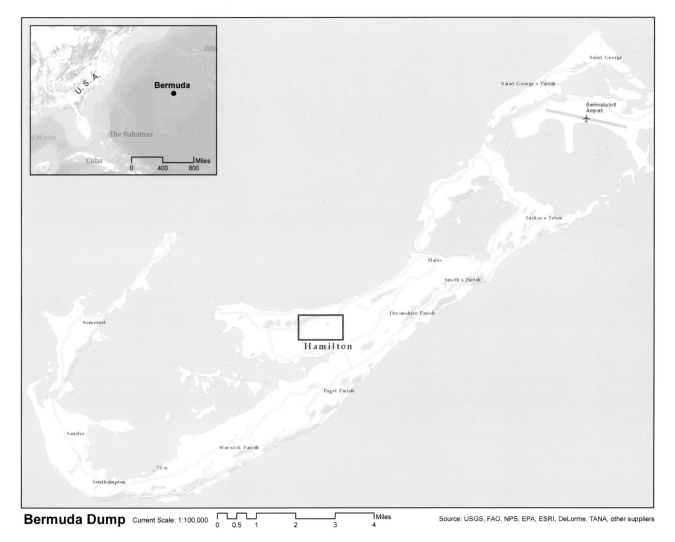

**Figure 7.30: The Bermuda dump study area.**

categorize the issues and prepare simple diagrams of every observation, idea and proposal that they had been offered or which they themselves had. These diagrams were all simple line drawings to a standard scale. *All* diagrams, whether proposed by local people, derived from historic examples, or invented by the students, were included, without any pre-judgment as to their value. The diagrams were presented anonymously: the process of selecting, combining, and interpreting diagrammed ideas into a design would later be available for any individual or group.

When we returned to Harvard, at our first working session the students agreed on a final list of about 20 issues that would have to be resolved in any design. These were of two kinds: the *constants* that had to be incorporated into every design, and the *requirements*, for which there might be several diagrammatic solutions. Pairs of students selected different required issues to address and produced between two and five solution-options for each required issue. This process generated approximately 80 diagrams, each drawn with permanent black marker on thin clear plastic so that they could easily be selected, overlain, and

reviewed together as a set or, as the students called them, a "sandwich." We then rank-ordered the issues and alternatives using a modified Delphi technique and displayed them in their prioritized sequence favoring upper and left positions in the summary diagram.

Using a system of numbered rows and columns to order, identify, and sequence the prioritized sketches was a very useful technique for communicating within the studio. As I have mentioned earlier in this book, learning how to communicate effectively and efficiently within the geodesign team is important. In our case, creating our layout of diagrams was completed at the end of the third studio class.

**Change**

In the next phase of the studio, each individual student was required to prepare an initial design by selecting a different sequence-set of the diagrams. We held a lottery and the winning student was able to choose first from among all of the variables (figure 7.32). Each subsequent student in the lottery ranking was required to choose a *different* set from all previous

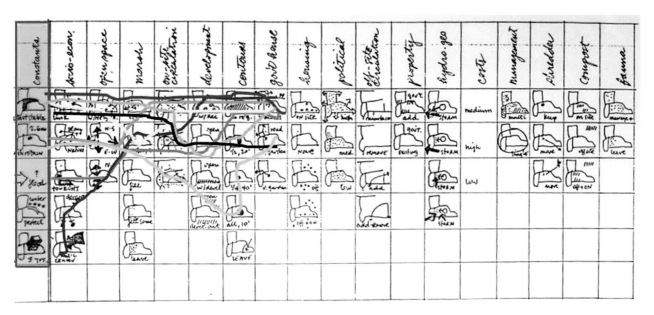

**Figure 7.32:** Selecting the sequence of diagrams. The student who picked number 1 in the lottery was able to select first among the variables; the choice is indicated with the red line. Subsequent students had to choose a different set of variables so that each collection was ultimately a unique combination. This is symbolically drawn here by different colors. | Source: C. Steinitz, ed., Alternative Futures for The Bermuda Dump (Cambridge, MA: Graduate School of Design, Harvard University, 1986).

students, so that each individual collection of choices was distinctive from the others. By the end, when the selected drawn-on-plastic diagrams were overlain, there were 14 substantially different diagrammatic and sequential initial design strategies. These were available after the fourth studio class, at the end of the second week of class.

This stage of the Bermuda study raises a special issue of pedagogic ethics. Even in the most organized or restrictive faculty-led studio, each student has an absolute right to explore his or her own ideas, and in his or her own way. However, one of my objectives is the teaching and testing of methods which are expected to be of interest and of use to the student, and the priority in this particular studio was not the encouragement of the students' idiosyncratic creative ways. The ethics of being a teacher require this to be openly stated, openly discussed, and somehow managed within the social contract between student and teacher. In this case, all the students chose the studio fully

aware of how it would be conducted and why. I am well aware that some colleagues and some students do not agree with this position.

Next, each student prepared a fully developed design and a model of that design to a single, pre-agreed format at a common scale using standard and mass produced materials, as organized by student subcommittees. Each of the 14 models could be segmented and placed in a cardboard shipping carton (figure 7.33).

**Impact, decision**

At the end of the sixth week of class, a small group of students returned to Bermuda and presented all fourteen of the student designs to the Bermuda Planning Committee, the people responsible for the redevelopment of the dump site. After careful consideration, the Committee selected three of the designs to move forward to the next stage.

**Figure 7.33: Four of the fourteen initial designs as built by the students, made to travel.** | Source: C. Steinitz, ed., *Alternative Futures for The Bermuda Dump* (Cambridge, MA: Graduate School of Design, Harvard University, 1986).

## Feedback

Once the class was reunited, each student whose design had *not* been chosen joined one of the three remaining design teams. The teams were of approximately equal size and each followed one of three very different design strategies (thereafter called A, B, and C), and prepared a final design (figure 7.34). At the end of the semester, the three designs were presented to and discussed with Prime Minister Swan and other representatives from Bermuda who attended a meeting at Harvard. Afterwards, the entire class was then invited to return to Bermuda and publically present the three final designs.

## Decision

Bermuda had a population of approximately 90,000 people in 1986, and about 10,000 of them saw at least one of the presentations and the exhibition made by the students. As luck would have it, the final designs were able to be on display for several weeks in a prime and central public location. Prime Minister Swan and the planning committee then decided to have the choice of one of the three park concepts placed before the electorate in a special poll. The intent was not to build one of the student designs specifically, but rather to identify the preferences of the general public for the strategies that were embedded in the design options. Several years later, an adaptation of that student design was eventually built by the government of Bermuda.

This adaptation of the sequential change model was used to purposely and rapidly generate a wide range of preliminary design options. It is a robust and effective method, and I have subsequently organized several studies which apply it. From an academic perspective, it works best when there is a substantial component of anonymity and a low personal involvement in the preliminary designs. It is not a test of the student's skill or intelligence. As can be seen from the final three proposals, this method can lead to a wide range of how proposed changes are expressed. It is interesting to note that the winning design (C in figure 7.34) was the one that most closely conformed to the sequence of upper row and left hand section of the diagram layout with which the studio got started (the red line in figure 7.32).

**Figure 7.34: Designs A, B, and C.** | Source: C. Steinitz, ed., Alternative Futures for The Bermuda Dump (Cambridge, MA: Graduate School of Design, Harvard University, 1986)

## Notes

1. Adapted from C. Steinitz, M. Binford, P. Cote, T. Edwards Jr., S. Ervin, R. T. T. Forman, C. Johnson, R. Kiester, D. Mouat, D. Olson, A. Shearer, R. Toth, and R. Wills, *Landscape Planning for Biodiversity; Alternative Futures for the Region of Camp Pendleton, CA* (Cambridge, MA: Graduate School of Design, Harvard University, 1996) [P. Bales, D. Barnard, H. Bidwell, J. Blomberg, D. Bowser, J. Crowder, D. Friedman, K. Goldsmith, G. Y. Han, B. Hoffman, M. Mildbrandt, K. Pickering, H. Quarles, C. Steinbaum, A. Tsunekawa, R. Winstead, E. Yovel]; C. Steinitz, ed., *An Alternative Future for the Region of Camp Pendleton, California.* (Cambridge, MA: Graduate School of Design, Harvard University, 1997) [C. Adams, L. Alexander, J. DeNormandie, R. Durant, L. Eberhart, J. Felkner, K. Hickey, A. Mellinger, R. Narita, T. Slattery, C. Viellard, Y.-F. Wang, E. M. Wright]; C. W. Adams and C. Steinitz. "An Alternative Future for the Region of Camp Pendleton, CA," in *Landscape Perspectives of Land Use Changes,* eds. U. Mander and R. H. G. Jongman, 18–83, Advances in Ecological Sciences 6 (Southampton, UK: WIT Press, 2000); E. Howard, *Garden Cities for Tomorrow* (London: S. Sonnenschein & Co., Ltd., 1902); D. White, et al., "Assessing Risks to Bio-diversity from Future Landscape Change," *Conservation Biology* 11, no. 2: 349–60.

2. E. Howard, *Garden Cities for Tomorrow* (London: S. Sonnenschein & Co., Ltd., 1902).

3. Adapted from J. C. Vargas-Moreno, "Participatory Landscape Planning Using Portable Geospatial Information Systems and Technologies: The Case of the Osa Region of Costa Rica" (D. Des. diss. Graduate School of Design, Harvard University, 2008).

4. The hardware used in the conducting of the field work was a regular laptop computer in which ArcView software was installed, and an interactive pen display. The interactive pen display used was the Cintiq 21UX by Wacom Companies. This display provides capabilities for drawing directly on the screen. It combines the advantages of a large-format LCD monitor with the control and productivity of cordless, battery-free pen technology.

5. Adapted from C. Steinitz, ed., *Alternative Futures for The Bermuda Dump* (Cambridge, MA: Graduate School of Design, Harvard University, 1986) [R. Choksombatchai, B. Cutting, R. Daimant, T. Dierker, M. Fry, M. Gerard, N. Gerdts, V. Jearkjirm, T. Johnson, E. Lardner, A. Mackin, S. Murphy, T. Oslund, M. Poirier, N. Rejab, N. Shapero, L. Thompson]; Bermuda, Department of Planning, *The Pembroke Marsh Plan 1987* (Bermuda: Department of Planning, Government of Bermuda, 1987).

# CHAPTER 8

# Geodesign under uncertainty

THE CONSTRAINING AND COMBINATORIAL change models share the assumption that stakeholder groups and/or the geodesign team is uncertain about how change for the future should come about. This may involve uncertainty about the assumptions, the requirements, or the design options for the requirements. While a confident designer is a commonly-held stereotype (and is an assumption of the anticipatory, participatory, and sequential change models described in the previous chapter), being uncertain should not be seen in a negative light. This is a normal condition faced frequently by geodesign teams and should be recognized as such by all involved. This recognition will profoundly affect the eventual choice of a change model and how it is used.

## The constraining change model

The **constraining** method, depicted in figure 8.1, is an appropriate choice when the geodesign team is not sure of the criteria for selecting among the several options for any single requirement, and has no preconceptions as to the final design or its alternatives. It is most useful when the relative importance of the objectives or requirements of the study's decision model are rank ordered and are found to approximate Zipf's law in their relative importance (figure 5.3). During the third iteration of the framework, the team then considers the options *in rank order of the importance of the requirement,* systematically narrowing options to the point where one is moved forward towards the final design.

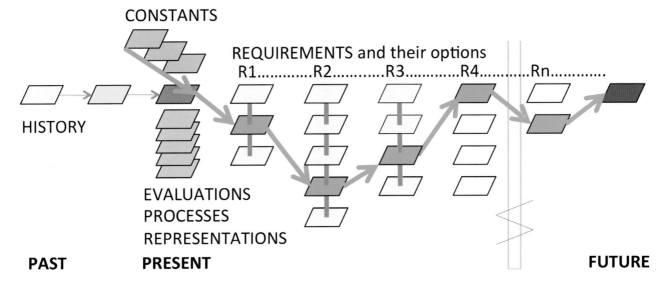

**Figure 8.1: The constraining change model.** | Source: Carl Steinitz.

The constraining approach is also frequently used when the design process is the work of a committee or part of a participatory process. The participants discuss one issue at a time, one objective or requirement toward which the future design is being directed, then after its options are compared, a decision is made and the group moves to the next objective or requirement needing deliberation. Eventually, successful design ideas may be reached. An advantage of this method is that it allows the designer to retain good partial solutions on the most important issues, and avoid serious errors along the way.

## Cagliari, Sardinia, Italy [1]

The international workshop "Alternative Futures for the Metropolitan Area of Cagliari, Sardinia" was held in Cagliari for a five-day period in March 2009. The full-time participants were twenty architecture and engineering students from the University of Cagliari and 12 landscape architecture students from the University of Hannover (Germany). The workshop was organized

by Professor Emanuela Abis, Claudia Palmas and Stefano Pili, University of Cagliari, and Professor Christina von Haaren, University of Hannover, Germany, and Christian Albert and Daniela Kempa, Leibniz University, Germany. The teaching team was led by me (Carl Steinitz), with Juan Carlos Vargas-Moreno, Tess Canfield, and the faculty organizers listed above. The "problem" focus of the workshop was to be the future growth of Cagliari, the capital of Sardinia, Italy (figure 8.2).

By definition, short workshops such as this one have little time available, compared to semester-long studio courses or a professional study. This limits the freedom of the participants, in this case the students, to define what they are exploring. During a workshop, the organizing faculty make many decisions in advance, whereas in my studios an important part of the students' education involves them defining the problem itself and selecting the methods that should be applied. For the relatively short (five-day) Cagliari workshop, the faculty decided several variables ahead of time, including the scope of the problem, its methods,

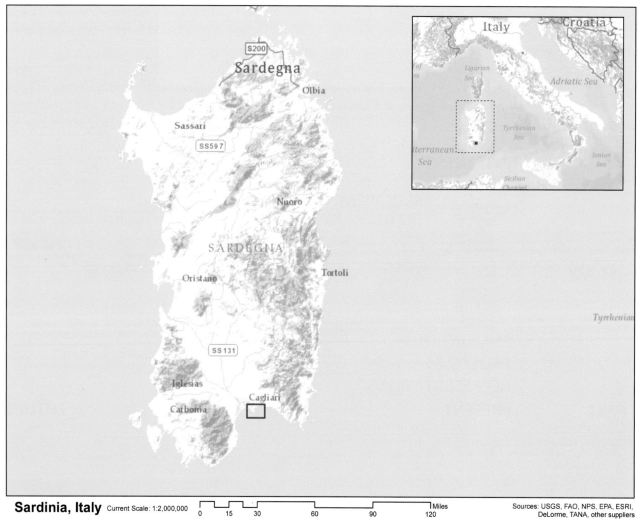

**Sardinia, Italy** Current Scale: 1:2,000,000

0   15   30        60        90        120   Miles

Sources: USGS, FAO, NPS, EPA, ESRI, DeLorme, TANA, other suppliers

**Figure 8.2:** The Cagliari, Sardinia, study area.

and its expected products. One early decision we made was that the design would follow a constraining change model.

## Representation

Cagliari has about 160,000 residents, and about 500,000 people live in the metropolitan region. Sardinia has a substantial tourism industry, with millions of visitors annually. Despite the fact that Cagliari is a modern city with an implemented system of planning, very little of the necessary workshop data were available in digital form. This is not an uncommon circumstance and one must always adjust expectations to the available resources. We did have access to current land use data (which we then generalized into a simpler classification), a terrain model, several sector plans, and the relevant section of the Sardinian Regional Landscape Plan. We also utilized the many photographs that students took on their site visit as well as aerial imagery that was available on-line.

The workshop began with two intensive days devoted to a general orientation to the study area (figure 8.3). We learned about its history, its current characteristics, how the city functions, its current issues, and future projections. Local experts shared this information with us during a series of brief, 20-minute-long presentation and question/answer sessions. During this time we also took a half-day guided bus and walking trip throughout the study area, to be as familiar with the local environment as possible.

## Process, evaluation

We created 10 process-evaluation teams of students, each devoted to evaluating a different process that was deemed central to the future of the region: habitat, the visual landscape, the cultural and recreational landscape, residential development, tourism, transport, hydrology, and because of a special interest on the part of the German students, geothermal energy, solar

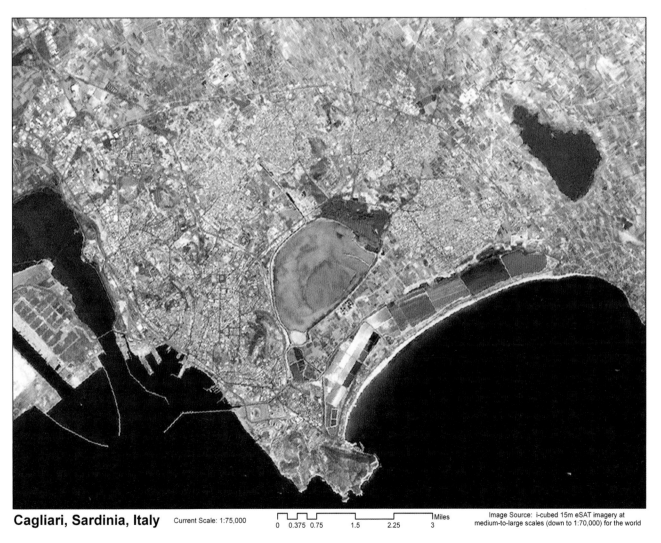

**Cagliari, Sardinia, Italy**   Current Scale: 1:75,000    0  0.375  0.75   1.5   2.25   3 ⌐Miles    Image Source: i-cubed 15m eSAT imagery at medium-to-large scales (down to 1:70,000) for the world

**Figure 8.3: The Cagliari metropolitan area.**

and wind energy, and biomass energy. Each team was charged with producing two items. The first was a simple two-color map drawn by hand on clear plastic, in which green represented highly valuable elements that had been identified as sustaining to that team's particular process of interest (and therefore which should be protected), while red showed areas of vulnerability to that process (and which would need improvement). Areas deemed to be unrelated to the evaluation were left unshaded.

A team's second product was a numbered set of geo-referenced diagrams with notes representing ideas for

projects and policies to change their process, either via the protection of valuable areas or the improvement of problem areas (figure 8.4). These were to be drawn on thin plastic sheets and color-coded uniquely for each of the 10 teams. Each group also rank-ordered their potential projects in terms of their importance and likelihood of producing beneficial impacts, as a pre-assessment for incorporation into a change-design.

Standardizing color codes, graphic scales, and styles of representation is a critically essential part of a geodesign study. I cannot emphasize that enough. Regardless of whether the

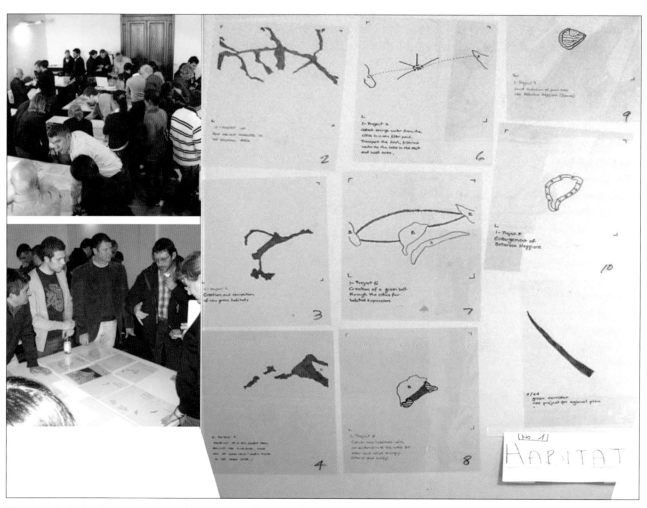

**Figure 8.4: Projects and policies that were drafted by the team whose process model was habitat conservation and enhancement.** | Source: C. Steinitz, "Teaching in a Multidisciplinary Collaborative Workshop Format: The Cagliari Workshop," in 2010 FutureMAC09: Alternative Futures for the Metropolitan Area of Cagliari, The Cagliari Workshop: An Experiment in Interdisciplinary Education / FutureMAC09 : Scenari Alternativi per l'area Metropolitana di Cagliari, Workshop di Sperimentazione Didattica Interdisciplinare, by C. Steinitz, E. Abis, V. von Haaren, C. Albert, D. Kempa, C. Palmas, S. Pili, and J. C. Vargas-Moreno (Roma: Gangemi, 2010).

leaders are a geodesign team or a professionally organized firm, or it is during a workshop or a semester-long academic studio, participants and visitors need to be able to rapidly comprehend each other's work. A shared graphic language is indispensable to ensure this task. Note the crudeness of the initial diagrams, a normal outgrowth of speed in production. The graphic qualities of such sketches have little to do with the quality of thinking behind them and everything to do with time and the technologies of data management and representation available in this case.

At the end of this stage, each of the 10 process-evaluation teams made a concise presentation of how it understood its assigned process, how it defined the priority areas of conservation and change, and what its initial rank-ordered set of potential projects was. The full workshop group observed these presentations in anticipation of later reorganizing themselves into different teams for the change-stages of the workshop. Everyone would need a full range of knowledge in order to best integrate all of the processes. All of the local experts who had given talks at the beginning of the workshop were present, and they then met with the student teams, presented their critiques, proposed revisions,

**Figure 8.5: The long table with all the proposed projects, classified by color.** | Photo by Tess Canfield.

and suggested additional potential projects. Afterwards, teams made a second, brief presentation of their modified evaluations and proposals. Here the standardized method of graphic representation that we had instituted again demonstrated its value as it enabled participants to rapidly understand what was happening without the need for extensive further clarification.

At this point in the workshop, the start of the third day, all of the proposed projects were uniquely numbered by rank order and systematically organized onto a long table (figure 8.5). This arrangement also enabled many additional potential projects to be contributed in the next stage of the workshop.

## Change

The faculty then re-organized the students out of their original ten process-evaluations teams and into six larger multi-disciplinary teams, each representing a different "stakeholder group" with interests in the future of the Cagliari metropolitan area. These new "change teams" were:

1. Team A, conservationists
2. Team B, residential, commercial, and industrial developers
3. Team C, a foundation for the support of renewable energy
4. Team D, several local governments in the area, each seeking reelection
5. Team E, the tourism development board
6. Team F, regional planners emphasizing the Sardinian Regional Landscape Plan

Each new change team first had to reach agreement among its members on the assumed objectives and requirements of its stakeholder group and envision a scenario of priority projects and policies that would enhance the interests of the client. Every team's overall task was to make a design for changes that would support those objectives over the next 20 years. Each team also had to accommodate a 4-percent growth in population and its concomitant land-use changes, and be as self-sufficient in energy as possible. Their respective resulting designs would be based on a selection of the projects presented by the process-evaluation teams plus any variations or additional projects proposed by the change team. The new or varied projects were to be drawn in the same graphic format as the prior sets, and once each one was complete, they were numbered and placed on the long table so that they were available for use by anyone else.

Each change team had the constraining task of selecting no more than 15 of the available projects from the full collection that now numbered approximately 150. In some cases change teams grouped and redrew projects related to a particular process, thus limiting the number of plastic sheets they had to overlay. For this part of the workshop, we had opted to use a low-tech, rapid and easy method for overlaying the drawings, using an overhead projector as a light table and a digital camera for recording (figure 8.6).

Then one person from each change team made a concise presentation to the rest of the class, while the other students returned as members to their original process-evaluation teams to comparatively assess the impacts of each of the proposed designs.

**Impact, decision round one**

The impact assessments consisted of each process-evaluation team evaluating each of the six stakeholder change proposals with a six-level scale. Though the scale was simple, it still required thoughtful internal discussion and judgment by the impact assessors. The teams assigned scores:

- +3 represented a much better circumstance for that process;
- +1 meant a better situation;
- 0 meant no change;
- -1 meant a worse situation;
- -3 meant that it was significantly worse, and
- -5 meant that the process was "lost."

An example of an impact deserving a score of -5 would be, for instance, if a project were to inadvertently eliminate

**Figure 8.6: Participants from the change teams, working on their first design.** | Source: C. Steinitz, "Teaching in a Multidisciplinary Collaborative Workshop Format: The Cagliari Workshop," in 2010 FutureMAC09: Alternative Futures for the Metropolitan Area of Cagliari, The Cagliari Workshop: An Experiment in Interdisciplinary Education / FutureMAC09 : Scenari Alternativi per l'area Metropolitana di Cagliari, Workshop di Sperimentazione Didattica Interdisciplinare, by C. Steinitz, E. Abis, V. von Haaren, C. Albert, D. Kempa, C. Palmas, S. Pili, and J. C. Vargas-Moreno (Roma: Gangemi, 2010).

the resident flamingo population of Cagliari. All numerical evaluations were then written on a chart we drew onto a whiteboard; scores circled in green meant the team was doing best among the six alternatives and a red circle meant the team was doing relatively worse (figure 8.7).

This graphic representation of the impact assessment was visible to all workshop participants but not subject to public discussion. Rather, it was intended for private consultation between the change teams and the impact assessment teams, with the known intent that the designs would be improved in a second stage. Particular attention was necessary for those aspects that had earned red circles. One important technical byproduct of

this first round of design and comparative assessment was that some projects were clearly more significant, either because they were central to the change proposals of one stakeholder team or they were common elements in the designs of several teams. A small group of students, one representing each process-evaluation team, then digitally redrew these projects and linked them to a spreadsheet.

### Feedback, change round two

On the fourth day, the participants were again regrouped into their stakeholder change teams, and we started a second change-design cycle. Each team could rapidly drop or add

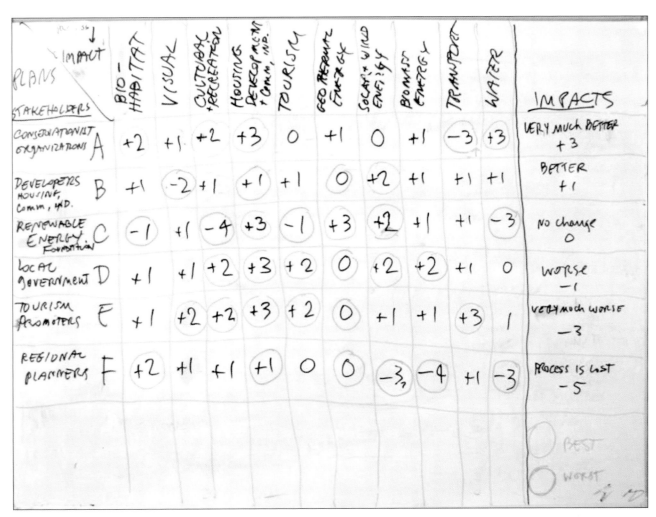

**Figure 8.7: The first impact assessment of the six designs.** | Source: C. Steinitz, "Teaching in a Multidisciplinary Collaborative Workshop Format: The Cagliari Workshop," in 2010 FutureMAC09: Alternative Futures for the Metropolitan Area of Cagliari, The Cagliari Workshop: An Experiment in Interdisciplinary Education / FutureMAC09 : Scenari Alternativi per l'area Metropolitana di Cagliari, Workshop di Sperimentazione Didattica Interdisciplinare, by C. Steinitz, E. Abis, V. von Haaren, C. Albert, D. Kempa, C. Palmas, S. Pili, and J. C. Vargas-Moreno (Roma: Gangemi, 2010).

projects. Several teams made new projects and variations that again were brought to the attention of the entire group, numbered, and placed on the long table for common use. New diagrams that were then part of any design were also redrawn digitally and added to the digital file of projects. Each team presented their designs a second time, and they were again assessed for their impacts by the process model teams. This time the presentation session was held in silence because everyone had become sufficiently familiar with the standardized graphic conventions.

## Impact, round two

A second round of comparative impact assessments was then made. At this time all work was assumed to be finished except for a very few last-minute changes that could be made within the briefest of time. Each change team delegated one person to convert its design to a digital format within a GIS so that all projects could be combined into a complete set of digital graphics for the final presentation on the fifth and final day of the workshop (figure 8.8).

## Decision, round two

The graphic product and format for the final public presentation was specified by the faculty. It would consist of the following:

1. three to five images presenting the change team's principal policy objectives in order of importance,
2. an image of the accumulated projects for each process, with the processes presented in rank order of importance,
3. an image of the existing conditions,
4. an image of the proposed changes in the design,
5. an image of the future state for Cagliari (the existing and changed conditions), and
6. a summary graphic showing only the proposed projects and the proposed alternative future, for comparative purposes.

Each of the teams used these materials during their respective 10-minute presentations to an audience that included the entire workshop group, all of the local experts who had participated, and many additional faculty and students from the University of Cagliari. All final presentations were conducted in Italian, and afterwards time was provided for questions, answers, discussion, and a friendly argument or two.

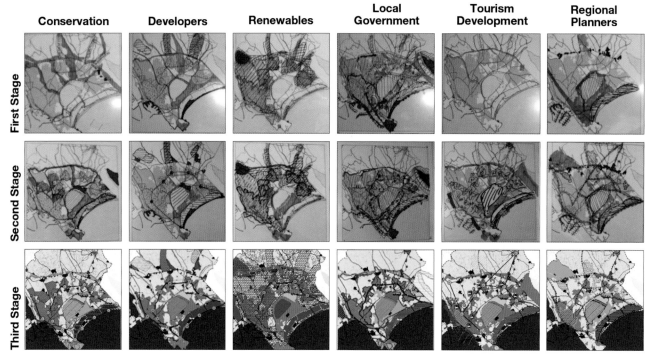

**Figure 8.8: The six final designs and their stages of design development.** | Source: C. Steinitz, "Teaching in a Multidisciplinary Collaborative Workshop Format: The Cagliari Workshop," in 2010 FutureMAC09: Alternative Futures for the Metropolitan Area of Cagliari, The Cagliari Workshop: An Experiment in Interdisciplinary Education / FutureMAC09 : Scenari Alternativi per l'area Metropolitana di Cagliari, Workshop di Sperimentazione Didattica Interdisciplinare, by C. Steinitz, E. Abis, V. von Haaren, C. Albert, D. Kempa, C. Palmas, S. Pili, and J. C. Vargas-Moreno (Roma: Gangemi, 2010).

Each of the local experts was invited to judge which of the six alternatives best met his or her expectations for the future of the Cagliari metropolitan area. In some cases people chose to reflect their real institutional stakeholder interests while others chose a broader personal perspective.

Towards the conclusion of the workshop, our discussion focused on the decision model. Should the decision makers select only one of the six alternatives, thus seeing the exercise as a zero sum game? Or, would it be possible to select popular elements from among the alternative designs and generate a new combined plan that joined (and possibly compromised) the interests of the stakeholder groups in developing a larger constituency for a negotiated design?

To provide additional information for this last discussion, we then conducted a very rapid exercise in real time. One of the workshop leaders, Christian Albert, had made a frequency assessment of the number of times each of the policies and its component projects had been selected by the six change proposals. Each was digital and linked to a spreadsheet of the components of each design. Another workshop leader, Juan Carlos Vargas-Moreno, then selected the most frequently used policies and projects and created a composite digital design from the selected project graphics (figure 8.9).

After viewing and discussing this composite design, the local experts and Cagliari faculty generally agreed that the proposal was a good one. With this we concluded our working

Conserve the Molentargius Wetlands (6x)

Protect the open water areas and the hydrological system (6x)

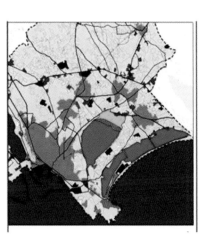

New transport network of metro/ train (5x)

Connecting habitats to a new green belt (4x)

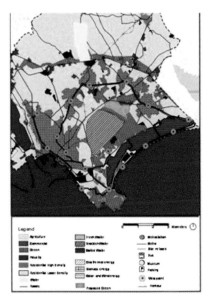

**Figure 8.9: The composite design and its major contributing policies and projects.** | Source: C. Steinitz, "Teaching in a Multidisciplinary Collaborative Workshop Format: The Cagliari Workshop," in 2010 FutureMAC09: Alternative Futures for the Metropolitan Area of Cagliari, The Cagliari Workshop: An Experiment in Interdisciplinary Education / FutureMAC09 : Scenari Alternativi per l'area Metropolitana di Cagliari, Workshop di Sperimentazione Didattica Interdisciplinare, by C. Steinitz, E. Abis, V. von Haaren, C. Albert, D. Kempa, C. Palmas, S. Pili, and J. C. Vargas-Moreno (Roma: Gangemi, 2010).

sessions and ended the workshop, apart from the excellent final social event held for all participants, especially the students who were a very satisfied but tired group by the end of this week.

For a short but intense workshop as this one was, the organizing faculty had agreed from the beginning on how to structure the activities of the participants. We knew we had to divide the geodesign process into clearly defined tasks, each to be accomplished within a fixed and concise time, since the biggest liability facing the workshop would be lengthy and irrelevant discussion. We wanted to produce and compare several alternatives based on different sets of objectives and requirements associated with different stakeholder interests. We also wanted to have at least one round of feedback and revision at the phase of the change model. The constraining method is the method which most efficiently generates a design strategy under the circumstances faced by the student teams. Without having had the students directed towards a final design using the constraining change model, I doubt whether we could accomplished as much as well.

## The combinatorial change model

The **combinatorial** change model is most useful when there are a very few requirements, or when the few main objectives are of similar importance (figure 8.10). The combinatorial way of designing is also a good choice when the geodesign team or the client is not sure of the appropriate choices among options in the sequence of decisions leading to the design.

In the combinatorial way of designing, the geodesign team first identifies the few most significant requirements of the scenario that will guide the design. Each of these requirements is likely to have a range of potential solutions, for example, for the route of a proposed highway. Consider the following as a set: an exit from the highway, a possible new shopping center and new high density housing. Several optional locations and arrangements can be selected, but not too many as the number of alternatives will propagate quickly. Useful sets to include are what can be considered the extremes of the possible range for each requirement. The method simultaneously combines these option-sets for the most important requirements and prepares

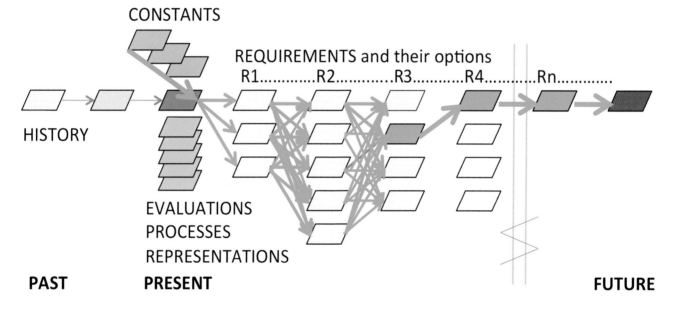

**Figure 8.10: The combinatorial change model.** | Source: Carl Steinitz.

partial solutions *of all combinations*. These alternatives are then systematically evaluated before one (or a few) is selected for further development.

   The combinatorial approach is commonly used to investigate alternative scenarios for the future. The great advantage of this approach is that it tests the most significant requirements before proceeding much further into the design and therefore helps the geodesign team avoid serious mistakes. However, its liabilities include the fact that it can be difficult to identify the most significant options a priori, and the number of designs that must be generated from the simultaneous combinations can become very large indeed.

## The Roncajette Park and the Industrial Zone, Padova, Italy [2]

This case study illustrates the combinatorial change model. La Zona Industriale di Padova (ZIP) is the largest "industrial park" in Italy, employing about 25,000 people (figure 8.11). The ZIP consortium owns a large adjacent area, the Parco del Roncajette. The park was initially conceived in the 1960s as a barrier between the old city of Padova and a new industrial zone, but by 2005 it was generally seen as a failed park, though it still continued to be an important link in a regional landscape system. The city of Padova and ZIP were both committed to building a new park on this land, but there were many unknowns.

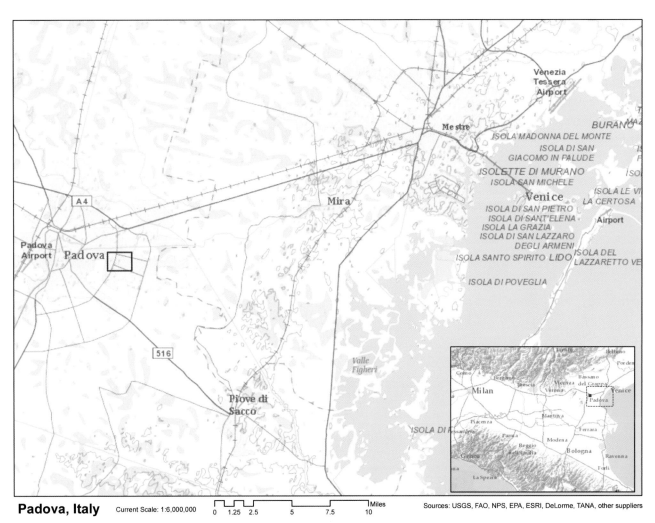

**Padova, Italy**   Current Scale: 1:6,000,000   0  1.25  2.5   5   7.5   10 ⌐Miles          Sources: USGS, FAO, NPS, EPA, ESRI, DeLorme, TANA, other suppliers

**Figure 8.11: Study area including the Parco del Roncajette and La Zona Industriale di Padova.**

ZIP was also dedicated to implementing a "Sustainable Industrial Area Model" consistent with recent directives from the European Union.

At the request of ZIP and the city of Padova, in 2006 I led a semester-long studio with Laura Cipriani, Juan Carlos Vargas-Moreno, and Tess Canfield which produced designs that tested different sets of requirements for the Parco del Roncajette, ZIP, and their urban study area (figure 8.11). The studio was organized as a collaborative effort with substantial self-management by 13 students from Harvard's programs in urban planning and design, landscape architecture, and architecture. The students' designs were intended to be the focus of what was expected to be intense local debate. ZIP and the city of Padova wanted the proposals so that they could clarify their assumptions, requirements and preferences before commissioning their own designs. Given the complexity of the problem, the many combinations of requirements and options, and our limited time frame, the geodesign team chose to use a combinatorial change model, to be applied at more than one scale, to generate alternative designs.

**Representation, process**

Both the Roncajette River, heavily polluted by both urban discharge and ZIP industry, and several large flood control channels all flowed through the study area towards the nearby Venice Lagoon (figure 8.12). Existing proposals to reduce pollution had yet to be implemented. The Roncajette site also contained the city's sewage treatment plant, the famous analog model of the Venice Lagoon, and residential and agricultural in-holdings. Padova had been trying to follow a "green spaces strategy" that included connecting many small "green areas" and a reconsidered future of an existing local airfield. Meanwhile, ZIP had major expansion plans on nearby farmland. Thus, all at the same time, a large new park was to be designed while an adjacent industrial zone was being ecologically reconsidered, and another industrial zone had to be

**Figure 8.12: Roncajette park and the industrial zone.** | Source: C. Steinitz, L. Cipriani, J. C. Vargas-Moreno, and T. Canfield. Padova e il Paesaggio-Scenarui Futuri peri il Parco Roncajette e la Zona Industriale / Padova and the Landscape — Alternative Futures for the Roncajette Park and the Industrial Zone. (Cambridge, MA: Graduate School of Design, Harvard University, Commune de Padova and Zona Industriale Padova, 2005). Photo by ZIP.

preplanned nearby, all in the context of the city's landscape and regional infrastructure strategies.

## Evaluation

During a first orientation and scoping visit to Padova, the students prepared a list of observations, evaluations and ideas for projects and policies as reactions to the daily meetings and discussions in which we engaged. They also reviewed data that had previously been organized. By the end of the field visit, the students had identified 250 possible projects and policies, each of which was represented by a simple hand-drawn diagram in a manner similar to those in the Cagliari case study (see figure 8.5 earlier in this chapter).

Once we were back at Harvard, we used a digital process (designed previously by Juan Carlos Vargas-Moreno), to store and access the diagrams: all of the policy and project diagrams were digitized and entered into a "project list" maintained on an Excel spreadsheet. For each project we listed its unique identifying number, the name of the person who had proposed it, and whether the project was a spatially specific physical change or a policy. Each was also classified according to its decision-level

and relevance for different types of policy: transportation, industrial, hydrology, heritage, utilities or ecological. All digital project and policy diagrams were then also organized as separate layers for use within ArcGIS. By simply selecting the numbers of desired layers via the spreadsheet in overlay-order, the students could quickly create different combinations of diagrams as needed.

## Change

Our next exercise involved the combinatorial testing of many of ZIP and Padova's most important change requirements in their many combinations of options. As examples, at the scale of the city, we overlaid the sets of potential projects that might combine into a connected system of green spaces (an example is shown figure 8.13A). We also combined sets of diagrams of potential actions to generate a new identity for the Parco Roncajette as a central park for the city (an example is figure 8.13B). These and other initial exercises allowed the students to rapidly combine, visualize and consider many different solutions for the most important requirements, albeit via simple diagrams.

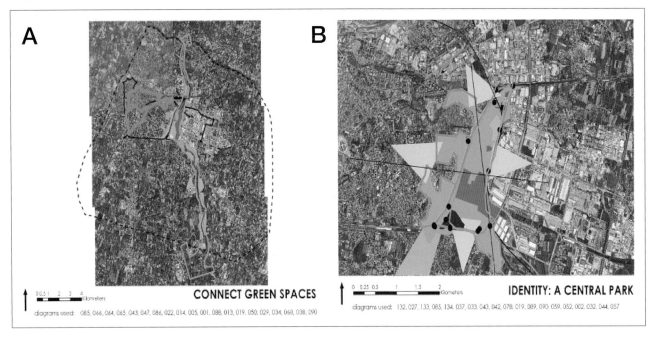

CONNECT GREEN SPACES
diagrams used:  085, 066, 064, 065, 043, 047, 086, 022, 014, 005, 001, 088, 013, 019, 050, 029, 034, 068, 038, 090

IDENTITY: A CENTRAL PARK
diagrams used:  132, 027, 133, 085, 134, 037, 033, 043, 042, 078, 019, 089, 090, 059, 052, 002, 032, 044, 057

**Figures 8.13A and B: Connected green spaces at city scale and a new Central Park, schematically designed by selecting and combining numbered diagrams to evaluate opportunities for change.** | Source: C. Steinitz, L. Cipriani, J. C. Vargas-Moreno, and T. Canfield. Padova e il Paesaggio-Scenarui Futuri peri il Parco Roncajette e la Zona Industriale / Padova and the Landscape—Alternative Futures for the Roncajette Park and the Industrial Zone. (Cambridge, MA: Graduate School of Design, Harvard University, Commune de Padova and Zona Industriale Padova, 2005).

Through further experimentation, the class used a combinatorial change model to produce strategic diagrammatic designs for the most important requirements. During studio discussions they comparatively assessed these, and then worked in their change teams to develop three scenarios by combining different projects and policy options. For these, we made preliminary designs and presented them to a visiting delegation from ZIP and Padova for their feedback. Everyone was in agreement that all designs would need to resolve six constants and integrate options for another six high priority requirements (figure 8.14).

With these constants and requirements now determined, three combined strategies (A, B, and C) were developed further as staged and more detailed designs (figures 8.15A, B, and C).

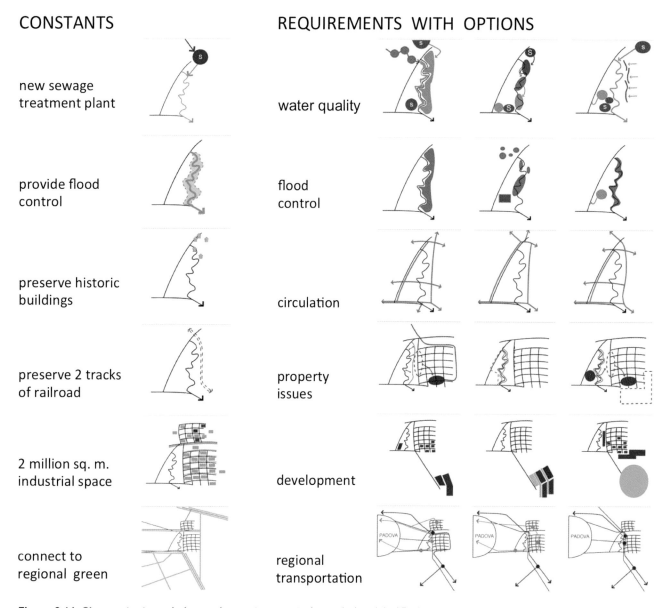

**CONSTANTS**

new sewage treatment plant

provide flood control

preserve historic buildings

preserve 2 tracks of railroad

2 million sq. m. industrial space

connect to regional green

**REQUIREMENTS WITH OPTIONS**

water quality

flood control

circulation

property issues

development

regional transportation

**Figure 8.14: Six constants and six requirements were to be combined into three alternative designs.** | Source: C. Steinitz, L. Cipriani, J. C. Vargas-Moreno, and T. Canfield. Padova e il Paesaggio-Scenarui Futuri peri il Parco Roncajette e la Zona Industriale / Padova and the Landscape — Alternative Futures for the Roncajette Park and the Industrial Zone. (Cambridge, MA: Graduate School of Design, Harvard University, Commune de Padova and Zona Industriale Padova, 2005).

Figure 8.15A, B, and C: Designs for scenarios A, B, and C for ZIP and the Parco Roncajette. | Source: C. Steinitz, L. Cipriani, J. C. Vargas-Moreno, and T. Canfield. Padova e il Paesaggio-Scenarui Futuri peri il Parco Roncajette e la Zona Industriale / Padova and the Landscape—Alternative Futures for the Roncajette Park and the Industrial Zone. (Cambridge, MA: Graduate School of Design, Harvard University, Commune de Padova and Zona Industriale Padova, 2005).

## Impact

The student teams that had made the original process-evaluations qualitatively compared the relative potential impacts of the three alternatives (figure 8.16). While all three designs performed somewhat similarly when measured in these ways, the inverse relationship between the cost and performance of these alternative designs was an unanticipated but nevertheless interesting finding and generated much discussion.

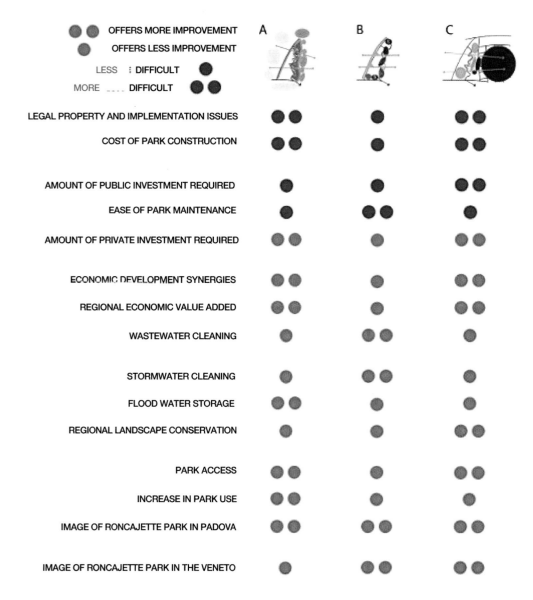

**Figure 8.16: Assessing the impacts of the three designs.** | Source: C. Steinitz, L. Cipriani, J. C. Vargas-Moreno, and T. Canfield. Padova e il Paesaggio-Scenarui Futuri peri il Parco Roncajette e la Zona Industriale / Padova and the Landscape—Alternative Futures for the Roncajette Park and the Industrial Zone. (Cambridge, MA: Graduate School of Design, Harvard University, Commune de Padova and Zona Industriale Padova, 2005).

**Decision**

We had the unusual opportunity to return to Italy to present the work to the people of Padova. The designs and their assessments were put on display for a month in a glass-fronted exhibition hall on the main shopping street, Via Roma. During that time, thousands of people saw the designs. Meanwhile, a private meeting was held among city and ZIP leaders and the studio team (figure 8.17), and we discussed and compared each alternative thoroughly.

**Figure 8.17: The exhibition and the meeting at ZIP.** | Source: C. Steinitz, L. Cipriani, J. C. Vargas-Moreno, and T. Canfield. Padova e il Paesaggio-Scenarui Futuri peri il Parco Roncajette e la Zona Industriale / Padova and the Landscape—Alternative Futures for the Roncajette Park and the Industrial Zone. (Cambridge, MA: Graduate School of Design, Harvard University, Commune de Padova and Zona Industriale Padova, 2005).

During these discussions, a proposal for a fourth design emerged, one that was based in large part on scenario C but which also combined elements from the other two designs. Because all of the representations of design elements in each of the three alternatives were organized as separate digital files to be digitally shared and combined, this new design could readily be generated and viewed by everyone (figures 8.18 and 8.19).

Upon further reflection and discussion by all at the meeting, this fourth design was deemed superior to the other three. ZIP and the city of Padova accepted it as the basis for their design strategy for the park and the "green" renovation of the industrial zone. The main features of the design are the renovation of the industrial zone, especially its water management, energy production, and urban and rooftop landscapes. A new regional rail link was added, and the Parco Roncajette was remade as a *smaller* central park once land near the industrial area was used for a new technical university as well as a new headquarters building for ZIP. This design strategy was later adopted by the Padova and ZIP as their preferred approach. It is being implemented as part of the plans associated with the fiftieth anniversary of the industrial zone.

Issues of time and project management for the complex and numerous requirements and options made the combinatorial design strategy the wisest choice for this geodesign project. This study was organized from the beginning to be managed by student subcommittees, each in turn responsible for the entire enterprise for approximately one month. The initial management team had the task of deciding how the change model would be selected. In this case, I lectured to students on the multiple possible ways of designing that seemed suitable for the scope of this particular geodesign problem that they were facing. After discussing the possible options, it was the students who decided to organize the initial phase of design by the combinatorial change model. It was clear to them that the combinatorial model would allow the representatives of ZIP and the city of Padova to focus on defining the constants, the requirements, and their options (which would later be developed into the three alternative designs) during their visitors' planned trip to Harvard. This had to be an efficient process under significant time restraints, and it turned out to be a very successful exercise.

**Figure 8.18: The existing conditions.** | Source: C. Steinitz, L. Cipriani, J. C. Vargas-Moreno, and T. Canfield. Padova e il Paesaggio-Scenarui Futuri peri il Parco Roncajette e la Zona Industriale / Padova and the Landscape — Alternative Futures for the Roncajette Park and the Industrial Zone. (Cambridge, MA: Graduate School of Design, Harvard University, Commune de Padova and Zona Industriale Padova, 2005).

**Figure 8.19: The design strategy that was decided for ZIP and the Parco Roncajette, as shown by the elements in color.** | Source: C. Steinitz, L. Cipriani, J. C. Vargas-Moreno, and T. Canfield. Padova e il Paesaggio-Scenarui Futuri peri il Parco Roncajette e la Zona Industriale / Padova and the Landscape — Alternative Futures for the Roncajette Park and the Industrial Zone. (Cambridge, MA: Graduate School of Design, Harvard University, Commune de Padova and Zona Industriale Padova, 2005).

# Notes

1.  Adapted from C. Steinitz, "Teaching in a Multidisciplinary Collaborative Workshop Format: The Cagliari Workshop," in *2010 FutureMAC09: Alternative Futures for the Metropolitan Area of Cagliari, The Cagliari Workshop: An Experiment in Interdisciplinary Education / FutureMAC09: Scenari Alternativi per l'area Metropolitana di Cagliari, Workshop di Sperimentazione Didattica Interdisciplinare,* by C. Steinitz, E. Abis, V. von Haaren, C. Albert, D. Kempa, C. Palmas, S. Pili, and J. C. Vargas-Moreno (Roma: Gangemi, 2010).

2.  Adapted from C. Steinitz, L. Cipriani, J. C. Vargas-Moreno, and T. Canfield.*Padova e il Paesaggio-Scenarui Futuri peri il Parco Roncajette e la Zona Industriale / Padova and the Landscape—Alternative Futures for the Roncajette Park and the Industrial Zone.* (Cambridge, MA: Graduate School of Design, Harvard University, Commune de Padova and Zona Industriale Padova, 2005) [A. Adeya, C. Barrows, A. H. Bastow, P. Brashear, E. S. Chamberlain, K. Cinami, M. F. Spear, S. Hurley, Y. M. Kim, I. Liebert, L. T. Lynn, V. Shashidhar, J. Toy]

# CHAPTER 9

# Geodesign when knowing the rules

THE FOUR CASE STUDIES IN THIS CHAPTER: rule-based, optimized, agent-based, and mixed, are all in one way or another based on rules. The typical rule-based approach requires the geodesign team to specify a set of formal rules as a set of computer algorithms for developing the design. These rules can be based upon vulnerability evaluation criteria and act as constraints to change, such as, "For hummingbird (and other protected bird species) habitat, conserve the riparian cottonwood vegetation in the Upper San Pedro river basin." Or they can be related to attractiveness evaluation criteria: "Build houses on flat dry land and between 20 and 100 meters from a two-lane paved road," for example.

The simplest form of a rule-based land use change model is commonly known as a "build-out" analysis, in which all legally developable land is simulated as being developed. In the rule-based study of alternative futures for La Paz, development was allocated in a sequence of rule-based allocations for several land uses based upon their ability to pay for land, and subject to a variety of rule-based policy constraints. For example, "proactive" policies excluded development on the most valuable species habitats, and from and within the most preferred public views. Since neither of these policies currently exist, these rules are prospective and the scenarios they generate are essentially spatial policy experiments. This allows the conceptualization and testing of policies which can be much more elaborate and spatially detailed than what is practical to draw by hand. It is therefore a mainstay of geodesign.

A second common yet different use of rule-based approaches in change simulation is to convert model values into a single

metric, most often money. This enables optimization. In the optimized case study of the Telluride regional study detailed below, a much more sophisticated rule base was used to simulate the interactions between two real estate submarkets which placed different economic values on proximity to landscape elements, and which had varying levels of economic power. The market for "second homes" was highly sensitive to environmental quality and proximity to skiiing, and insensitive to land price and access to schools. In contrast, the market for "primary homes" was highly price-sensitive, but also placed value on access to community assets not important to seasonal visitors. In this case, the conceptual model of real estate submarkets was developed in consultation with local planners and other stakeholders, implemented using viewshed and travel time analyses, then validated using parcel-level development history and real estate transactions data. In general, this form of rule-based approach uses historical data to calibrate a change model whose goal is to replicate typical human behavior within a particular cultural and geographic study area.

Agent-based models inherit many characteristics from rule-based models. In particular, they typically have an explicit rule base calibrated to historic data or purposefully include changes in policy. However, agent-based models are distinguished by their overarching organization into computer "agents" designed to mimic real-world objects or people. Each agent is independent, they are social in that they react to each other, they interact with their environment, and they are goal-oriented. The agents often maintain history and "learn" from it, and compliance or behavior is assumed to vary at the individual level.

# The rule-based change model

**Rule-based** change modeling in general is spatially sophisticated, but behaviorally simple. People or land uses are divided into behavioral classes. Each member of a class can be influenced by site or locational conditions, but behaves deterministically and identically given those conditions. The proportional level of effort expended in various phases of implementation is different in rule-based modeling than in other methods. The generation and testing of a rule-base is an elaborate and sometimes difficult process. For example, while general models exist, these almost always require local calibration, and historic spatial data of uniform quality can be scarce. However, once rules are generated, rule-based change models are very easy to run and to adjust. Dozens to thousands of iterations can be automated, allowing the performance of "sensitivity testing." The ability to systematically and rapidly generate and test variants on policies in scale, location and time is an important advantage to this approach.

The rules for each requirement (represented in figure 9.1 as differently colored arrows) are combined in a sequence of design decisions comparable to that in a sequential approach. However, rules can also be made to be dependent on evaluations, leading to more complex formulations.

Because a rule-based approach is frequently expressed as a sequence of computer algorithms (the differently colored arrows in figure 9.1), it is particularly suitable for experimental use in which sensitivity analysis is applied to variability in assumptions, requirements, or options underlying any of the rule sets (figure 9.2). Different options for an early and important design requirement will lead to significantly different designs.

## La Paz, Baja California Sur, Mexico[1]

This study investigated how economic performance, demographic changes, private and public investments, and public policy choices could influence urban growth and land use change in the region of La Paz of Baja California, Mexico, over a 20-year period (figure 9.3). The case is adapted from C. Steinitz, R. Faris, M. Flaxman, J. C. Vargas-Moreno, G. Huang, S.-Y. Lu, T. Canfield, O. Arizpe, M. Angeles, M. Cariño, F. Santiago, T. Maddock III, C. Lambert, K. Baird, and L. Godínez, *Futuros Alternativos para la Region de La Paz, Baja California Sur, Mexico/Alternative Futures for La Paz, BCS, Mexico* (Mexico D. F., Mexico: Fundacion Mexicana para la Educación Ambiental, and International Community Foundation, 2006).

Using a rule-based change model, a range of scenarios for the region of La Paz was developed. The scenarios were applied using models that evaluated the locational attractiveness for the major land use types of the area, based on data from sales of local real estate. These projected a range of alternative futures through the year 2020. Computer-based models, built on expert knowledge, assessed the economic, ecological, hydrological, and visual impacts of the alternative futures and were used to analyze the consequences of the range of policy choices embedded in the scenarios.

### Representation

La Paz, the capital of the state of Baja California Sur, is located on the shores of the Bay of La Paz in the Sea of Cortez, named for the Spanish conquistador Hernán Cortez who visited La Paz in 1535. The city has a long history of settlement and its 2002 population was approximately 200,000 people. At the time of the study and continuing to today, their diversified economy

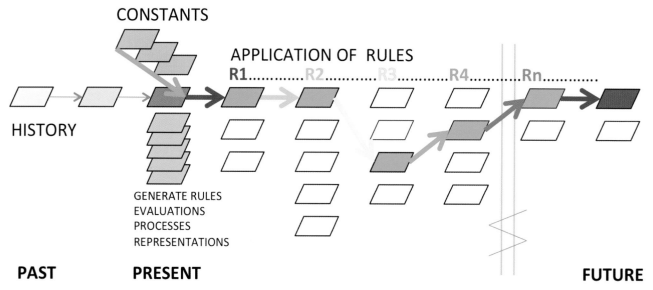

**Figure 9.1: The rule-based change model.** | Source: Carl Steinitz.

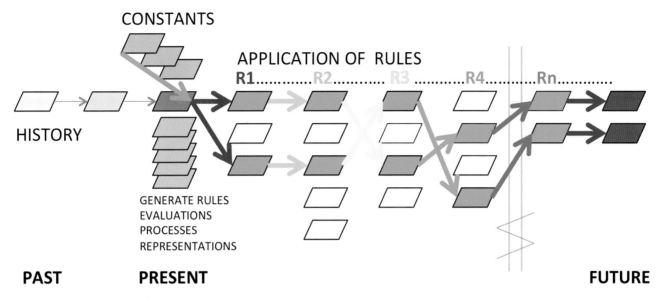

CONSTANTS

APPLICATION OF RULES

R1............ R2............ R3 ............ R4............ Rn............

HISTORY

GENERATE RULES
EVALUATIONS
PROCESSES
REPRESENTATIONS

PAST        PRESENT                                                    FUTURE

**Figure 9.2: Rule-based sensitivity analysis leading to different designs.** | Source: Carl Steinitz.

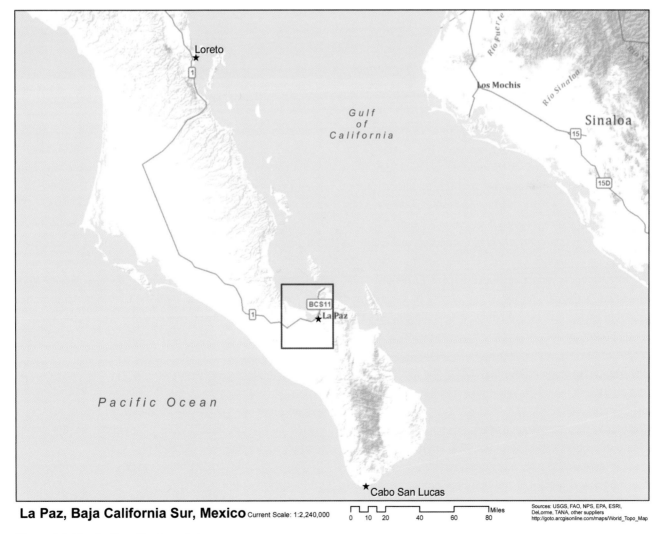

**La Paz, Baja California Sur, Mexico** Current Scale: 1:2,240,000

0  10  20    40    60    80  Miles

Sources: USGS, FAO, NPS, EPA, ESRI,
DeLorme, TANA, other suppliers
http://goto.arcgisonline.com/maps/World_Topo_Map

**Figure 9.3: The La Paz, Mexico, study area.**

**Figure 9.4: La Paz, BCS, Mexico.** | Source: La Paz geodesign team (2006); photo by Michael Calderwood.

has been supported by industry, agriculture, commerce, real estate, tourism, and government services. The quality of life for residents in La Paz is considered to be excellent, compared to elsewhere in the country, and the traditional feel of the city and the surrounding landscape have provided a major draw for tourism and real estate development (figure 9.4). Like many growing cities around the world, decision makers in La Paz are facing a number of major challenges: providing adequate drinking water, ensuring public access to beaches and marine areas, safeguarding the visual quality of the city and surrounding areas, reducing poverty while managing substantial in-migration, maintaining the economic health of the historic core of the city, enhancing tourism, attracting new ideas and innovation, managing development for the benefit of both current and future residents, and protecting fragile marine and terrestrial ecosystems.

The study relied heavily on existing scientific research, data, and the professional expertise of the Mexican members of the geodesign team. A GIS was used to organize the data spatially and to model and represent the complex processes at work in the study region. Interviews and discussions with relevant individuals and groups informed the study, both to help determine the types and extent of the conservation and development

strategies to be studied, and to help define the economic, hydrological, visual, and ecological assessment models. One of the results of this effort was the compilation of the first digital information base for the La Paz region, including its first digital land use/land cover map for the years 2000 to 2002, referred to here as 2000+ (figure 9.5). During development of the geographical data base, some deficiencies in available data became apparent. For example, no digital property ownership information was available, nor was there sufficient spatially detailed information to develop more than general models of impacts on terrestrial and near-shore marine ecosystems.

**Process**

Process models were developed for regional economics and demographics, new land use development, hydrology, terrestrial and marine ecology, visual quality, and recreation. Just as issues facing the region were interrelated, so the computer models were interlinked (figure 9.6).

The economic models projected the likely composition and performance of the region's economy. Economic performance was measured by gross regional product and employment levels. The scenarios also drew upon demographic projections that were linked to the various alternatives. These forecasts

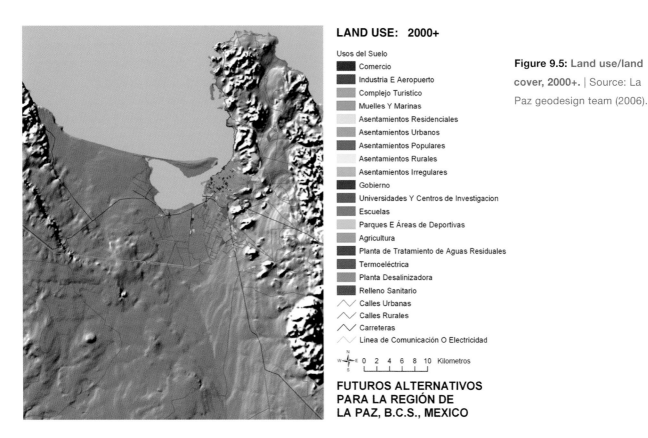

LAND USE: 2000+

Usos del Suelo
- Comercio
- Industria E Aeropuerto
- Complejo Turístico
- Muelles Y Marinas
- Asentamientos Residenciales
- Asentamientos Urbanos
- Asentamientos Populares
- Asentamientos Rurales
- Asentamientos Irregulares
- Gobierno
- Universidades Y Centros de Investigacion
- Escuelas
- Parques E Áreas de Deportivas
- Agricultura
- Planta de Tratamiento de Aguas Residuales
- Termoeléctrica
- Planta Desalinizadora
- Relleno Sanitario
- Calles Urbanas
- Calles Rurales
- Carreteras
- Línea de Comunicación O Electricidad

0  2  4  6  8  10  Kilometros

**FUTUROS ALTERNATIVOS PARA LA REGIÓN DE LA PAZ, B.C.S., MEXICO**

**Figure 9.5: Land use/land cover, 2000+.** | Source: La Paz geodesign team (2006).

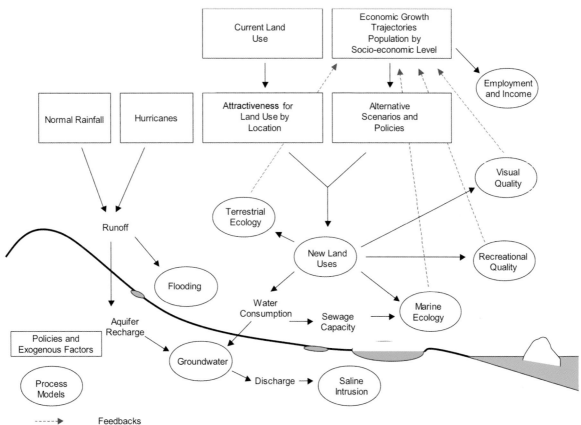

**Figure 9.6: The suite of process models are in black, and their impact-driven feedbacks are in red.** | Source: La Paz geodesign team (2006).

produced estimates of the demand for new housing and for commercial, industrial, and tourism-related development.

The development model for new land uses was based on models of the attractiveness criteria for five different types of housing as well as new commercial, industrial, and tourism-related development. The model evaluations directed the computer allocations of these developments to economically preferred locations in the study area.

The hydrological model assessed both ground and surface water. The groundwater model predicted the impact of increasing water demands on the quantity of groundwater storage in the aquifer underlying the region. It also located the extent of saltwater intrusion for each of the scenarios, and identified private and public wells at risk. The level of future water demand was linked to the economic and demographic projections. The surface water model assessed the risk of flooding from hurricanes.

The terrestrial ecology model assessed the biodiversity of the region's vegetation and habitat types. The marine ecological model assessed the potential impact of land-use changes on the lagoon of La Paz.

The visual model used the results of a photographic survey to define the scenic preferences for visual qualities of the landscape, as evaluated by local residents and tourists. The model applied these preferences to describe the existing scenic preference throughout the study area and formed the basis for measuring changes associated with each of the alternative futures. The recreation model identified areas of highest recreational value.

## Evaluation

The team evaluated existing conditions in the study area in terms of the parameters inherent in each of process models listed above, and were assisted by close coordination with an advisory group of local and regional representatives. The output of each of the evaluation models was a map of the baseline conditions in 2000+.

## Change

Scenarios for change were based upon wide ranging discussions with the advisory group and were intended to represent the broadest spectrum of foreseeable futures. Each of the scenarios was projected over a 20-year time horizon, in two 10-year stages. Each scenario was defined by a unique combination of variables. The demand variable reflected economic

projections and population growth forecasts. The supply variable determined the amount and location of land assumed to be available for development given different sets of constraints. The public resource variable was based on the assumed amount of public financing that was available for investments to address public needs. In addition, infrastructure project assumptions varied by scenario.

The demand variable was defined by three possible economic trajectories, based on different growth forecasts for each of the major sectors of the economy. Each of these economic trajectories included sub-models that predicted future population growth using current trends in population growth and predicted future employment.

A. *Trend growth* assumed moderate economic growth, projected to average 3.2 percent per year over the 20-year period, with the sectoral growth rates based upon the trends observed in the recent past.

B. *Medium growth* was based on higher overall economic growth compared to the trend trajectory, with higher population growth rates drawing upon strong performance in the real estate sector and higher economic activity in the commercial and service sectors. This trajectory assumed that La Paz actively fostered economic growth by enhancing the region's educational and research institutions and by capitalizing on opportunities in the real estate market.

C. *Rapid growth* was based on rapid growth in the tourism industry, similar to that experienced in nearby Los Cabos. Tourism was projected to grow at an annual rate of 8 percent per year for the first decade, and at 4.5 percent in the second decade, accompanied by strong growth in the commerce, services, real estate, finance, and construction sectors.

Land available for development was influenced by the implementation of legal restrictions on location and type of development as well as policies designed to maintain the environmental, cultural, historical, and visual integrity of the study area. There were three possibilities based on increasingly restrictive supply criteria:

1. *Unrestricted*–All land was assumed to be available for development, including land that was currently protected by law. Lands that were excluded from new development were those that had already been developed, or were covered by surface water, or were areas unsuitable for development under any circumstance, such as areas within the annually flooded major arroyos.

2. *Laws*–All land was available for development except those areas that were protected by current law, plus the land already excluded in the *Unrestricted* supply option, above. Legally protected areas at the time of the study included the islands in the Gulf of California, areas of mangroves, and the federal maritime zone.

3. *Proactive*–All land was open for development except those areas that were excluded as per *Unrestricted* and *Laws*, as well as add*itional areas* subject to new cultural, histori-cal, visual, safety, and environmental conservation policies. These additional areas included agricultural land, areas at risk of flooding from hurricanes, all flood prone arroyos, areas with important biodiversity, steep slopes, and high-quality view corridors.

In addition to the demand and supply variables, the study considered two scenarios of public financial capacity for new infrastructure projects. Each scenario incorporated assump-tions about new infrastructure development, including improve-ment of existing roads, construction of new roads, enlargement of flood-control levees, and expansion of the sewage and water supply systems. Investments slated to be completed in the first 10-year period were assumed to have an immediate influence on land use choices and therefore contributed to the develop-ment patterns that emerged during this period.

### Creating the scenarios

The combination of supply, demand, and public financial resources variables produced 18 possible scenarios. From these, ten priority scenarios were selected for analysis (figure 9.7).

The first and second scenarios represented the assumed extremes of change to the region. Scenario 1 assumed the high-est rate of economic expansion and population growth and the lowest level of constraints on development, with a high level of public funding available for project implementation to encour-age growth. This scenario was expected to result in the most change in land use and the highest impacts, combined with high overall economic benefits. Scenario 2 modeled the lowest level of population and economic growth and the most restric-tive set of conservation policies to shape the location of future growth, with high levels of government resources available for policy-implementation. This scenario was expected to produce the lowest environmental impact and least landscape change. The remaining eight scenarios were chosen to provide a range of incremental policy changes, providing the basis for sensitiv-ity analysis of the several sets of assumptions.

### Change

The economic projections from each scenario were converted into demands for new land uses in eight categories: tourism, industry, commerce, and five kinds of housing. A computer program then defined the areas that were constrained from development by the relevant policy set. Subsequently, the development attractiveness model for each development type was implemented based upon infrastructure investments and policies that either attracted or repelled development. The pro-gram allocated the new land uses required in the first 10 years, in the order that they were assumed able to pay: tourism, indus-try, commerce and the several housing types. This process then repeated for the second 10 years.

| Scenario | Economic and Demographic Trajectory | Public Policy Context | Availability of Public Financial Resources |
|---|---|---|---|
| 1 | Rapid growth | Unrestricted | High |
| 2 | Trend growth | Proactive policies | High |
| 3 | Rapid growth | Unrestricted | Low |
| 4 | Trend growth | Unrestricted | Low |
| 5 | Trend growth | Following existing laws | Low |
| 6 | Moderate growth | Unrestricted | Low |
| 7 | Rapid growth | Following existing laws | Low |
| 8 | Rapid growth | Proactive policies | Low |
| 9 | Rapid growth | Proactive policies | High |
| 10 | Moderate growth | Proactive policies | High |

**Figure 9.7: Summary of scenario specifications.** | Source: La Paz geodesign team (2006).

The resulting land use patterns varied in terms of the extent of growth, the direction of growth, and the pattern of growth. Figure 9.8 shows alternative future 1, the extent of land use change in the year 2020 resulting from scenario 1, which was the alternative with the greatest projected change in land use with high economic and population growth, unregulated land use, and a high level of public resources.

In contrast, figure 9.9 presents the opposite extreme from scenario 2, with low economic and population growth, a proactive set of public policies designed to protect ecological, recreational and visual assets, and a high level of public resources for policy implementation. Actual land use in 2020 was very likely to fall between these two projections, depending upon the economic context and the choice of policies that would be put into place.

## Impact

The new land uses of the alternatives were assessed for their potential impacts associated with construction, maintenance, and use in normal local practice. These were measured by each process-impact model after the first 10-year allocation, and again at 20 years.

The economic model estimated gross regional product by economic sector, employment, and income by socio-economic class.

The hydrology model estimated the impact of changes in water demand and land cover on groundwater storage in the region and forecasted the wells at risk of saltwater intrusion for each of the scenarios. The surface water component of the model estimated the areas at risk of flooding in major hurricane events.

The terrestrial ecology model assessed the impacts on different vegetation and habitat categories. The marine ecology model assigned impacts from land use changes in each of the scenarios on the lagoon of La Paz using five criteria: eutrophication, direct impacts, indirect impacts, pollution, and stability. The levels of impact in each of these five criteria were combined to produce a summary impact index.

The visual model assessed the impact of future development and resulting landscape changes on visual preferences. The study team measured the impacts of land use change using the visual preferences of local residents and visitors as recorded in interviews carried out during a site visit.

The recreation model evaluated the impact of future land use change on sites of high recreational value.

The impacts of the ecological, visual, and recreation models were reported by location and we mapped the degree of change in five summary levels:

- Beneficial: positive effect
- Compatible: no significant change
- Moderate: natural mitigation possible
- Severe: mitigation possible with major engineering
- Terminal: no possible mitigation

## Some conclusions

The construction and upgrading of roads exerted a strong influence on the pattern of growth, leading to greater sprawl. The high public resource scenarios, which included higher investments in roads, led to even more significant sprawl. The scenarios that assumed lower availability of public resources produced land patterns with more development in areas closer to the historic core of the city (and less sprawl).

Existing laws provided little constraint on the pattern of future development and correspondingly little protection for the ecology of the region, the quality of its visual landscape, or its public recreational opportunities. The effect of these laws was primarily in keeping development out of the federal marine zone and away from dangerous locations. These laws did little to influence the general shape and direction of growth.

However, new land use policies and related regulations could have a dramatic influence on the pattern of future land use. For example, a regulation that limited the spatial extent for future growth by requiring residential development to be served by the sewage system showed a dramatic influence on future land use patterns. The proactive alternatives showed the impact of implementing this constraint on development, with extensions of sewerage along the edge of the existing service area, and with an extension of the sewage system to the west. These alternatives contrasted sharply with others, where growth continued to the south, following the major roads out of the city. Infill policies, as included in the Laws and Proactive alternatives, only moderately reduced the amount of new development located beyond the existing urban areas.

The ecological, visual, and recreational impacts of these 10 alternatives varied according to the projected new land use pattern. Alternative future 1 showed extensive damage to the ecological, recreational, and visual quality of the region. Alternative future 2 showed environmental impacts that were small in comparison. This alternative resulted in a lower overall level of economic activity, accompanied by higher per capita economic benefit. La Paz depends on groundwater for its water supply. Scenarios with greater economic activity and population generated increased groundwater demands, which in time would result in decreased aquifer storage capacity, increased recharge of effluent, and increased saline intrusion. The study showed that degradation of the ecological, visual, and

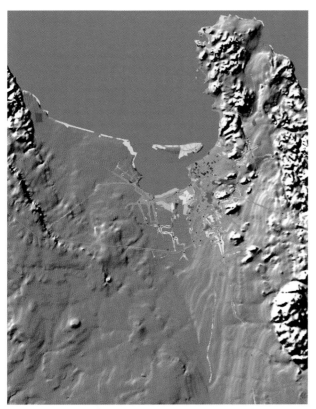

**FUTUROS ALTERNATIVOS PARA LA REGIÓN DE LA PAZ, B.C.S., MEXICO**

## LAND USE  2020

### ALTERNATIVE FUTURE 1
·TREND GROWTH
·PROACTIVE
·HIGH PUBLIC RESOURCES

- Redensificacion de viviendas

Usos del Suelo

- Comercio
- Industria E Aeropuerto
- Complejo Turistíco
- Muelles Y Marinas
- Asentamientos Residenciales
- Asentamientos Urbanos
- Asentamientos Populares
- Asentamientos Rurales
- Asentamientos Irregulares
- Gobierno
- Universidades Y Centros de Investigacion
- Escuelas
- Parques E Áreas de Deportivas
- Agricultura
- Planta de Tratamiento de Aguas Residuales
- Termoeléctrica
- Planta Desalinizadora
- Relleno Sanitario
- Calles Urbanas
- Calles Rurales
- Carreteras
- Línea de Comunicación O Electricidad

 0  2  4  6  8  10  Kilometros

**Figure 9.8: Land use in 2020 for alternative future 1 based on scenario 1.** | Source: La Paz geodesign team (2006).

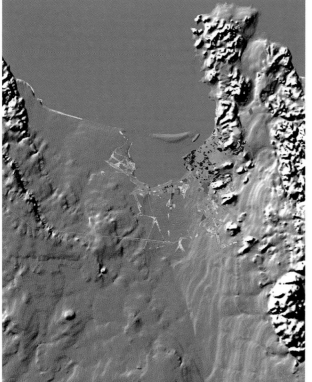

**FUTUROS ALTERNATIVOS PARA LA REGIÓN DE LA PAZ, B.C.S., MEXICO**

## LAND USE  2020

### ALTERNATIVE FUTURE 2
·TREND GROWTH
·PROACTIVE
·HIGH PUBLIC RESOURCES

- Redensificacion de viviendas

Usos del Suelo

- Comercio
- Industria E Aeropuerto
- Complejo Turistíco
- Muelles Y Marinas
- Asentamientos Residenciales
- Asentamientos Urbanos
- Asentamientos Populares
- Asentamientos Rurales
- Asentamientos Irregulares
- Gobierno
- Universidades Y Centros de Investigacion
- Escuelas
- Parques E Áreas de Deportivas
- Agricultura
- Planta de Tratamiento de Aguas Residuale
- Termoeléctrica
- Planta Desalinizadora
- Relleno Sanitario
- Calles Urbanas
- Calles Rurales
- Carreteras
- Línea de Comunicación O Electricidad

 0  2  4  6  8  10  Kilometros

**Figure 9.9: Land use in 2020 for alternative future 2 based on scenario 2.** | Source: La Paz geodesign team (2006).

recreational landscape might have profound consequences for the future of the tourism and real estate sectors, as well as the quality of life for the residents of La Paz. If growth were directed by a well-coordinated set of regulations, as reflected by the Proactive alternative futures, there would be enough land for La Paz to grow over the next two decades without major loss of public amenities. This was true even under conditions of rapid economic growth.

## Decision

The most important question, "How should the study area geography be changed?" had to be answered by the actions of the decision makers of La Paz. As always, political will and public interest would decide the evolving future of La Paz. It was the aim of this study to provide the basis for informed decision making, in the hope that the future La Paz reflected the values and priorities of its people. While each alternative was made by a rule-based change-allocation program, albeit on the basis of a different set of assumptions, selection of the "best" alternative from among the 10 possible ones was a question of judgment. To graphically display the aggregate performance of each of the alternative futures, using summary indices for economic and environmental performance, we linked a spreadsheet to an aggregated set of impact models (figure 9.10). The alternatives

are plotted with codes referring to the scenario numbers and their names (see figure 9.7 earlier).

The economic index was constructed using gross regional product and per capital income, weighted equally. The environmental index was based upon the results of the visual, recreation, marine ecology, and terrestrial ecology models, weighted equally. Moving from the upper left to the lower right of the graph implied a trade-off between economic performance and environmental quality. For example, with a given policy set, increased economic output coincided with a drop in the environmental quality index. Movements from the lower left to the upper right indicated an improvement in both economic and environmental terms. Within a given economic trajectory, the scenarios based on the proactive policy set (e.g., scenarios 2, 8, 9, and 10) led to better economic and environmental results.

At a heavily attended public meeting, the then-Governor of Baja California Sur, stated that he considered "the economy and the environment to be equal in importance." If so, then alternative 10 (as seen in figure 10.8) was the best design in his definition of "best." The figure also illustrates the triangular "territory" in which the best solution is likely to be. Scenario 9 generated the economically best alternative, while scenario 2 produced the best environmental one. This spreadsheet "product" also illustrated a situation that is relatively common in geodesign

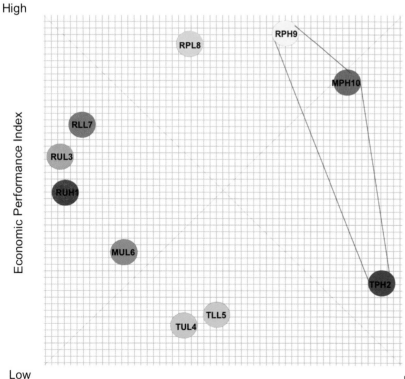

High

Economic Performance Index

Low

Environmental Quality Index          High

**Figure 9.10:** A summary comparison of the ten alternative futures. The alternatives are plotted with codes referring to the scenario numbers and their names (figure 9.7). Moving from the upper left to the lower right of the graph implied a trade-off between economic performance and environmental quality. Movements from the lower left to the upper right indicated an improvement in both economic and environmental terms. | Source: La Paz geodesign team (2006).

studies: Governors, mayors, and heads of major businesses frequently do not want to be told what they should do. Therefore, and perhaps even more useful, the study revealed the much larger set of alternative scenarios which should *not* be pursued.

One decision that the mayor of La Paz made during the time of the study, and under the direct influence of intense public response to this study, was the protection of the bay and beaches of Balandra as well as its hinterland from being changed into an enormous private tourism and recreation development. These have long been the region's most significant recreational and environmental resources (figures 9.11 and 5.26 through 5.28).

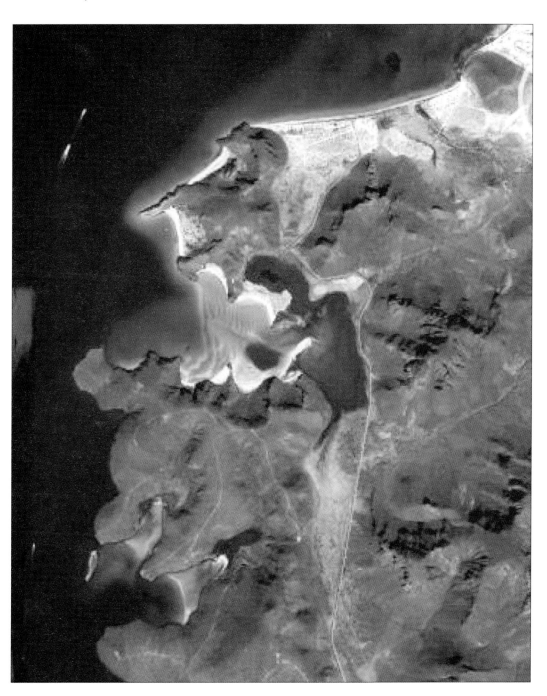

**Figure 9.11: Aerial view of Balandra Bay, La Paz, Mexico.** | Source: La Paz geodesign team (2006).

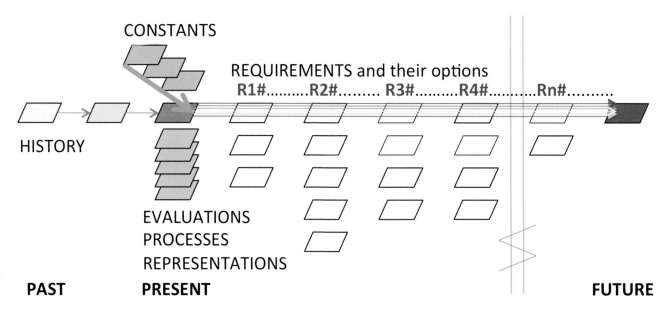

**Figure 9.12: The optimized change model.** | Source: Carl Steinitz.

## The optimized change model

The **optimized** approach requires that the client and the geodesign team understand the relative importance of the desired requirements and also their decision criteria (figure 9.12). This approach also requires these criteria to be comparable in a single metric, such as financial rate-of-return, energy needs, potential votes, etc., in order to be able to declare a design to be "optimal." Optimization is perhaps the most difficult of all of the above design methods to implement. The optimized approach makes the assumption that the geodesign team can link and integrate the decision model's criteria (which will eventually decide whether the design is approved and implemented) with the design actions that best fulfill those criteria.

A principal advantage of the optimized way of designing is that it doesn't waste time. It can be specifically directed toward the articulated objectives and requirements as presented by the decision makers. Another advantage (like that of a rule-based change model) is that it is a computer program that can be used

efficiently in sensitivity analysis, testing the relative importance of the requirements. A principal liability is that it forces decision makers to articulate their objectives, values and criteria a priori, before actually seeing any alternative designs, and that can be difficult.

### The Telluride region, Colorado, USA[2]

This optimized geodesign example is adapted from M. Flaxman, C. Steinitz, R. Faris, T. Canfield, and J. C. Vargas-Moreno, *Alternative Futures for the Telluride Region, Colorado*. (Telluride, CO: Telluride Foundation, 2010). This study forecast and assessed future development patterns for San Miguel County and parts of Montrose and Ouray counties in Colorado (figure 9.13). Nine alternatives based on different combinations of assumed population growth and public policies were simulated in a 20-year projection, and spatially allocated via rule-based models at two different geographic scales. The alternatives were assessed and compared for their economic, demographic, traffic, visual preference, and ecologic consequences to the region and its major towns. The Telluride Foundation funded our research team from the Graduate School of Design at Harvard University and the Massachusetts Institute of Technology to inform its long range grant making strategy and assist itself and regional community leaders in decision making that might affect the future of the region.

**Representation**

The Telluride region is located in southwestern Colorado (figure 9.13). The study area is contained within a rectangle measuring 85 miles east to west and 40 miles north to south. It was designed to include areas in Montrose, Ouray, and San Miguel counties that are most directly influenced by the towns of Telluride and Mountain Village.

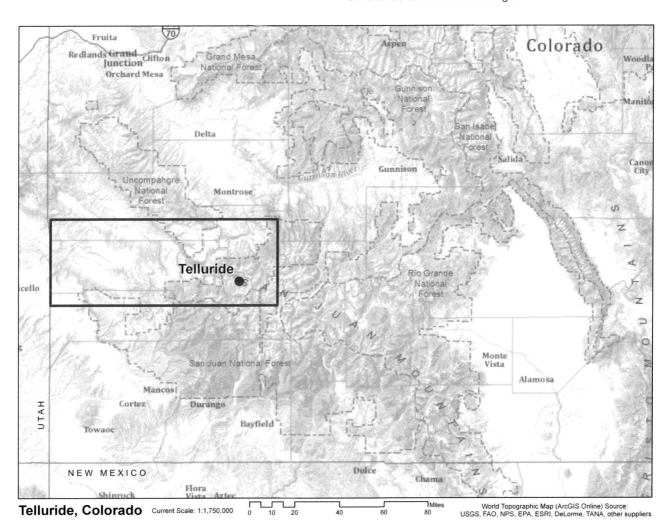

**Telluride, Colorado**   Current Scale: 1:1,750,000

World Topographic Map (ArcGIS Online) Source: USGS, FAO, NPS, EPA, ESRI, DeLorme, TANA, other suppliers

**Figure 9.13: The Telluride region of Colorado.**

The area is famous for its outstanding mountain scenery, and towns such as Telluride and Ouray are surrounded by snow capped peaks reaching 13,000 feet (figure 9.14). Skiing is a major attraction and a regional annual average of 300 inches of snowfall provides for a season from November to April. The Bureau of Land Management and the USDA Forest Service manage large tracts of land around Telluride region. The San Miguel River, a tributary of the Dolores River, drains the study area.

For this region, there were numerous spatial data sets already publically available, and a GIS was organized with approximately 100 map layers. We included information on physical, hydrological, climatic, and ecological characteristics of the area, as well as socioeconomic data, including census demographics and digital property parcels information including sales and tax data. Because of the nature of the study area, it was necessary to integrate and coordinate information from sources across multiple political and jurisdictional boundaries.

**Figure 9.14: Views of the Telluride region and the surrounding mountain areas.** | Photos by Tess Canfield.

We adopted a standard format and areal extent of maps to show the entire study area (figure 9.15).

Land use and ownership were important variables in this study. Figure 9.15 shows the 2008 land use/land cover of the Telluride region, presented in 12 categories. The red areas are locations of existing development and the white areas represent the more mountainous parts of the region, above the tree line. The vast majority of land is used for agriculture or is covered by some form of vegetation. Figure 9.16 shows the various categories of publically owned lands in the study region, the most significant of which are managed by the USDA Forest Service and the Bureau of Land Management. One of the central assumptions of this study was that all future residential development will occur on private property, shaded in gray.

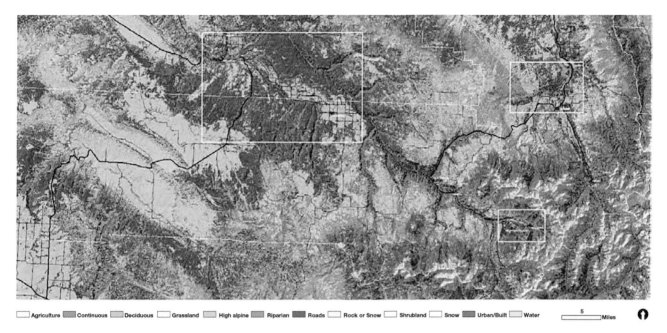

**Figure 9.15: Land Use/Land Cover, 2008. In addition to this broader regional review, we specifically analyzed the three major development areas: the Norwood, Nucla and Naturita zone, the Telluride-Mountain Village zone, and the Ridgway zone. These are indicated by white rectangular outlines.** | Source: Telluride geodesign team (2010).

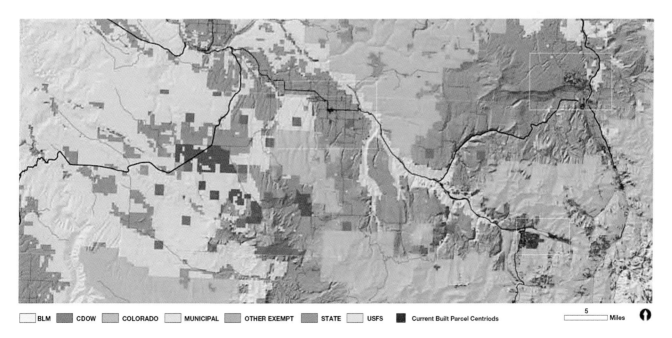

**Figure 9.16: Land ownership.** | Source: Telluride geodesign team (2010).

## Process, evaluation

Process models were developed for housing and employment economics, demographics, transportation, visual preferences, and terrestrial ecology. Just as issues facing the region are interrelated, the computer models developed for the analysis of these processes were interlinked (figure 9.17). The economy of the Telluride region is based on recreation. The expenditures by second home owners and tourists, along with a construction industry that is largely driven by the second home market, were estimated to be responsible for more than half of the jobs in the area, approximately 56 percent in San Miguel County and 49 percent in Ouray County. Under the then-current zoning laws, the amount of privately-owned and developable land could have more than doubled the future supply of housing stock, which at the time was about 10,000 existing housing units. The importance of the future housing markets made it the most critical model and therefore the "optimal" allocation-design was

defined by the geodesign team and the advisory committee as being based on simulating the market economics in the housing markets for second homes and full time residences.

The money that drives Telluride's economic growth, mainly from tourists and second home owners, comes from outside the region. These exogenous forces help to generate jobs that in turn translate into regional housing needs for the workforce. These exogenous demands also contribute to rising land and housing prices that result in displacing portions of the population who have been "priced out" of the area. Surveys were conducted to determine the structure of the local real estate markets and to evaluate their relationship to various amenities. We used statistical analysis and GIS tools to estimate a housing attractiveness model based on prior development and housing economic values in the region. We applied this strategy to modeling two separate sub-markets, one for full-time residents and one for second-home owners. For full-time residents,

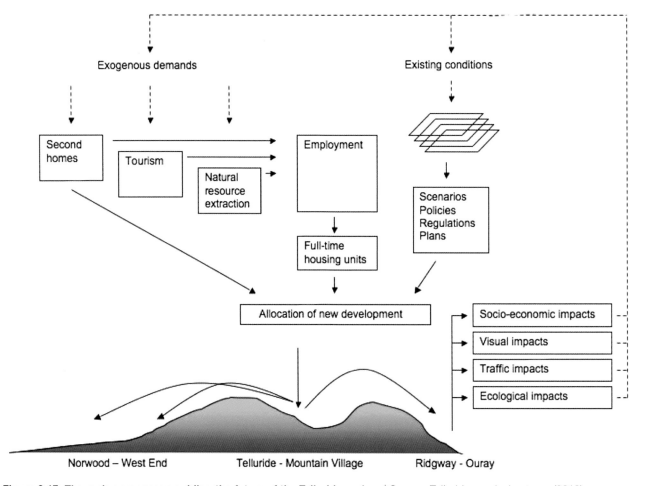

Figure 9.17: The major processes guiding the future of the Telluride region. | Source: Telluride geodesign team (2010).

attractiveness is mainly a function of proximity to roads, commerce and employment. They would like a nice view and land for their children to run around on, but travel efficiency is most important. For second homeowners, attractiveness is a function of proximity to the resort amenities of Telluride and Mountain Village, their respective nearby recreation assets, and the high visual qualities of the mountains. With both of these populations in mind, we mapped evaluations of all existing conditions as well as for several other process models: traffic, visual preference from all parcels of private land and from public roads, and species habitats for the bald eagle, the bighorn sheep, and the Gunnison sage-grouse.

### Change

The geodesign team then developed four policy sets intended to guide future change in the region. These were defined in consultation with a group of stakeholders, convened by the Telluride Foundation, and they provided a synthesis of the best available local knowledge of key land use, development and conservation policy options. The future of the region will be shaped not only by exogenous forces but also policy choices. Persons seeking to build are subject to public policies

under the control of county and municipal governments. For example, each town has regulations for defining developable areas, including zoning regulations and allowable densities. Affordable housing policies, particularly in the case of Telluride and Mountain Village, are additional policy levers that will help to shape the future of the region. We generated sets of policies defining where development may and may not take place and the allowable densities of that development.

The first policy set assumes that the current regulations in the region are applied and that all private lands are available for development, except for areas that are legally protected. So all local zoning laws would be applied, and there would be development restriction on public land, private and local conservation areas, water and wetlands, road rights of way and buffers that are legally required for power lines and other such infrastructure, and terrain slope constraints.

After consultation in our local meetings, we created a second "proactive" policy set that added protection of the most preferred views from main roads, increased the riparian and wetland buffers based on riparian vegetation, restricted mineral extraction on public lands, and enhanced protection of significant historic landscapes (figure 9.18).

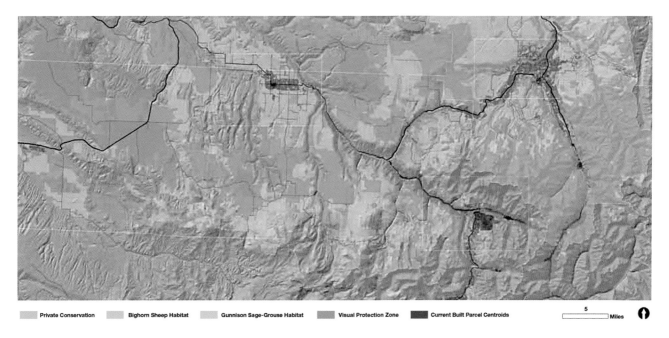

| | Private Conservation | | Bighorn Sheep Habitat | | Gunnison Sage-Grouse Habitat | | Visual Protection Zone | | Current Built Parcel Centroids |

**Figure 9.18: Proactive development constraints.** | Source: Telluride geodesign team (2010).

Offering affordable housing to the region's workforce is one of the region's most important current and future challenges, something about which we heard widespread agreement during our many conversations and meetings with regional participants. Therefore, a third land use policy option we proposed allowed for higher density development, increased by 50 percent in those developable parcels that are between one and five acres in size and lie within or near to the existing urban areas. The fourth and final land use policy combined the proactive policy set with higher allowable densities.

At this stage we had maps of legally developable parcels, the constraints based on the policy sets, the attractiveness for second and full-time home locations, and the anticipated future demand for second and full-time homes. With local advice, we determined the level of subsidized housing and set the level of mineral extraction for each of the scenarios. Because each of these scenario components has the potential to independently vary, there was the possibility that we would generate a great number of combinatorial scenarios. The report presents nine, all of which resulted from community discussions in which it was decided to test the region's sensitivity to the widest ranges of "reasonable" assumptions and policies (figure 9.19).

A rule-based allocation model was designed and applied to predict the spatial locations of development growth and redevelopment, based on a simulation of how economically-driven market demand will operate in response to a particular scenario.

Allocating new houses was based on the assessments of the economically measured attractiveness for the current and potential resident groups, each which has different preferences for housing types and locations, as well as abilities and willingness to pay. This model enabled the consideration of development over several time periods and also related processes such as "spillover development", a consequence of development which is not under local control, but nonetheless may have significant impacts on the community.

The regional allocations for housing were made to developable parcels of land without regard to political boundaries. The allocation of housing followed a sequence that reflects willingness to pay, with second home owners choosing first from the most desirable properties. Full-time residents then select from the remaining available properties. This general process took place over four stages. The first stage identified the developable private land parcels based on existing policy constraints and set the overall level of housing demand across the regional scale. In the second step, the amount of housing permitted in Telluride and Mountain Village were determined, based on both current density assumptions (a total of 950 new units in these two towns) and higher density scenarios (space for up to 1,500 units). Depending on the level of demand and the supply of available land as determined by policy choices, there may be insufficient housing sites in the most attractive areas for both second home owners and full-time residents. This is particularly likely in the

| Scenario | Economic trajectory | Land Use Policy | | | High-subsidized housing | Mineral extraction | New Housing Units | | |
| | | Current regulations | Proactive | Higher density | | | Second homes | Full-time residences | Subsidized housing |
|---|---|---|---|---|---|---|---|---|---|
| 1 | Low growth | • | | | | | 1738 | 1159 | 600 |
| 2 | Low growth | | • | | | | 1738 | 1159 | 600 |
| 3 | Low growth | | • | • | | | 1738 | 1159 | 600 |
| 4 | High growth | • | | | | | 4193 | 2795 | 600 |
| 5 | High growth | | • | | | | 4193 | 2795 | 600 |
| 6 | High growth | | | • | | | 4193 | 2795 | 600 |
| 7 | High growth | | • | • | | | 4193 | 2795 | 600 |
| 8 | High growth | • | | | • | | 4193 | 2795 | 900 |
| 9 | High growth | • | | | | • | 4193 | 3295 | 600 |

Figure 9.19: Nine scenarios for change: Scenario number one is based on the low growth projection and current regulations. This approximates current regional trends. The second scenario is constructed using low growth and the proactive set of regulations. The third scenario is simulated under low growth, proactive policies, and the addition of higher density development to lessen impacts on the landscape and to make it more efficient for public transport. The fourth scenario is based on the high growth projection and current regulations. The fifth is the high growth and proactive policies scenario. The sixth scenario is based on low growth, current regulations and higher densities. The seventh is based on high growth, current regulations and higher densities. The eighth scenario is based on high growth, current regulations, and increased subsidized housing. The ninth is based on high growth, existing regulations and mineral extraction for oil, gas and uranium to the full extent of currently leased lands. This was hypothesized as the "worst case" scenario from an environmental perspective. | Source: Telluride geodesign team (2010).

Telluride and Mountain Village area where most of the jobs are located. In this situation, existing residents are induced or forced to move to less desirable locations farther from their workplace, following a process of gentrification-dislocation that has been happening in the region for more than a decade.

The third stage of the allocation sequence was to allot subsidized housing units in Telluride and Mountain Village to the chosen level in the scenario. The modeling sequence assumes that Telluride and Mountain Village are built-out before second home demand spreads to other areas. Next, second home demand fills in the remaining allowable housing development in Telluride and Mountain Village. This is followed by any excess demand being allocated to other locations which are most attractive for second homes. Finally, full-time residents are allocated to the remaining locations that they find most attractive. Three of the resulting future patterns of development, ones that generated the most discussion, are shown below.

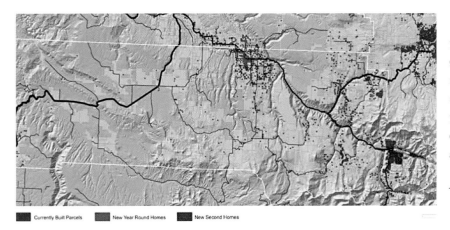

Figure 9.20: Alternative future 1, in the year 2030, based on scenario 1, low growth, current regulations. Red represents existing development, the new second homes are in purple, and the year round residences are blue. Each dot is a new house and its surrounding area, and has been expanded in size to increase legibility on the map. | Source: Telluride geodesign team (2010).

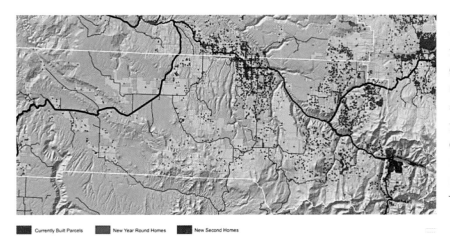

Figure 9.21: Alternative future 5, in the year 2030, based on scenario 5, high growth, proactive regulations. Red represents existing development, the new second homes are in purple, and the year round residences are blue. Each dot is a new house and its surrounding area, and has been expanded to increase legibility on the map. | Source: Telluride geodesign team (2010).

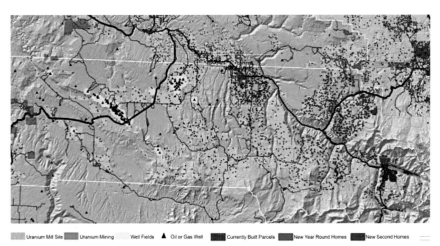

Figure 9.22: Alternative future 9, in the year 2030, based on scenario 9, high growth, current regulations, mineral extraction. Red represents existing development, the new second homes are in purple, and the year round residences are blue. Each dot is a new house and its surrounding area, and has been expanded to increase legibility on the map. Mineral extraction is shown in yellow. | Source: Telluride geodesign team (2010).

A second rule-based allocation model was designed to allocate roads and houses *within* parcels developed in the future. Homes were located on the single most attractive 50 meter grid cell on a given lot. Driveways and residential feeder roads were then allocated to connect the new houses, based on least cost paths to the nearest existing paved road. Greater costs were assumed for steeper slopes and lower for being near parcelization lot lines, while publically-owned lands were given a very high cost to cross. An example of this more detailed scale allocation showing new roads and houses is seen in the next two figures showing projected change from 2008 to 2030, based on the high growth (HG) scenarios.

**Impacts**

Along with the resulting land use changes and their consequent socio-economic impacts, the models for traffic,

**Figure 9.23:** View towards Telluride and Mountain Village, 2008. | Source: Telluride geodesign team (2010).Simulation by Michael Flaxman. Visualization by Andy Thomas, O2 Planning + Design Inc. Calgary. Building and road locations were simulated using Python scripting in ArcGIS software and visualized using Visual Nature Studio 3 (VNS).

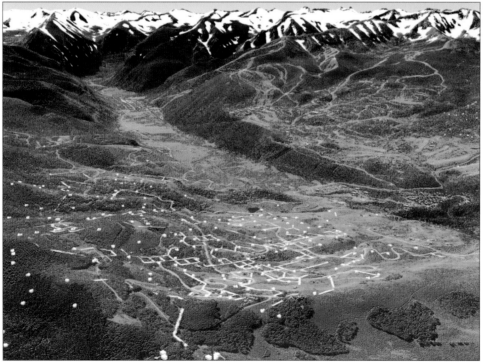

**Figure 9.24:** View towards Telluride and Mountain Village, 2030, based on the high-growth scenarios. | Source: Telluride geodesign team (2010).Simulation by Michael Flaxman. Visualization by Andy Thomas, O2 Planning + Design Inc. Calgary. Building and road locations were simulated using Python scripting in ArcGIS software and visualized using Visual Nature Studio 3 (VNS).

visual preferences from all private lands and public roads, and three selected species habitat models were organized to assess regional impacts out to the year 2030. To facilitate the comparison of the model results, their summary values were organized within a spreadsheet, and values such as market economic performance against ecological and visual preference could be graphed (figure 9.25). In this example, the scenario of low growth and the proactive constraints to development performed best in both summary assessments.

In all of the scenarios, Telluride and Mountain Village will be built out to their current legal capacity. Second homes and year-round homes were consistently allocated first to the region's existing urban areas: Telluride/Mountain Village, Ridgway, and Norwood. In the high growth scenarios, second homes and some year-round homes proliferated in unincorporated areas. As expected by the optimized model, this illustrated the attractiveness priorities for visual amenities and proximity to tourist and recreational areas for second home owners, and the more affordable land which will attract full time residents.

The lower growth scenarios are able to more easily accommodate a majority of new second-home owners and year-round residents within the existing communities. In the low growth scenarios, our model predicts that a majority of new residents in Norwood will be full time residents. In the high growth scenario, however, the majority of new entrants are second home

owners. Ridgway shows a similar pattern, except with a higher proportion of new units going to second-home owners because of acute competition for buildable land that has both high quality views and access to local amenities. The displacement of year-round residents by more affluent second-home owners will influence the ultimate distribution of households in the region. Policies that increase land scarcity, including the proactive set of policies modeled in this study, will push working families farther from the most attractive communities, highlighting the likely trade-offs between policies designed to protect natural amenities and those intended to further the social and economic well-being of the region's workforce. This is demonstrated in alternative future 5 which predicted that most new development in Ridgway and Norwood will be for second-home owners (figure 9.21).

The consequences of the scarcity of developable land are already being felt as increases in land value occur throughout the region. When Norwood and Ridgway become too expensive, many full time residents will move into more remote and unincorporated locations. Increased commuting distances, travel times, and traffic congestion will lead to personal hardship and financial costs for workers. Because of more widely spread development, costs borne by the towns and counties to provide infrastructure and public services for the sprawling low density development will rise disproportionately. Loss of

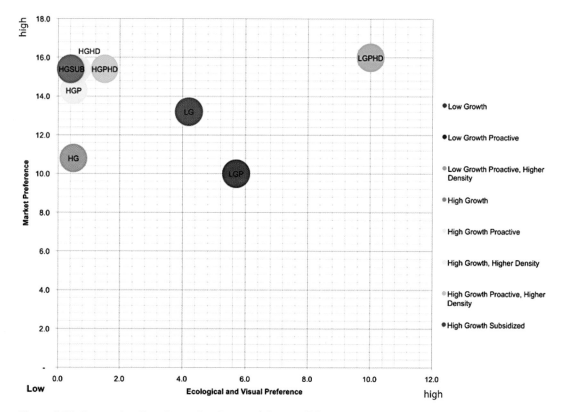

**Figure 9.25: Comparing the alternative futures.** | Source: Telluride geodesign team (2010).

full-time residents will have also social consequences for the region's communities.

Because of the region's demanding topography, it is extremely difficult and costly to increase capacity on the major roads, especially those that access Telluride and Mountain Village. Parking will become increasingly difficult, especially in Telluride, where parking, public services and subsidized housing compete for the same limited land. The traffic problem in Telluride and throughout the region cannot be solved if transit continues to be composed primarily of private vehicles.

The ecological, economic and social effects of any future mineral resource extraction will be felt primarily in the western areas of the region, where these resources are located. Oil, gas, and uranium exploitation may benefit the nation, the mining companies and their employees, and would provide substantial economic benefit to the towns of Nucla and Naturita. However, development of these resources will have a profoundly harmful effect on the quality and the character of the landscape of the western portion of the study area. Management of the visual quality of this part of the region is particularly challenging because of the easily disrupted long views across open ranch lands.

The present landscape presents the image of isolated urbanized areas separated by beautiful natural landscapes. It will be transformed to a more generally urbanized landscape. There will be few if any views that do not contain houses and these will be particularly visible from the region's public roads. The loss of desirable vistas will in turn have a negative impact on the region's long-term economic future.

**Decision**

The critical issues facing the Telluride region must be recognized as regional in nature. While the various towns and counties have legal rights and responsibilities, distribution of new housing, transportation, provision of services, and protection of the environment are at their core regional issues. Furthermore, actions to deal with these issues must be carried out over periods of time that are much longer than the electoral cycle. Because of its outstanding natural attractiveness, its reliance on potentially fickle tourism, and its vulnerability to damage by poorly coordinated development decisions, the potential risks to the Telluride region are particularly acute.

There are several major regional-scale policy issues facing the Telluride region which were identified in this study and which will require future decisions by stakeholders:

- Planning, providing and paying for regional public transport centered on Telluride and Mountain Village;

- Adopting a regionally coordinated approach to the challenge of workforce housing;
- Identifying opportunities for higher density development as a complement to and in coordination with regional transportation and workforce housing planning;
- Establishing visual management policies, especially in areas seen from main tourist routes;
- Establishing stronger environment-derived development constraints, particularly to protect Gunnison sage grouse and riparian vegetation zones;
- Managing the conflicts between mineral extraction and environmental quality and natural habitats.

As population increases and development sprawls, other issues will emerge such as planning for, providing, and financing water, sewer, education, public health and safety, and other public services in the counties. All of these issues will require an effective process for inter-jurisdictional planning, decision making and implementation, which will require much greater coordination and cooperation among the different towns and counties, and also with the several public agencies that control large amounts of land in the Telluride region.

It was the purpose of this study to draw together existing information about the Telluride region, and organize it into models for evaluating future, alternative scenarios. This study and its technical infrastructure are being used via the Telluride Foundation to inform the decision making process, by helping stakeholders to have a shared understanding of regional issues, and to help them choose policies more likely to yield desired outcomes. These decisions must be made by the region's stakeholders. It is they who will be most directly affected by these decisions, and who have the political power to implement them.

During the early scoping phase of the Telluride study it had quickly become clear that the driving force of change in the region was a combination of second homebuilding for recreation-oriented visitors and for the permanent residents who service the recreation and tourism industries. The Telluride region functions as a regional development market. It was also clear that the study area did not function as a single planning unit and that none of the towns or counties had full policy control over what future development changes would bring. Furthermore, the consequences of policies in one town would potentially radically transform a neighboring jurisdiction. As a result, the research team recommended and implemented a model based on mimicking the profit oriented performance of the regional housing market, and this economically driven optimized model became the central component of the several simulations of future change.

# The agent–based change model

**Agent-based** models are rule-based approaches that assume all members of a class or group behave individually instead of identically. The structure of agent-based models (ABM) is often considered to be more intuitive than other forms of modeling, since agents correspond to well-known objects such as people, households or land parcels. The range of behaviors of individual agents can be tracked over time and explained. The challenge in this approach is appropriate parameterization and testing. For example, much larger sample sizes are needed to reliably explain *individual* variations in human behavior rather than *average* behavior. Because such models tend to be temporally as well as spatially explicit, a second characteristic of such models is that behavior can be influenced by dynamic events, even those occurring at very different time scales.

The simplest form of agent-based (yet rule-based) change models are known as a "cellular automata" or CA. In this formulation, individual cells within a uniform "grid" are individually influenced and potentially change state as a consequence of the state of their immediate neighbors. In an example of this

approach as applied to fire modeling, three rules govern the transitions that each individual cell makes from one time period to another (figure 9.26). Fires, structures, flammable and inflammable vegetation, and bare soil can all be assigned rule-based behaviors and modeled for changes over time.

In actual planning practice, CA models are not commonly used, since change influenced only by the state of the immediate neighbors is typically too simplistic. Working models usually consider a combination of immediate and more general influences. For example, working fire models take into account wind speed and direction, which are of regional influence and not strictly a function of adjacency. Besides being applied in biophysical change simulations, this approach is frequently used to simulate land cover change. In this type of application, two kinds of rules are common: those which reflect market forces and those which simulate policies.

The agent-based approach assumes that the future state of the study area is the result of interactions among policy and design decisions that direct, attract or constrain the independent (but rule-based) actions of independent "agents," for example, home seekers or developers and conservationists.

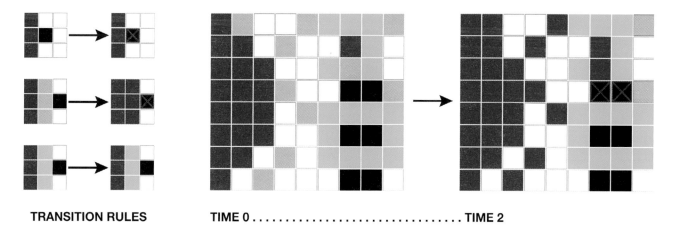

**TRANSITION RULES          TIME 0 . . . . . . . . . . . . . . . . . . . . . . . . . . . . . . . TIME 2**

**Figure 9.26:** A cellular automata-style rule-based model of fire. Three rules govern the transitions that each individual cell makes from one time period to another as indicated on the left side of the figure. Fire (red) adjacent to a structure (black), causes the structure to ignite (black with red X). Flammable vegetation (orange) propagates fire. Inflammable vegetation (green) or bare soil (white) constrains fire.

The maps to the right represent two points in time within a simulation, and show that complex and variable behavioral outcomes can be simulated by applying simple rules to relatively complex spatial landscapes. | Source: M. Flaxman, "Multi-scale Fire Hazard Assessment for Wildland Urban Interface Areas: An Alternative Futures Approach" (D. Des. diss., Graduate School of Design, Harvard University, 2001).

Their different rules of location and interaction are embedded into a computer model for each agent-type, and the changes occur simultaneously and adjust themselves in reaction to the sequence of requirements for the design (figure 9.27). The construction of novel or complex spatio-temporal change models still typically require scripting or programming ability, a potentially significant barrier to adoption of this design approach. However, simpler applications of such rules can be specified using graphical user interfaces, and such improvement in software usabilty is leading to increased use of such techniques.

The ABM approach been demonstrated in the natural sciences, and it has been applied in several case studies in geodesign. Its principal advantage is the strength of its theoretical position, in that it models the location-responses of many independent actions in reaction to each other, or to prior designed actions. This is a much more reasonable position for the planning of large and complex geographical study areas than the assumption that all actions can be normatively designed.

The following case study illustrates an agent-based model that links geodesign of land management policy and natural systems. It is edited from M. Flaxman, "Multi-scale Fire Hazard Assessment for Wildland Urban Interface Areas: An Alternative Futures Approach" (D. Des. diss., Graduate School of Design, Harvard University, 2001). I was a principal thesis adviser.

## Idyllwild, California, USA[3]

Tightly coupled human-natural systems offer a major challenge to traditional policy analysis and the design of management approaches for natural resources. From the point of view of policy analysis, the problem is that within such systems even simple and clear policies can have very complex effects, including significant and unanticipated consequences. These include large spatial or social differences in adoption or compliance, as well as adverse impacts on systems not considered by the policy. From a natural resources management or biophysical sciences perspective, the challenge is that the roles of people within such systems are too significant to ignore, and difficult or impossible to predict. Opportunities for participation and learning within the planning process itself can affect outcomes. The case of fire management policy-making is a good example of a contested human-natural system in which many of these issues must be addressed. Managing fire hazard is in some ways similar to many other forms of natural disaster mitigation, such as protection from flooding. The threat is rare enough to prompt complacency, but severe enough to warrant significant public effort.

As an example of this, consider figure 9.28, the fire model diagram below. It is a revision of the diagram shown previously, the rule-based modeling description in figure 9.26, with two additions. The first, represented with black outlines, is the

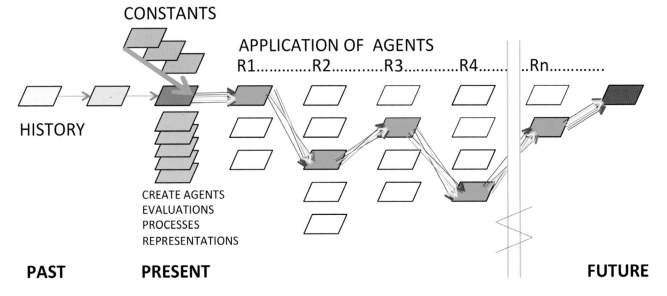

Figure 9.27: The agent-based change model. | Source: Carl Steinitz.

concept of a household "agent" managing a particular area autonomously. The second is that each of the two agents in this case chooses a different approach to managing the residential landscape. Thus, fire is no longer considered as a purely physical phenomenon, but instead interacts with a second-level model of human decision making.

Fire hazard in urban-wildland interface areas has three important characteristics that make it particularly difficult to manage. The first is that the areas at risk do not fall within a simple, contiguous and easily-understood boundary. The second is that human management has direct consequences on fire hazard, but that the accumulation of "fuels" in the form of shrubs and dead woody debris occurs very slowly, almost imperceptibly. The third is that even though the general public has an understandable fear of fires, frequently recurring small fires are characteristic of, and necessary to, the ecological health of many ecosystems, including this one.

These kinds of management and planning situations require a careful approach to characterizing the problem, representing it in forms that allow public comprehension of the issues, and developing policies that protect human life, safety, and property while also maintaining ecological health. A number of approaches are possible, but this is clearly a situation in which empirical testing of policies is impractical and undesirable, therefore some form of simulation is appropriate. Whatever simulation approach is taken, it must consider the impact of human activities on the land, and the impact of landscape characteristics on humans. This relationship is dynamic and iterative as well as spatially variant, and so the approach must be able to consider and visualize such patterns.

Spatially explicit agent-based modeling is one such simulation design approach. The technique has roots in two fields: conventional spatial modeling, as implemented through GIS, and object-oriented programming, in which computing "objects" are organized so as to reflect real-world objects or classes of objects. In an agent-based model, the agents often represent individual actors or institutions, such as homeowners or land management agencies. In spatially explicit agent-based models, the agents can "sense" the digital environment around them, and can act individually based on that information. In other words, there is some degree of autonomy and local context in which actions are undertaken, by whom, and where.

This study used an agent-based modeling approach in which both policy-level decisions and household choices were

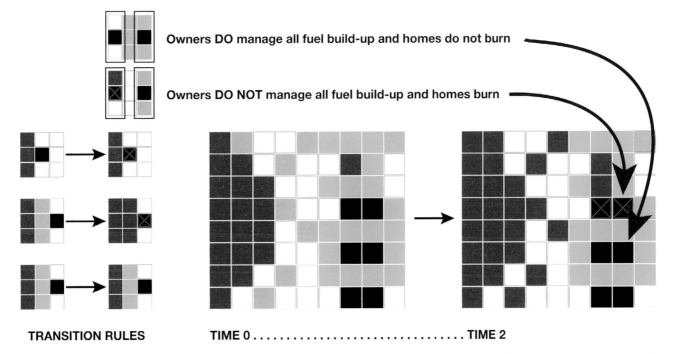

**TRANSITION RULES          TIME 0 . . . . . . . . . . . . . . . . . . . . . . . . . . . . . TIME 2**

**Figure 9.28:** An agent-based model of fire in which households facing similar choices make different decisions. | Source: M. Flaxman, "Multi-scale Fire Hazard Assessment for Wildland Urban Interface Areas: An Alternative Futures Approach" (D. Des. diss., Graduate School of Design, Harvard University, 2001).

considered. It examined a planning situation in which an agent-based modeling and visual simulation system was applied to the assessment and management of fire hazard in the area of Idyllwild (figure 9.29). Simulation modeling was used not only to understand the natural fire regime in space and time, but also to understand how the current human-influenced fire regime evolved and might be managed via the design of spatially explicit fire management policies.

### Representation

This study investigated alternatives for fire management in three southern California mountain communities, Idyllwild, Pine Cove, and Mountain Center. The Idyllwild study area also consists of parts of the San Bernardino National Forest, and the Mount San Jacinto State Park (figure 9.30). The Idyllwild region receives only 25.5 inches (645 mm) of precipitation a year, is heavily vegetated, and has a high fire regime in which dangerous wildfires are common.

Prescribed fire is a common mechanism on public lands, though always controversial because it has both positive and negative adjacency effects. While lowering long-term fuels hazard significantly, it carries significant short-term risk and annoyance to neighbors. Private land policies are controversial for other reasons: they restrict development on lots with the best views, they add to construction costs by requiring particular building techniques, and they intrude significantly on a domain traditionally considered personal—the management of front, back and side yards. Because public and private land ownership is frequently interspersed, there are significant interaction effects (figure 9.31).

The Idyllwild study simulated fire and landscape-processes at three scales: regional, neighborhood, and household. Land use/land cover was used as an integrating variable. Determining the appropriate representation of land cover was a major component of the study, since the landscape classification needed to reflect both human behavior and environmental conditions.

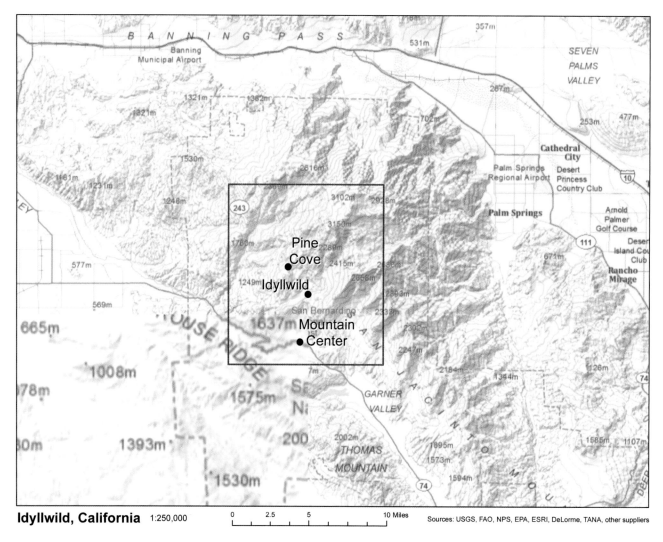

**Idyllwild, California**  1:250,000     0   2.5   5         10 Miles     Sources: USGS, FAO, NPS, EPA, ESRI, DeLorme, TANA, other suppliers

**Figure 9.29:** Idyllwild, California, study area location, about 70 miles (43 km) east of Los Angeles.

Therefore, rather than starting with a conventional land cover or vegetation map, the study considered landscape from a fire-management perspective. In this context, the major manageable component is "fuel load." This is related only loosely to dominant vegetative cover, something that is often mapped using satellite images or air photos, because the significant fuel load variation occurs in the understory and shrub layers that are not typically visible from such imagery. Fuel load is also

**Figure 9.30: Idyllwild is a mountainous, fire-prone area.** | Source: Shutterstock, courtesy of Steve Minkler.

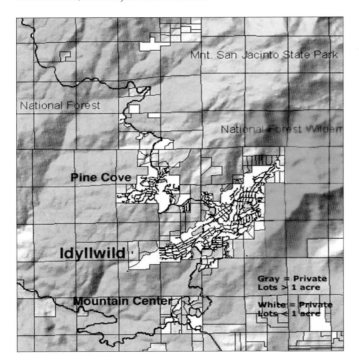

**Figure 9.31: Idyllwild, California land ownership and parcelization pattern showing public lands by management agency (colors), and large private parcels).** | Source: M. Flaxman, "Multi-scale Fire Hazard Assessment for Wildland Urban Interface Areas: An Alternative Futures Approach" (D. Des. diss., Graduate School of Design, Harvard University, 2001).

highly affected by human management practices, both current and historic. Therefore an extensive ground-based survey was conducted, involving a parcel-level survey of several thousand individual parcels. For each parcel, a dozen of the primary variables known to effect fire hazard were collected. Several other data components linked directly to fire risk included a set of variables related to terrain and solar exposure, as well as atmospheric variables relating to how winds flow through mountain landscapes.

The combination of all of these factors produces an enormous multidimensional "fire hazard" space. In order to reduce this complexity to a manageable and understandable set of discrete classes, a statistical technique known as "cartographic analysis of regression trees" (CART) was used. The end result was a discrete set of a dozen or so classes that reflected the most common combination of factors influencing fire behavior in such systems. Parcel survey, GIS and remote sensing data were classified using the CART technique, producing a discrete classification of current conditions.

**Process, evaluation**

Multiple models were required in order to appropriately simulate the processes of interest in the study area. Both human and natural dynamics needed to be considered, and these occurred at a range of spatial and temporal scales. Disaster mitigation planning requires the ability to simulate the discrete events in question, in this case large fires. These typically occur over a period of days and were simulated using hourly time steps. However, human management of fuel loads and building construction processes were also critical, and these took place continuously over a period of years.

Urban intermix fires involve a combination of processes that have historically been studied and simulated separately, including wildland fire behavior and structural ignition, or how buildings and other structures begin to burn. Since wildfire behavior has been relatively well studied, several simulation models already exist and the Idyllwild study used a model named "FARSITE" (Finney 2004).[4] As its input, FARSITE required a description of terrain, land cover, fuels and atmospheric conditions. In addition, one or more fire start locations had to be specified. The model produced gridded predictions of fire characteristics over time, including not only which areas were predicted to burn, but also the intensity and nature of the fire in each location.

Structural ignition is a variable that has also been independently studied, but no mechanistic models were available at the time of this study. Instead, a custom model was built that used a statistical approach, relating structural and landscape characteristics to the probability of an ignition. The spatial zone around a structure turned out to be of critical importance, and this was not simulated well by the regional fire model being otherwise used in the study, due to the spatial granularity of data required. Therefore a third model was constructed that looked at the 40–100 meter zone immediately surrounding structures.

These three models were coupled so that a fire event flowed from regional to neighborhood to structural scales. The characteristics of a fire front were passed from model to model using GIS as an integration tool. The resulting output predicted the consequences of fire on both ecosystems and on structures. The modeling approach could distinguish between low-intensity ground fires, which are generally ecologically beneficial and of negligible threat to well-maintained structures, and "crown" fires, which are disastrous in both ecological and structural consequences.

The fourth and final process model used was a custom-developed model of fuels-accumulation and fuels management (FAFM) (Flaxman 2001). This simulated the effects of policy and human behavior on fuels accumulation over long periods of time. For this study, the model was run in annual time steps for 20 years. This was structured as a decision-tree model that recorded transitions between discrete states of land cover and associated fuel loads. It also incorporated a background of natural transitions due to vegetative succession and fuels accumulation. These default transitions were modified by human interventions at the policy and household levels. Household-level actions were probabilistically simulated based on historical relationships between site characteristics, policies, and enforcement actions. These relationships were calibrated based on a roughly 10-year history of legislative policies and public awareness campaigns, as well as fire and fuels hazard inspection records. The model considered all known household characteristics that could be inferred from census and parcels data, but the only variables that proved to be predictive of human fuels management behavior related to the size, slope, and natural characteristics of the parcels themselves.

## Change

Four scenarios were considered at the regional scale. These scenarios reflected the major public policy choices related to fire hazard management in the context of both public and private lands, where different kinds of actions are often taken (figures 9.32A, B, and C).

Change simulation in this study took place at two time scales. First, a set of policies were put into place based on management scenarios that varied by land ownership. Second, the consequences of these policies on human behavior and on fuels accumulation were simulated over a 20-year period using the FAFM decision-tree model. Third, discrete fire events were simulated across the future landscape. This is a complex formulation that is difficult to organize, since it requires the development and coupling of multiple independent models. However, it allows for the consideration of future events occurring over a period of hours to days, with base conditions influenced by the accumulative effects of policies and natural processes over periods of years.

The FAFM model results indicate that over a 20-year time span, the policies tested would have very significant impacts on base fuel loads (figure 9.32B). Land ownership and management patterns interacted with topography and biophysical factors to create a complex mosaic of fire hazard conditions.

## Impact

Two general forms of impact could be considered. The first was the effectiveness of a policy set to protect against future threats to human life, safety, and property. In the context of an urban wildland fire, life and safety were directly correlated with fire characteristics simulated by the FARSITE model. These included rate of fire spread, fire height, and burn intensity. Property as well as safety aspects were also addressed by the structural ignition prediction model.

The simulated fire simulation results are shown below in two ways. In figure 9.32C (above) fire from each scenario is shown at a single point in time. This format facilitated judgments about the differences among fuels management policies.

**Scenario 1:**
**Mitigation on**
**Public and**
**Private Lands**

**Scenario 2:**
**Public Lands**
**Fuels Reduction**

**Scenario 3:**
**Private Lands**
**Fuels Reduction**

**Scenario 4:**
**Fuels Accumulation**
**on Public and**
**Private Lands**

**A**

**Fuel Accumulation and Fuels Management Model (FAFM) Outputs**

**B**

**Fire Height**

**C**

**All Scenarios at One Point in Time (10 hours post-ignition)**

Figures 9.32A, B, and C: Fuel accumulation and fuels management model (FAFM), fire height, and ten hours after ignition. The colors in the upper row of maps (9.32A) represent the unique "fuel models" that resulted from the combination of vegetative succession and fuels management policies. The most flammable chaparral fuels are in light brown, while dark blue shades represent moist forest types that do not burn except under extreme conditions. The middle row maps (9.32B) show increasing potential fire flame height as a gradient from yellow (ground fire) to dark red (canopy crown fire). The bottom row of images (9.32C) shows the fire for each of the scenarios ten hours after ignition. | Source: M. Flaxman, "Multi-scale Fire Hazard Assessment for Wildland Urban Interface Areas: An Alternative Futures Approach" (D. Des. diss., Graduate School of Design, Harvard University, 2001).

**Figure 9.33: Scenario 4 (Public/Private Fuels Accumulation) from 5 to 9 hours after ignition.** | Source: M. Flaxman, "Multi-scale Fire Hazard Assessment for Wildland Urban Interface Areas: An Alternative Futures Approach" (D. Des. diss., Graduate School of Design, Harvard University, 2001).

In figure 9.33, a single fire is shown over time. This type of visualization is more appropriate in the development of disaster evacuation plans and emphasizes the rate of and location of fire-spread.

**Decision**

Spatial visualization can significantly influence decision making, especially when the decisions are decentralized. In the case of this study, one goal of spatial visualization was to build professional and public understanding of the complex relationships between human behavior, natural conditions, and fire hazard. These occur over time as well as space, and involve three-dimensional aspects of forest structure. In order to convey this information succinctly, and in a non-technical but technically-accurate form, specific visualization methods were developed and tested with target audiences.

The technique that proved to be most effective was a form of animated geo-visualization. Landscape-scale topography and vegetation structure was simulated photo-realistically, and rendered from a series of low-altitude aerial oblique perspectives. Semi-transparent maps of fire risk were overlaid on these 3-D scenes, using a method known as "layer tinting." This allowed spatial context information such as the pattern of roads and structures to be visualized simultaneously and in register with abstract risk information. A similar graphical technique was used to simulate discrete fire events and structural ignitions. However in this case, fires were animated over time. One second of animation time represented one hour of fire event time. This allowed people to understand the different fire spread rates and intensities over various scenarios, with each animation lasting 30–45 seconds.

One frame from such an animation is shown below (figure 9.34). In this case, yellow was used to represent low intensity "ground fire" and orange higher intensity "shrub fire." In the top left of this particular fire, some unshaded chaparral vegetation is burning more intensely but most of the fire is low intensity. On the right of the image, however, is a discontinuous "spot fire" caused by embers from the main fire being carried aloft by prevailing winds.

The results of this case study were complex, as were the implications for planning and decision making. They indicated that neither public lands management policies alone nor private actions were sufficient to eliminate risk of high-severity fires involving large structural losses. However, private land management overall was almost 10 times more effective in terms of reducing structural fire risk. The combination of both policies showed a nonlinear increase in benefits.

The human behavioral aspects that turned out to be of highest significance related not to demographics or social factors, but rather to land management and parcel patterns. The large, steep, and mostly vacant parcels surrounding these mountain communities turned out to contain by far the highest fire hazard. This was of concern to both natural resource managers concerned with protecting the forests from urban fire starts, and to urban dwellers concerned with wildfires spreading into town. This observation was unanticipated in the original planning, policy, and model formulation, and it turned out to have a major influence on potential future policy and enforcement actions. This particular class of parcels had been exempted from previous urban fire hazard legislation, and from wildlands management. In part as a result of this study, the mountain communities created a new fire hazard ordinance specifically addressing large vacant parcels, and required their fire hazard mitigation by owners. Owners who did not maintain their lands to the legal standard are now subject to significant fines, and to tax liens to pay for mandatory risk reductions in extreme hazard cases.

Within these broader conclusions, the agent-based simulation modeling included a wealth of information on which individual structures and neighborhoods were at significantly higher fire risk. The existing fire hazard management program used this information to target enforcement actions in areas of higher risk. Fire managers were originally nervous to act on this information, lest their enforcement be perceived as selective law enforcement. However, they sought and received assurance from public officials that as long as enforcement activities were targeted based on risk assessments, they had the full support of the community.

Beyond the specifics of this case and location, we could also consider how agent-based modeling and visualization performed relative to substantive and procedural aspects of policy and plan revision. The evidence from this case was that such

techniques could indeed be effective in influencing public policy and management, and that the specific policies and benefits may not be apparent at project initiation. It was also clear from this case that ABM could allow for the more effective spatial targeting of plans and could be an appropriate environment within which to test potential design solutions. The disadvantage of the approach was in its complex technical requirements, in this case involving custom computer programming both to create new models and to link existing models together. However, in cases where stakes were high, this level of effort may well be justified. Planning costs, even using elaborate methods, were very low in comparison to ongoing management costs.

While the environmental benefits of such approaches could be difficult to quantify or monetize, they were certainly highly significant. On the human systems side, the risk reduction achieved in this case involved over a billion dollars of real estate value, and the lives and livelihoods of several thousand people. The study concluded that ABM techniques should be considered as an important new tool for spatial policy design and assessment. They were particularly valuable in cases where human-natural systems were tightly coupled, and for those problems where more complex geodesign and visualization methods were warranted.

**Figure 9.34:** **Layer-tinted geovisualization of modeled fire intensity over simulated landscape. Yellow represents low intensity "ground fire" and orange higher intensity "shrub fire." In the top left of this image, some unshaded chaparral vegetation is burning more intensely but most of the fire is low intensity. On the right of the image is a discontinuous "spot fire" that the model generated.** | Source: M. Flaxman, "Multi-scale Fire Hazard Assessment for Wildland Urban Interface Areas: An Alternative Futures Approach" (D. Des. diss., Graduate School of Design, Harvard University, 2001).

# Mixed: sequential and agent-based change models

As I discussed in chapter 5, the several ways of designing can be combined deliberately in whole or in part in an almost infinite number of ways. In the example that follows (figure 9.35), multiple geodesign teams, of their respective times, designed West London's transportation infrastructure using what most likely was a sequential change model (or possibly a constraining or combinatorial approach). Different transportation solutions were then transformed into the attractiveness evaluation-inputs for changes brought about by many independent development actions, as simulated in this research case study research

with agent-based change models for different land uses. This **"mixed"** model then continues through subsequent time-stages to model the historical growth of West London. Thus we can consider that the design model is "mixed" since it combines elements from several basic change model approaches.

## West London, United Kingdom, 1875–2005[5]

The following case study is edited from Kiril Stanilov and Michael Batty, "Exploring the Historical Determinants of Urban Growth through Cellular Automata" (*Transactions in GIS* 15, no. 3, [2011]: 253–71). This research studied the past urban growth of West London (figure 9.37) and explored a specific theoretical assumption regarding the spatial determinants of

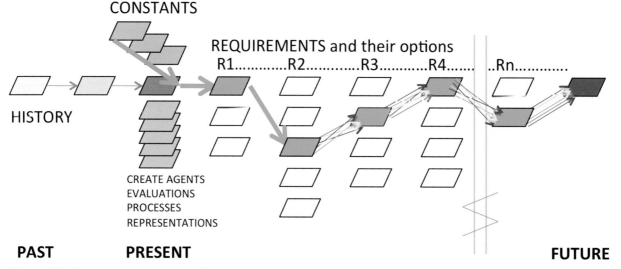

**Figure 9.35:** A mixed example: sequential and agent-based change models. | Source: Carl Steinitz.

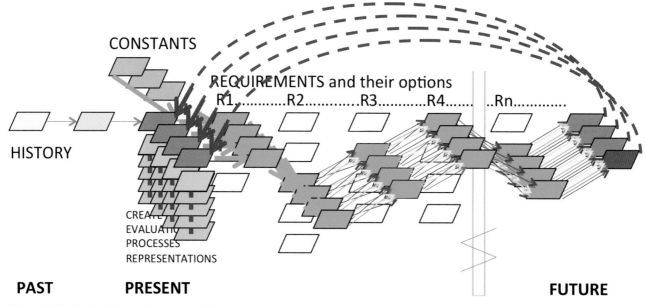

**Figure 9.36:** A mixed example: sequential and agent-based, in a time series. | Source: Carl Steinitz.

land use patterns. It is grounded in detailed empirical data that document the historical growth of West London at an unusually high level of spatial and temporal resolution. The results of the study provided support for a radical hypothesis which states that: (1) the spatial relationships between land uses and the physical environment are remarkably consistent through time, showing little variation relative to changes in historical context, and (2) that these relationships constitute a basic genetic code of urban growth which determines the spatial signature of land development in a given metropolitan area, and (3) that the resulting patterns of change can be "shaped" by designed elements such as those of major infrastructure.

This study explored the notion that at the core of what matters most in structuring the patterns of urban growth are a set of enduring spatial relationships. These relationships are defined by the forces of attraction and repulsion existing between the major land use classes, as well as by a number of key spatial characteristics of the built environment, some of

which, like infrastructure, are designed. A key argument of this study was that these relationships transcend socio-economic circumstances in the sense that they precede and operate to a large extent autonomously from shifts in economic, political, and technological regimes. In a fitting biological analogy, the spatial relationships analyzed here can be described as the genetic code of urban development, a set of fundamental rules that govern the shape and growth of an urban area over the course of its existence. Socio-economic factors exert an influence on the patterns of growth as an overlay agency superimposed on the primary set of fixed spatial relationships. To continue with the biological analogy, social agents alter the patterns of urban growth in a way similar to how the environment impacts the development of an organism whose structure and shape are defined a-priori by its genetic material.

The fundamental spatial relationships shaping metropolitan growth patterns operate on two separate but interrelated levels. On the first level (the local scale) they are defined by the

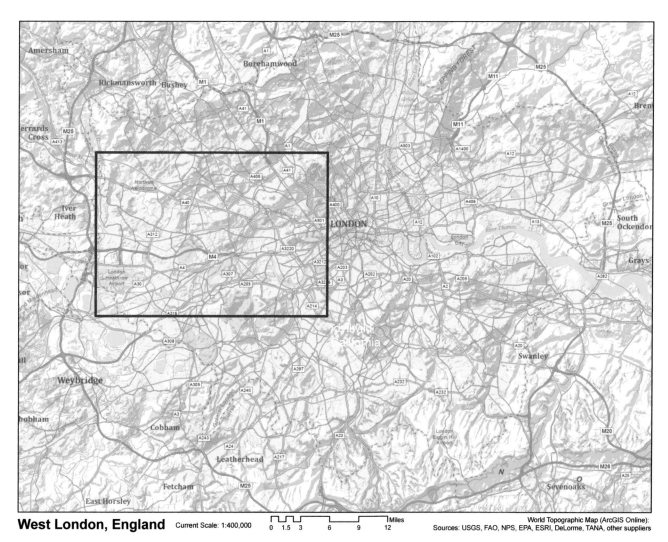

**West London, England**   Current Scale: 1:400,000

**Figure 9.37:** The study area of West London.

forces of attraction and repulsion exhibited between the various categories of urban land uses. Thus, for instance, all land use classes are attracted to themselves (resulting in the formation of homogeneous land use clusters); some are attracted to each other (e.g., high-density residential and commercial and recreational, etc.); while others are not disposed to co-location (e.g., residential and industrial). On the second level (the regional scale) land use patterns are conditioned by the physical properties of the overall urban spatial frame, which consists of the main elements of the transportation infrastructure (major roads and transit nodes) and the network of activity centers (the central business district (CBD) and suburban activity clusters). Physical geography such as steep terrain, water, etc. and legal constraints such as public lands, parks, etc. also play a significant role. The patterning of infrastructure elements and activity centers determines the regional accessibility of every location within the metropolis, exerting decisive influence on the spatial patterns of land use distribution. It is these elements of urban structure that are largely exogenous to the code of development and once determined, the code adapts to the form that is laid down from above.

In order to test this hypothesis, this study built an exploratory model that assessed the validity of assumptions based on solid empirical data covering an extended timeframe. It seemed that the only way to meet these challenges was to reverse and redefine the thrust of traditional urban growth models. What if rather than trying to predict the future we stepped far back in time and tried to predict the present? What if we pretended that the year is 1901, Queen Victoria has just died and the Victorian world is ending, the peace in Europe continues to be fragile with World War I in sight? What if we tried to determine what cities would look like in the beginning of the twenty-first century based on data from the late Victorian period? We would have the natural advantage of knowing what has actually happened, and a powerful tool in the form of a model that would allow us to test the validity of our assumptions about the consistency and importance of key spatial relationships across time using hard historical evidence rather than speculation.

## Representation

With this general conceptual framework in mind, a cellular automata model of West London's historical growth was built that simulated its patterns of land use changes over the course of the last 130 years. The development of the model was based on time series maps that were generated with high spatial and temporal resolution derived from detailed historical Ordnance Survey (OS) records. The idea was to calibrate the model based on data only from the first three map series (1875, 1895, and 1915) and then let the model run all the way to 2005 without changing its initial parameter values. The fit between the post-1915 patterns generated by the model and those recorded from OS maps served as a test for the validity of the model assumptions. The results confirmed the hypothesis, showing a surprisingly robust and accurate "prediction" of West London's growth patterns for 1935, 1960, 1985, and 2005, thus supporting the argument that a limited set of spatial variables can be read as an urban genetic code, determining to a large extent the long-term physical evolution of an urban area.

A consideration in selecting London as a case study, besides its key role in urban history and its well-documented past, was related to the characteristics of London's planning regime. The decentralized and fragmented approach to managing urban development had been a consistent feature of London's history (Hall, 1989),[6] thus making it easier to isolate the impact of planning on metropolitan development patterns to a limited number of key interventions. In the case of West London, these were related to the establishment of the Green Belt and a few infrastructure projects of regional significance. A unique feature of the database employed by this project was the extensive time coverage, which spanned the last 130 years of London's urban growth. The data set included time series maps showing slices in the evolution of West London's metropolitan fabric in 20-year increments, starting from 1875 onwards.

For the documentation of land use change, a highly detailed historic OS map, at a scale of 1:2,500, was used to identify a wide range of land use categories and building types with high spatial resolution, allowing for the identification of close to 60 land-use classes and building types with an accurate representation of actual parcel boundaries (figure 9.38). Ultimately, the number of land-use classes included in the model was reduced to 9, leading to an optimized modeling environment cognizant of the general requirements of parsimony.

Land-use polygon coverages were created for all seven map series. The vector-based maps were then converted to grid coverages with a cell size of 25 by 25 meters. In addition to the development of the land use database, we recorded the evolution of the infrastructure network in the study area. For each one of the map series, this process included the digitization of each roadway, railway, and waterway; and a recording of the location and opening date of each railway and underground station. In addition, the center of the major suburban clusters was identified using the neighborhood function of ArcGIS spatial analyst. These data were important components in the development of the urban growth model.

**Process**

The selection of cellular automata as a modeling approach for this project was based on CA's proven ability to deal with spatial phenomena and their capacity to handle high-resolution applications easily. This study used METRONAMICA, a modeling system developed by RIKS. METRONAMICA has the capacity to model a wide range of urban land uses (the current limit is set to 26 classes). It has the ability to interactively set parameter values and explore the model behavior visually and in real time. This ability of the modeling system encourages experimentation, offering immediate feedbacks through built-in

features particularly suitable for the calibration of exploratory models in which the impact of determinant forces is tested through a method of trial-and-error.

Following the modeling concepts embedded in METRONAMICA, the nine land-use classes were divided in three groups. The first group was composed of three classes (residential, commercial, and industrial uses) that were actively modeled. The dynamics of these land uses, called *active functions*, respond to exogenous demand for land. In this case the amount of development, or the number of cells in each of the three classes, was set by the area of these land uses as recorded in

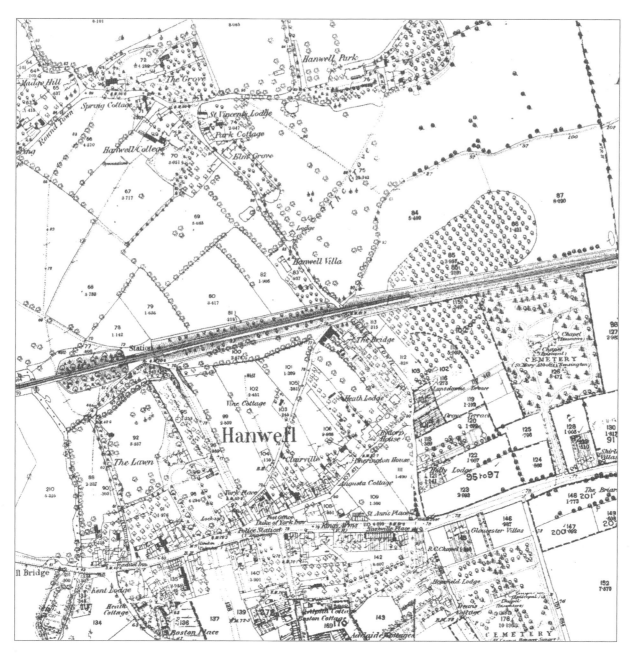

**Figure 9.38:** Hanwell, West London, 1875. Due to the high resolution of the original data sources, the maps come in tiles, each one covering 1 sq. km. The West London study area covers 200 of these tiles. | Source: Kiril Stanilov or UK Ordinance.

the map series. In other words, the model took the number of cells in each one of the study periods and for each one of the three active land uses as a given exogenous constraint, and allocated this growth in the study area for each time step (one year increments).

The second group of land uses, called *passive functions*, was comprised of the land use classes that were not controlled by exogenous demand. To this group was assigned the vacant uses and a class called soft development, which is comprised of estates, farms and other types of land particularly prone to urban conversion. These passive functions appear or disappear as a result of land being taken or abandoned by the growth or decline of the active functions listed above.

Finally, a third group of land uses was composed of the *static* classes, which are designed and appear instantaneously in the landscape and change little over time. Airports, transportation, water, recreation, and large institutional uses (military bases, large hospitals, prisons, etc.) were placed here reflecting the fact that these developments are not driven by processes of organic growth but are known to be (or at least appear to be) a result of centralized decisions at certain moments in time. These land uses were therefore introduced in the model at the time they first appeared on the OS maps. In this sense, these uses were "designed" and not actively modeled, but they influenced the location of the other land uses through their attraction or repulsion effects.

## Evaluation

A next critical step in the development of the model was the integration of accessibility parameters, a modeling function that METRONAMICA handles by introducing various infrastructure elements as polyline shapefiles overlaid on top of the land-use maps. For the road network, only the major roads were included, which were classified as primary arterial roads and secondary collector roads. The accessibility parameters included also the main transit nodes (railway and underground stations) and the location of the CBD and major suburban activity clusters.

To the extent that the model was calibrated on data from 1875, 1895, and 1915, an era largely preceding the first Town Planning Act of 1909, development regulations were not included as a determinant of land use patterns. This decision was in line with the main goal which was to test to what extent the patterns of growth in West London could be explained strictly by spatial characteristics inherent in the built environment. However, there were restrictions on land development imposed by the establishment of the Green Belt, which was first advanced as a planning concept in the Greater London Plan (Forshaw and Abercrombie 1944)[7] and first implemented

comprehensively in the 1950s by the Ministry of Housing and Local Government.

## Change

METRONAMICA's built-in allocation algorithms controlled the transition of agent-cells from one land use state to another, based on a value called *transition potential*. The calibration of the model involved the refinement of parameter values related to the interaction among various land uses across distance and the influence of various elements of the accessibility network on the active land use functions. The initial assignment and refinement of parameter weights was done through an interactive process by verifying visually the spatial effects of the parameter weights on the patterns generated by the model. In order to test the hypothesis about the significance and consistency of the analyzed spatial interactions between land uses and the built environment, the 1875 map was used as a starting point and calibrated the model parameters with reference to the land use patterns recorded in the 1895 and 1915 map series. Having implemented the calibration based on this 40-year period (from 1875 to 1915), the model ran from the initial year of 1875 to 2005. Running the model beyond the calibration period was driven by the project's objective to develop a model that would allow comparisons between the model's predictions and reality.

Finally, it is important to underscore that the model is a constrained cellular automata in the sense that the simulated land use dynamics are influenced by exogenous input. Through the course of the simulation run, spanning 130 years, the model was updated every 20 years with information derived from the map series related to 1. the demand for development for the next 20-year period for each of the three active functions (residential, commercial, and industrial); 2. changes in the accessibility network (new major roads, railway, and railway stations, emerging suburban centers); and 3. the introduction of new static land use features (airports, recreation, large institutions). This type of constraint is traditionally employed in most CA-based land-use models as a mechanism for adapting the abstract mathematical CA apparatus to the realities of the urban development process, leading to substantial improvement in model outcomes. In the end, the results produced by the model far exceeded the most optimistic expectations.

## Impact

The analysis of West London's growth patterns, documented in the historical map series, revealed a highly dynamic and complex land use configuration. A comparison of the maps featuring the areas of land absorbed by new development during the six study periods indicated clear qualitative shifts in the patterns of urban growth. Three distinct periods were discerned, characterized by patterns of nucleation (1875 to 1915), diffusion (1915 to 1960), and infill (1960–2005).

The results of the spatial analysis of the land use dynamics, performed in ArcGIS, helped to support the hypothesis. It confirmed the presence of systematic and consistent relationships between the distribution of land uses and their proximity to major roads, railway stations, suburban activity clusters, and London's CBD. When new residential development (1915 to 1935) was plotted on land which was available in 1915 (excluding already developed cells), its distribution relative to distance to the CBD and railway stations remained surprisingly similar to the previous periods (figures 9.39A and 9.39B). The enduring influence of accessibility to key elements of the metropolitan spatial structure on the patterns of growth was even more pronounced in the plots showing the distribution of residential uses relative to arterial and connector roads (figures 9.39C and 9.39D).

## Decisions

The ultimate test of the hypothesis about the importance and consistency of key spatial determinants of urban growth was provided by the outcome of the simulation. The map of predicted land uses for 2005 generated by the model (figure 9.40) demonstrated a surprising degree of correspondence with the actual land use patterns for that year as recorded in the map series. The evaluation of the model results considered the "correctness" of the overall patterns exhibited by characteristics such as the general distribution of land uses across the study area, the degree of dispersal relative to the city center, the location and size of clusters, and the general level of spatial affiliation between pairs of land use classes (residential and commercial, residential and industrial, recreational and residential, commercial and airports, etc.). The application of more sophisticated quantitative techniques for evaluation of the fit between model outcomes and real data would be inappropriate in this case. Indeed, the popular suite of statistical measures (kappa and fuzzy kappa coefficients, fractal dimensions, etc.) could hardly be considered relevant in a case when the simulation stretched to cover almost a century past the last period of calibration and two-thirds of the predicted development is new growth. Location-specific estimates based on landscape metrics may not be as useful as having the model reproduce realistic patterns: the outcomes of models "must look right". In that regard this study was very successful.

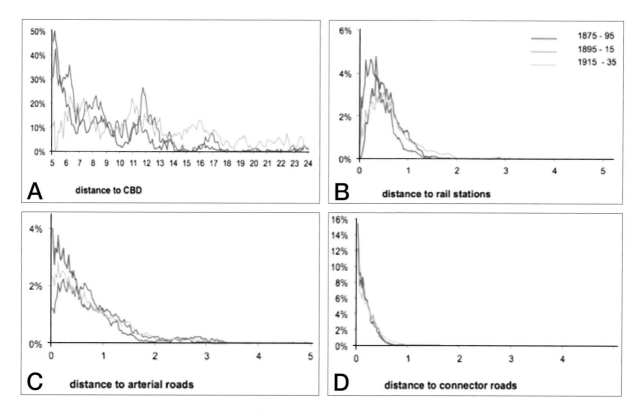

**Figure 9.39A, B, C, and D:** Distribution of residential uses relative to (A) CBD; (B) railway stations; (C) arterial roads; and (D) connector roads. | Source: K. Stanilov and M. Batty, "Exploring the Historical Determinants of Urban Growth through Cellular Automata," *Transactions in GIS* 15, no. 3 (2011): 253–71.

What is more, the simulation of West London's growth not only generated realistic results for the year 2005 based on data from the nineteenth century, but it captured important properties of the urban growth dynamics characterizing the evolution of the urban pattern. The model predicted with high degree of spatial and temporal accuracy the allocation of land uses in each one of the study periods capturing the transitions in urban growth from nucleated, to diffused, to infill (figure 9.40).

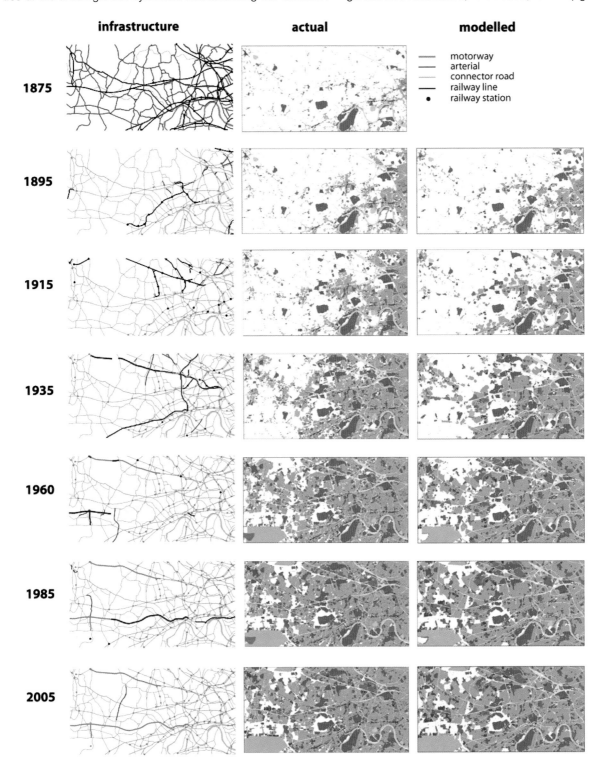

**Figure 9.40: Comparison of designed transportation changes, and actual and predicted land uses by time-periods.** | Source: K. Stanilov and M. Batty, "Exploring the Historical Determinants of Urban Growth through Cellular Automata," *Transactions in GIS* 15, no. 3 (2011): 253–71.

In addition, the simulation successfully reproduced the emergence of industrial corridors in the first half of the twentieth century (figure 9.41A) and the emergence of commercial clusters in the suburban outskirts towards the century's end (figure 9.41B).

In this study of the history of West London, the emergence of industrial corridors and commercial clusters was explored by linking two streams of cellular automata, developing a system that tested a specific theoretical assumption using high-resolution empirical data. The spatial analysis documented the historical growth of West London by providing strong support for this hypothesis. The patterns of urban growth are underlined by enduring spatial relationships that define the interactions between land uses and accessibility parameters related to the designed infrastructure and physical framework of the built environment. These results can be interpreted as proof of the enduring nature of the spatial relationships that underlie the patterns of urban growth regardless of changes in particular socio-economic circumstances.

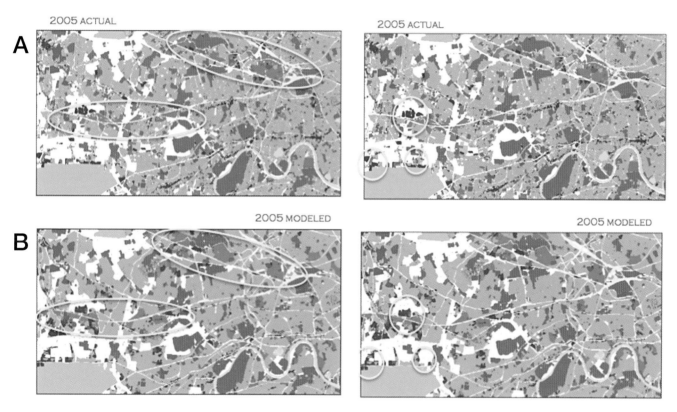

**Figure 9.41A and B:** Emergence of industrial corridors (A) and suburban commercial clusters (B) as predicted by the model.

| Source: K. Stanilov and M. Batty, "Exploring the Historical Determinants of Urban Growth through Cellular Automata," *Transactions in GIS* 15, no. 3 (2011): 253–71.

The four case studies presented in this chapter share several characteristics. In one way or another, they are all rules — based, yet each one has varied the way in which it has developed and applied rules describing the central processes of the study. They have all been applied to relatively large study contexts and to complicated issues of public policy and geodesign. They have all been relatively more difficult to implement as change models because of the need to describe the rule-based processes algorithmically. Yet they also share two characteristics which may be their most significant: they are all based upon calibration using present and past data, and with the exception of the West London study which applied a "back-casting" research strategy, they all applied their change models in several time-stages looking towards the future.

## Notes

1. C. Steinitz, R. Faris, M. Flaxman, J. C. Vargas-Moreno, G. Huang, S.-Y. Lu, T. Canfield, O. Arizpe, M. Angeles, M. Cariño, F. Santiago,T. Maddock III, C. Lambert, K. Baird, and L. Godínez, *Futuros Alternativos para la Region de La Paz, Baja California Sur, Mexico/Alternative Futures for La Paz, BCS, Mexico* (Mexico D. F., Mexico: Fundacion Mexicana para la Educación Ambiental, and International Community Foundation, 2006); C. Steinitz, R. Faris, M. Flaxman, J. C. Vargas-Moreno, T. Canfield, O. Arizpe, M. Angeles, M. Carino, F. Santiago, and T. Maddock, "A Sustainable Path? Deciding the Future of La Paz," *Environment: Science and Policy for Sustainable Development* 47 (2005): 24–38.

   In Japanese in *Landscape Research Japan* 69, no.1 (2005): 66–67.

2. M. Flaxman, C. Steinitz, R. Faris, T. Canfield, and J. C. Vargas-Moreno, *Alternative Futures for the Telluride Region, Colorado*. (Telluride, CO: Telluride Foundation, 2010).

3. Edited from M. Flaxman, "Multi-scale Fire Hazard Assessment for Wildland Urban Interface Areas: An Alternative Futures Approach" (D. Des. diss., Graduate School of Design, Harvard University, 2001).

4. M. A. Finney, "FARSITE: Fire Area Simulator — Model Development and Evaluation" (Research paper. RMRS-RP-4. Ogden, UT: US Department of Agriculture, Forest Service, Rocky Mountain Research Station, 2004).

5. Edited from K. Stanilov and M. Batty, "Exploring the Historical Determinants of Urban Growth through Cellular Automata," *Transactions in GIS* 15, no. 3 (2011): 253–71.

6. P. G. Hall, *London 2001* (London: Unwin Hyman, 1989).

7. Forshaw, H., and L. P. Abercrombie. *County of London Plan, 1943*. Westminster, England: Town Planning and Improvements Committee, 1944.

# PART IV

# A future for geodesign

Successful geodesign requires an integrative approach. Separating tools, techniques, and methods from values and theories, and problems from applications in research, education and practice, is necessarily difficult. I have never believed in teaching separately the aspects of what clearly must be integrated in geodesign practice. We want to make wise choices so that we have a higher probability of achieving a better design, one that has a better chance of producing a better environment. I believe that this is the ultimate purpose of our work.

Part IV of this book explores three areas on which the future of geodesign and its participants ultimately will depend: research, education, and practice. Chapter 10 focuses on research needs for geodesign, while chapter 11 contains a proposal regarding education. I believe there are two aspects of geodesign that are necessary components for the performance of any of our geodesign-related tasks, as well as for education in geodesign, and that both are currently underrepresented in our schools and in our professional settings. The first involves developing *integrated* tools and techniques for handling relevant information for the six geodesign framework questions. The second is an under- emphasis on history and precedent, a topic that I will return to later in chapter 11. In chapter 12, I speculate about the future of practice in geodesign.

# CHAPTER 10

# Implications for research in geodesign

## Tools, techniques, and methods[1]

I do not have *the* all-encompassing list of tools, techniques, and methods that must be taught, understood, adapted, and used for effective geodesign. No one does. Certainly, there are already many tools and techniques that we can apply to the various aspects of geodesign. Diverse tools include countless combinations of computer hardware devices, information-management programs, packaged models, and many equivalent nondigital tools. There are also all manner of techniques: interviews, Delphi methods, mnemonics, and heuristics like the "Escape of Tigers" that I wrote about in chapter 4, basic skills in drawing, writing, and speaking, etc. In the case studies of this book I have already highlighted several methods and combinations of tools and techniques.

Rather, it is performance and personal experience (and sometimes theory) that allows us to designate a tool, a technique, or a method as "better" or "more appropriate" in a given situation. Those collaborating in geodesign have their own legitimate experiences regarding tools and techniques. I would, therefore, like to limit my discussion to some related but general observations, and then to what I see as necessary in the six questions that organize our geodesign activities. I find these to be at the essential core of our work and they can be applied at different scales, contexts, and content areas, and situations that geodesign represents.

If we believe that our work is largely based upon individual intuitive interpretations of problems and solutions, or if we want to focus on well-understood, clearly defined, and repetitive problems, then we may already have perfectly adequate tools and techniques. It is only when we begin to recognize the limitations of such approaches that we see the needs for new tools and techniques to arise in the first place. At that point we have a very serious problem because the more complicated we perceive problems to be, and the more we recognize complexity

(and the desirability of complexities) in proposed "solutions," the more we must necessarily rely on tools and techniques that will give us shortcuts to more verifiably efficacious results.

Members of geodesign teams need to multiply their individual efforts in handling information, within the framework and the chosen methods, towards some concept of overall project efficacy. The purpose of tools and techniques is to support these efforts. They serve as shortcuts to avoid the painful process of having to begin each problem anew with no concept of precedent, no concept of past knowledge, no concept of experience, no concept other than having to invent everything again each time. They are basically designed to increase our efficiency towards an improvement in the products of our efforts, towards the best possible design.

Tools and techniques that are successfully useful are ones that help us either eliminate options or select from among them. When we acknowledge that complexity is a necessary aspect of the world in which we are attempting to act, we recognize that a large design problem doesn't have two or three or four or five alternatives, it has thousands or millions. Thus we need things that help us eliminate and sort through, quickly and massively, those multitudinous options. Then we can arrive at a number that is conceptually manageable, feasible to be evaluated and compared, and capable of being understood by the decision makers. It will be from this group that final selections are made and implemented. Efficiently determining the *WHERE, WHEN, and HOW* changes which will be most beneficial when compared to an existing condition is the central issue, so the tools must provide essential impact assessments as feedback and help us and the decision makers rapidly evaluate proposals.

A critical role of tools and techniques is enabling the use of inference. Some might call this analysis, but it is often mixed with a substantial amount of inferential interpretation. We seek to identify the limits and opportunities of the situation with which we are faced. I am not satisfied with our mastery of the many techniques available to assist in this often complex task. How many of us who talk in our proposals about "maintaining water quality" actually understand the means by which water quality is measured? How many of us with a carefully honed sense of visual awareness have an understanding of how his/her neighbor perceives a beautiful or an ugly view?

Most of the techniques that we use are directed at avoiding potential future problems. Unless we have theory to describe the geodesign study area and how it will perform under changed conditions, it is foolish for us to turn to and rely on tools and techniques. Basic tools and techniques involve simple logic expressed graphically or verbally. Accordingly, more complex tools and techniques involve far more complex logical links, including fuzzy logic, and may be expressed in terms of linked spatial and temporal models. For educational and professional work, the absolute mastery of inference techniques using simple logic is essential. When the requirements become more complex, the more our roles will become specialized and part of larger team efforts. Then, a shared understanding of the more complex modeling techniques available in the design professions and the geographic sciences for analyzing limits and opportunities of geodesign problems becomes very useful.

Designers who are accustomed to teaching and practicing with fairly simple methods may be very surprised to realize the amount of modeling work being done in the geographic sciences that has direct relevance to our work and our perceived "territory." This is a critical issue for the future of geodesign and the collaboration between the geographic sciences and design professions. As design students become more aware of the limitations of their current practices and the advantages gained by leveraging the tools, techniques, and approaches from other science fields, I believe the benefits to our disciplines will outweigh the costs. This infers that students of the design professions *and* the geographic sciences must develop a basic understanding of the content and processes of our environment that each considers central to its roles. Then we all must continue to strive for effective collaboration, the fundamental but challenging step that is critical for the success of geodesign.

# Research needs for geodesign

## Representation

For each of the six fundamental questions of the geodesign framework, there are important and relevant research needs. One central area is data itself and its inadequacies and inappropriateness for geodesign projects. Though it will often be necessary to "go beyond information given" while making geodesign

decisions, we first have to master information available. We invariably collect unnecessarily large quantities of data. Instead, we should acquire and use the *minimum of relevant data* with a maximum of efficiency. It is incredible how much data is acquired and then either misused or not used at all. The tools and techniques for data acquisition can and should become more formalized, both in our education and professional practice. At one end this includes procedures for field surveys, and at the other, a knowledge and use of the most advanced remote sensing and data acquisition and management technologies.

Our data sets are overwhelmingly focused on items that are relatively easy to define and measure, usually with quantitative scales. Most spatial data within a GIS are based upon sharply defined polygons with uniquely defined characteristics and measurements, or upon regular geometrical divisions with similar attributes, or upon single points whose locations are allegedly precisely determined. During these processes one rarely encounters fuzzy boundaries and fuzzy definitions, though the world is in fact full of these. We are often more uncertain about what we are characterizing and measuring than we care to admit, and I doubt that anyone understands the implications of this uncertainty upon geodesign (in general) and ways of designing (in particular). We have very little experience with social science data that record feelings and emotions, yet these undoubtedly enter into the decision models which are so critical to shaping geodesign processes, products and decisions. And as digital data become standardized and ubiquitous, will we be in danger of losing the sense of place gained from the direct experience of our many geographic contexts?

We can also identify research needs for all of geodesign's technical information-management infrastructure. While the information technologies themselves are improving and expanding at extraordinary rates, most continue to lack easy and intuitive ways of interacting for the many people who must participate in collaborative geodesign. Designers and scientists can easily understand the advantages of managing increasingly large and complex geographic information systems in increasingly rapid time, but we consistently underestimate how long it takes for us to truly digest and comprehend what we are doing when it is happening and evolving so fast.

## Process

As I discussed in chapter 5, our process models and therefore our impact models are almost always seen as separate from one another. Yet we know that the geographic contexts for geodesign are interrelated systems, with complex attributes that are connected to each other, as was shown in figure 5.32. We know that if you make a big change to one part, you will inevitably change the other parts of the system via complex chains of interaction. This realization is well understood among the geographic scientists who use *nonspatial* systems-oriented models. However, it is extremely rare to see a set of interacting *spatial* process models in a geodesign study, and organized in a manner so that they interact among themselves over space and time. This is exactly what we should be developing in research and in application.

## Evaluation

Our evaluation models overwhelmingly emphasize themes and criteria that can be evaluated in quantitative scales. Yet remember that the famous physicist Albert Einstein (1879–1955) said "Not everything that can be counted counts, and not everything that counts can be counted."[2] We need to emphasize (and discover innovate ways to measure and represent) the qualitative characteristics of the environment far more than we currently do in computer-based geodesign activities. Contributions from the psychological and perceptual sciences are largely absent from geodesign projects, and this also needs remedying through research and practice.

## Change

Our change models and the tools and techniques that support them are unnecessarily and inappropriately idiosyncratic. Once we recognize that there are far more than a few "alternatives" to a given problem, we can accept a wider diversity of synthesis approaches. Two that I believe are potentially the most useful (and also underrepresented in our teaching and professional practice) are trial and error and optimization.

Trial and error, with its constant seeking to improve, is extremely useful when a formal and rapid impact assessment and feedback procedure exists as part of the geodesign infrastructure. This requires efficient links between change and impact models. If we cannot efficiently assess our trials, we cannot hope to improve on our errors. Recent developments in applying computer modeling to the efficient evaluation of design trials have been remarkable, yet our educational and professional procedures too often see this as an *inefficiency*. We place far too great an emphasis on our students' initial trials (their "concepts" and preliminary designs), rather than focusing on how they can improve their final outcomes by making more trials more easily, and lowering the emotional cost along the way. This is also true in geodesign practice. Increasing the opportunities to experiment with tools and techniques, to add to the numbers of trials for a given problem, will benefit out decisions and outcomes. "Hill climbing" toward a good design via rapid

assessment feedback may mitigate the choice of inappropriate methods choices elsewhere in the geodesign study.

At the other extreme, I believe that our students and practitioners should be much more aware of the many algorithmic procedures applicable for geodesign, especially those already used widely in industry and engineering. Our problems are not so uniquely different that they cannot align with rule-based, optimizing and agent-based procedures. Once we accept rule-based procedures for evaluation, we will be better positioned to apply more formal methods and techniques to our change models. And you can still always stand back and say that you don't like the way something has come out.

Because change models are rarely recorded, they are not easily adapted to other geographic contexts or transformed for linking to different stages of a geodesign process. For any specific circumstance, we need far more experimentation and comparative research to understand the potential efficacy of choosing to design in one way over others. For example, we should organize a series of "geodesign problems" that vary in size and scale, and have different groups try to make designs using all eight change models as initial ways of designing, and compare the results. Until we do such systematic methodological experiments several times and achieve a greater understanding of these relationships, we do not really have the evidence to say that geodesign's ways of designing matter (even though I for one believe they matter a great deal).

## Impact

We need to master many more formal procedures for the environmental, social, and economic assessments of geographic study areas and the impacts of our designs. I find it strange that so much of our education in design is based upon review and criticism by faculty and clients who are essentially using informal and experience-based opinions. At the same time, our professional practitioners are having their designs, particularly the larger project work and regional policy work, evaluated by formal predictive impact models. To a surprising and unsettling extent, our design students and professionals are not being educated to master, develop, and apply these more rigorous methods themselves.

Our impact models are overwhelmingly quantitative because of the quantitative focus of most process models and their underlying data. Let me give a simple example from the realm of visual assessment models: the spatial mathematics of measuring inter-visibility between two points is not the same thing as assessing the perception of beauty. Both are needed in geodesign.

## Decision

Finally, decision models in the real world of geodesign almost always do *not* follow idealized decision models, such as those common within the political science literature. They are frequently personal, highly political, messy, sometimes greedy, sometimes corrupt, rarely transparent and rarely democratic. And yet we persist, as we must, in the belief that geodesign (in Herbert Simon's definition of design) is a means toward a better future. This is a hope and an ideal certainly worth striving for.

## A research question: which level of spatial-analytic complexity?

Assuming that all eight cumulative levels of process model complexity that I described in chapter 5 can be applied to major geographic processes, including hydrology, ecology, microclimate, and human activity, we still face a dilemma regarding which complexity level we should choose for any given geodesign problem. As we move down the levels of complexity, the amount of science and effort that are required increases while the public understanding moves in the opposite direction (figure 5.46). Should we use complicated ways to understand similarly complicated processes, or should we use simpler ways because the general public (and we) will have greater understanding of the model and therefore possibly provide greater political input towards and support for a decision?

Scale and size surely matter, but do we really know which levels are most appropriate for which scales and sizes and for which processes? I don't think we do. This lack of knowledge can be especially risky when we are trying to link models of different aspects of the landscape in a particular study. There cannot be only one answer. At its simplest, the direct personal experience of the designer may be sufficient to proceed without *any* formalized spatial and temporal analysis, especially for smaller projects. At the other large size extreme, very complicated and costly efforts are likely to be required, and yet the project may still suffer from a lack of public understanding. Answering this dilemma and deciding on the appropriate methods and their level of complexity requires judgment and experience. At this time there is no other way or substitute.

However, there is a potentially useful research study that addresses this particular situation. We have access to many existing models for processes such as erosion, hydrology, forest succession, traffic, air pollution, noise, and visual preference. Comparing both the efficiency and efficacy of such process models, across scales and levels of complexity, would result in a better understanding of which combinations are the most appropriate fit

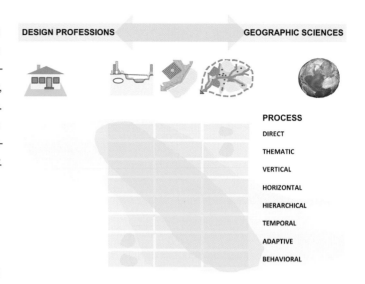

**Figure 10.1:** A hypothesis regarding the relationship between geographical study area (size and scale) and process model complexity. | Source: Carl Steinitz.

for any design problem. My hypothesis is that there is a fuzzy diagonal relationship (with outliers) between geographic size or scale and appropriate process model complexity (figure 10.1).

Conducting this type of comparative research, and preliminarily categorizing the applicability of many existing analytic models, would be a significant step towards increasing geodesign's efficiency and efficacy. Basically, if we know the content of the design problem, its size(s) and scale(s) and its required analytic complexities, we would begin to know the capabilities of the spatial analysis methods which are available and required for that particular application. We could start making more-informed selections of methods. In the process we might also identify important further research needs for geodesign.

## A research question: which ways of designing?

The change models, the eight ways of designing described in chapter 5 and in their related case studies, are not equally efficient and they are not equally effective. Furthermore, none of these methods is typically used on its own. However, each can provide the starting point and the central approach that guides the development of a design. The choice depends greatly on the scale(s) of the design problem, the decision model and its needs for information from impact models, the consequent needs for complexity in the study's process models, the technologies available to the geodesign approach, and the skill and experience of the geodesign team.

The availability of these several ways of designing raises important research questions: How does a design resulting from a participatory approach compare with one resulting from applying an optimizing approach to the same objectives and relative weights, or with an agent–based modeling approach in which there are feedback updates to all assessments between stages of development? Or how does it compare to any of the other methods? And if these results are significantly different when compared against their relative impacts, then why? And which design product should then be chosen?

Again, my hypothesis is that there is a fuzzy diagonal relationship (with outliers) between geographic size and scale and appropriate change models (ways of designing), and this is linked to the appropriate process model complexity. Just as for research related to model complexity, this will be affected by differing contributions among the geographic sciences and the design professions. These interactions, characterized by their diagonal relationship across scale, is where I think that many of the advantages of collaboration in geodesign are located and where I believe research and experimentation should be concentrated.

## A research question: which ways of visualization and communication?

Communication has three basic elements: the message, the medium and the meaning. Most designers (including the designers of GIS-derived maps) believe they have a message and need to give it expression. The medium is how the design is abstracted, transformed, and visualized in a map, graph, animation, etc., although the medium could also be a policy, a law, or an investment. The viewer is assumed to gain an impression from the medium and (one assumes) obtain the meaning. This is certainly the most common expectation of our students and professional colleagues, and it frequently does not work as communication.

Effective two-way communication will increasingly be a paramount need for effective geodesign. We must assume that a viewer, such as a stakeholder, knows what meaning is being sought. The viewer actively seeks the meaning from his or her impression of the medium, and the geodesign team must provide that expression. It is not the designer's message which is paramount, but rather the message being sought by the decision-making viewer.

It is only when the messages go in both directions that real communication for geodesign can exist. This must be based on a shared knowledge of the subject, shared assumptions

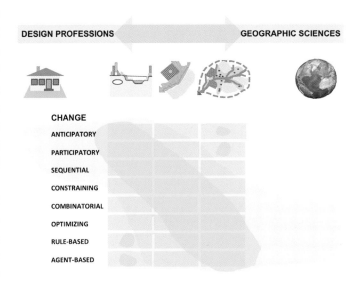

**Figure 10.2:** A hypothesis regarding the relationship between geographical study area (size and scale) and change models. | Source: Carl Steinitz.

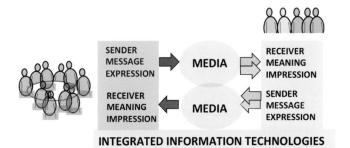

SHARED KNOWLEDGE OF THE SUBJECT
SHARED ASSUMPTIONS
SHARED LANGUAGE

# COMMUNICATION

**Figure 10.3:** Two-way communication between the stakeholders and the geodesign team is essential. | Source: Carl Steinitz.

and a shared language including a shared language of visual representation. The central role of integrated information technologies, the media, will be to enable collaboration and the implementation of the framework for the geodesign team, but perhaps even more important, it also enables visualization and communication with the people of the place. In this regard, I believe we are focusing too much of our professional, educational, and research resources on promoting visualization without thinking enough about essential issues of communication. Many designed aspects in geodesign are not easy to visualize, such as conservation, or the deliberate decision *not* to do something as part of a geodesign strategy.

Furthermore, I think that too much time of our time is spent on idiosyncratic and pyrotechnic expression using the latest visualization technologies. We place far too much faith in the assumption that people will understand our visualizations just because they see them. In the words of the great English painter John Constable (1776–1837): "We see nothing truly until we understand it."[3] He believed that you must understand *before* you see. He did not believe the reverse, that just because you see it you will understand it.

To this end, we need to develop much more adaptable, reliable, and *integrated* computer-based technologies, and we need to adopt many more standardized communications conventions such as words, symbols and land use and other color codes that *all* can easily comprehend and share. We also need more and easier ways of user-determined visualization within geodesign studies. There is an entire existing research field of cartographic cognition with which designers are largely unfamiliar, and this should change. Consider the alternative — visualization, but a lack of communication. *Visualization is not the same as communication,* and communication matters more.

# A support system for geodesign[4]

The following section is adapted from a paper by Stephen Ervin, "A System for Geodesign," in *Teaching Landscape Architecture,* eds. E. Buhmann, S. Ervin, D. Tomlin, and M. Pietsch (Proceedings, Digital Landscape Architecture, Anhalt University of Applied Sciences. Dessau, Germany, May 2011), 145–54.

To progress through the framework effectively and efficiently, a geodesign team requires a new system for technical support, and determining how best to envision and construct this tool is an essential area of applied research. Such a geodesign support system (GDSS) will likely combine the best of various legacy tools (CAD, GIS, BIM, e.g.), and some new and best-practice techniques, such as object-oriented diagrams and key-indicator "dashboards." These will be obtained not by perfecting any one software product, but by leveraging interoperability and providing essential modularity and flexibility in component design. Such a system could entail at least fifteen essential and interrelated components (figure 10.4).

These fifteen components fall roughly into three groups of five each: meaning and linkages, parts and relations, and behavior and performance. Each is described briefly below.

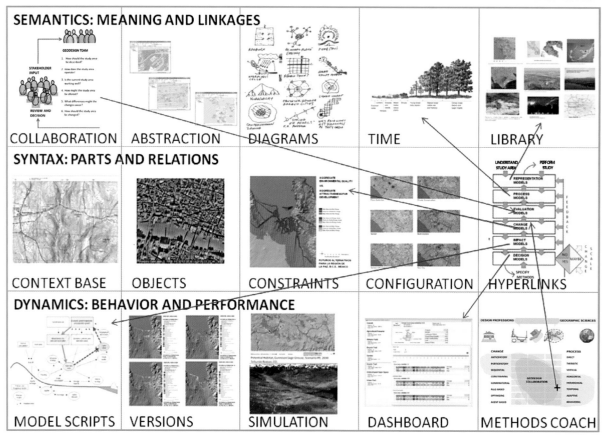

## A GEODESIGN SUPPORT SYSTEM: INTEGRATED TOOLS AND HELPERS

**SEMANTICS: MEANING AND LINKAGES**

COLLABORATION | ABSTRACTION | DIAGRAMS | TIME | LIBRARY

**SYNTAX: PARTS AND RELATIONS**

CONTEXT BASE | OBJECTS | CONSTRAINTS | CONFIGURATION | HYPERLINKS

**DYNAMICS: BEHAVIOR AND PERFORMANCE**

MODEL SCRIPTS | VERSIONS | SIMULATION | DASHBOARD | METHODS COACH

**Figure 10.4: The elements of a geodesign support system.** | Source: Carl Steinitz, based upon ideas from Stephen Ervin.

Meaning and linkages are the sources of the ideas supporting geodesign:

1. Collaboration tools: Interfaces, communications, and record-keeping tools are needed to enable teams of (possibly geographically and temporally-remote) participants to effectively work together on shared documents.

2. Level of Abstraction (LOA) Manager: A mechanism is needed for distinguishing various levels of abstraction, from high-level, abstract schematics (where constraints may play a major role), to low-level, most concrete (where specific dimensions, objects, materials may play a more important role). These are not the same as, but are related to, "scale."

3. Diagram Manager: An important form of high-abstraction design layout is the family of "diagrams," in which high-level assertions and constraints are embedded in more-topological-than-geometric configurations.

4. Time/Dynamics Manager: Configurations and contexts are not always static, and may change over time. Explicit recognition of time as a dimension in geodesign is essential.

5. Library: A stored, searchable, indexed and annotated archive of elements, configurations, study area information, etc. that can be retrieved and added-to as needed should be accessible. These may be personal or shared, and supports a the geodesign team's all-important "case memory," as described in chapter 7.

Parts and relations are the specifics of a geodesign study:

6. Context-Base: Information about the geographic context or setting that is expected to be important to consider and relate to, but that will not directly be changed by the geodesign activities is essential. This may consist of representation models such as maps or demographic data, etc., including GIS and CAD data.

7. Objects: The "elements" of geodesign, ranging from assemblies like "parking lot" to individual items like "tree"; should be instantiated in the "Object-Oriented" sense that each has attributes that can be queried and modified, and exist within a network of classes, instances, methods, inheritances, etc.

8. Constraints: Geometric and logical relationships or "rules" desired for and among elements should be implemented ("one parking space per dwelling unit," or "front doors facing south," etc.). They can be used to automatically generate elements and configurations, or test them for compatibility.

9. Configuration: The geometric arrangement of objects with attributes in a design is the central role of geodesign. Configurations may be more or less abstract (see Abstraction-Manager); a "schematic diagram" or a "construction document," a 2D "plan" or 3D "model," etc.

10. Text/Media (Hyper-Links): The ability to connect relevant material to any object, or configuration, which leads to related textual, or multi-media descriptive material, and possibly even more links (via the Internet) is important for rich digital design documents.

Behavior and performance are what we normally do in geodesign:

11. Modeling/Scripting Tools: Traditional full-fledged languages such as C, or Python, or simpler embedded scripting facilities in drawing or modeling software, to enable automation of repetitive tasks, and algorithmic / interactive generation of forms and solutions, will be needed.

12. Version Manager: A set of facilities for managing disparate versions of design configurations, over time ("Plan A," "Plan B," "Jim's Plan, Monday 5 PM," etc.) is essential.

13. Simulation Tools: Assessing and visualizing consequences (quantitative, qualitative, visual, and others) of design configurations, especially over time, is critical to the comparison of design alternatives.

14. Dashboards: Monitoring the status of a design over time, with reference to key-indicators (such as total area or number provided versus target desired, resultant carbon footprint, results of simulations, etc.), is very important. Dashboards provide essential real-time, visual, and other feedback during design sessions, or when comparing versions, etc.

15. Geodesign Methods Coach: Recognizing that various distinct design methods exist within many problem domains, and drawing upon emergent experience with their suitability and efficacy, this automated 'coach' can comment upon, critique, and suggest design approaches as part of the geodesign process.

Development of methods and tools that can be easily integrated is a clear priority for geodesign-related research and development. Without these, and without further research on the appropriateness of selecting process models of differing complexities, on choosing differing ways of designing, and on effective ways of communicating (and especially with the people of the place), our efforts will continue to be dominated by ad-hoc choices as we organize and manage geodesign. The serious issues that we all face require and deserve more predictable, efficient, and effective methodologies.

# Notes

1. Adapted from C. Steinitz, "Tools and Techniques: Some General Notes but Precious Few 'Hard' Recommendations," in Proceedings, Council of Educators in Landscape Architecture Conference, 1974.

2. Attributed to Albert Einstein.

3. Attributed to John Constable.

4. S. Ervin, "A System for Geodesign," in *Teaching Landscape Architecture,* eds. E. Buhmann, S. Ervin, D. Tomlin, and M. Pietsch (Proceedings, Digital Landscape Architecture, Anhalt University of Applied Sciences. Dessau, Germany, May 2011), 145–54.

# CHAPTER 11

# Implications for education and practice in geodesign

GEODESIGN AND MUSIC share a corresponding need for both soloists and conductors. Education for the design professions is largely directed towards training soloists. Despite the entry level employment towards which most students aim, employment which can be characterized as being similar neither to a soloist nor a conductor, the majority of students still see themselves as (eventually) becoming soloists. For these students the goal is to master *all* of the skills and knowledge needed for effective professional activity: to identify problems, analyze them, propose solutions, and see them built to the satisfaction of self, clients, and peers. This attitude is not just egocentric. It is a reflection of our system of design education and a central product of that system. In countries that have professional registration, it is an assumption of and a requirement for that recognition. Nor is it so different in the sciences, once the scope of specialization is selected by a student.

All design professionals are familiar with the traditional format and structure of project-oriented design education (the studio system) in which a problem statement is given, students typically work as individuals, and their work is reviewed by expert juries in a somewhat competitive and defensive presentation format. We have all participated in this process as students and as faculty. I suspect that we all have an understanding of the great strengths of this system and some of its weaknesses. Some of the survivors of this teaching method do indeed become highly effective soloists. Many, probably the majority, remain useful "second trombonists" throughout their careers.

My purpose here is not to attack the traditional studio system upon which most of the design professions base their education. Nor is it to attack the educational patterns in the sciences. We need first-rate hydrologists, ecologists, sociologists, and geographers, as well as architects and landscape architects and civil engineers. Rather, it is to ask other questions:

From where will the conductors emerge? Who will lead and guide the collaborations needed for effective geodesign?

## Educating conductors vs. training soloists [1]

Relatively few students see their long-term objective as preparing to conduct, that is to lead or manage teams that collaboratively share an enterprise and the responsibilities for its success or failure. The vast majority of my graduate students had some teamwork experiences during their prior education, though these were usually neither systematically organized nor particularly successful. Yet a surprising number of these same students are now in professional practice as "conductors." They are partners and associates in larger firms, often functioning as leaders of project teams. They are in policy-making levels of public agencies. Some of them are teachers. Their professional success is due as much to their critical, judgmental, organizational, and managerial skills as it is to their actual design and production capabilities. All too frequently they have undergone a difficult and sometimes painful transition between the roles for which they were initially trained and towards which they entered their profession, and their current, more responsible roles, often involving fewer direct design activities.

For many reasons, I teach in a manner that requires students to work in (often large) multidisciplinary teams. This has been consistent for the more than 40 years that I have taught at Harvard's Graduate School of Design, where I often lead studios that focus on problems associated with change in large, complex and valuable landscapes. Moreover, I have led dozens of related workshops at other universities. Several have been profiled as case studies in this book and others are listed in the bibliography. For the last 30 years or so, these studios and workshops have been organized by versions of my geodesign framework that I have described here in earlier chapters. They have always had participants from diverse fields, sometimes in teams as small as three people, and sometimes involving a studio class of 12 to 18 people acting as "a team of the whole."

Participants in studios and workshops alike are typically organized as if they were a large, multidisciplinary geodesign team. This arrangement is optimal for focusing on the scope and complexity of the design problem at hand, as well as the need for many individual tasks to be coordinated. The students themselves are responsible, to the greatest extent possible, for the entire project. Unlike the more traditionally organized studio, in which the students are given a site, a client, and a program, students in my studios are responsible for problem identification, much of the design of the methodological approach, product definition, production and presentation of work, and all aspects of project management, including budget allocation and chairing of meetings and reviews. In this book, the Padova case study exemplifies my studio teaching style and the Cagliari case study is typical of one of my workshops.

In terms of student-to-faculty relationships and student-to-student relationships, the sociology of my class is quite different than that of the traditional design studio. Of special importance is learning to publically review, comment upon, and organize the work of others. Students manage the enterprise in small teams, so that each one gains leadership experiences. The faculty responsibilities are diverse but emphasize the roles of "producer," "consultant," and "presence." Ultimately, the educational experience for both teacher and student may be different from a typical one, yet I would characterize these experiences as being generally successful and positive ones, both from my perspective and those of my students (though I concede that these experiences are not without occasional pain). Clearly, one of my central purposes is to help educate some future conductors.

The difference in education, styles, and skills required of conductors versus those demanded of soloists should be reflected in our educational institutions for design professionals. Soloists continue to need training; after all, they are essential and geodesign will require many more of them. However, I would also argue that no one should escape without having had some well organized education directed towards the conductor's role, not only because of the many large and crucial geodesign problems which will require team approaches, but also because such a lack can seriously hinder our students' future professional careers. Simply stated, I am more interested in educating future employers than in training future employees. Geodesign needs conductors!

# The roles of history and precedent[2]

I have worked long enough in geodesign studies to know that a surprising majority of *new* work accomplished is based upon *previous* work accomplished. In other words, people make responsible decisions based both upon their personal experiences and whatever insight they can gain from others, including that which was acquired in the past. That is one reason why history and precedent are important for geodesign.

Content matters, and the study of history and precedent are essential in teaching *any* geodesign-related field. Geodesign methods and skills should be available to people in *any* of the geographically-oriented sciences, to GIS and computer science specialists, and to designers who are in *any* of the geodesign professions — architecture, urban design, landscape architecture, urban and regional planning, civil engineering, etc. More opportunities for having shared or experienced any common curricula will increase the chances for productive collaboration in the future.

Design professionals share their desire to be instruments of change (for the better, we hope) with people from many other disciplines. Moreover, the relationship between historical precedent and our future-oriented activities is not really different from such relationships in other fields, including economics, political science, or law. So here I will outline some roles for the study of precedent in the education and professional activities of those who are interested in geodesign in particular. I will also comment on what may be the central question: of all the history and precedent that may be relevant to geodesign, upon which aspects should we focus as being the most important?

A person active in a future oriented field such as geodesign, whether a student or an experienced practitioner, balances three human tendencies while they are working: intuition, emulation, and investigation. History has an inevitable and important place in each.

Intuition, the "great leap forward," is clearly a valuable part of any creative activity. However, intuition does not exist in a vacuum. It works best when it is carefully nurtured and based on experience. Case memory matters. This is as true for a scientist framing a hypothesis for research as it is for a designer. Where can this intuition-guiding case memory come from? Usually the answer lies in one of two places. It can be derived from the past and depends upon a highly valued and often personal capacity for historical analysis. Or, it comes from a view of a better future, which is itself intuitive but requires for its own life a comparison with a clear view of the past. This is not unlike any other social movement. If the future is its attraction, it is only because it promises a better condition. Even the most inventive, farsighted, "intuitive" approach to design thus fundamentally rests upon the knowledge of the past and cannot be accepted unless it holds forth the promise of a better condition than what precedent would have provided.

Emulation is a surprisingly commonplace perspective in design, though few will admit to it. Emulation goes against the ego of the designer (or the research scientist) seeking to be considered a creative person. And yet in many fields of endeavor, emulation is a standard and respected approach. Consider the case of open heart surgery. There are standard procedures (albeit named after their inventors), and the replicability of cases and surgical procedures is basic to the professional ethic. For geodesign, emulation is a legitimate and effective approach that succeeds to the extent that precedent is understood. The essential aspect of an emulation approach to design is having something meaningful to understand and emulate. The "case study" approach and the "prototype" approach both have as their clear purpose the study of precedence, so that the designer can learn from the advantages and disadvantages of past experience, build a vocabulary, deepen the case memory, and when the situation calls for it, adapt or replicate the solutions that are now within one's knowledge.

Investigation as a working tendency tends to emphasize a more empiric attitude towards the creation of proposals for change, and a more scientific outlook towards creative methodologies. In my view, investigation becomes particularly beneficial as problems become larger, more complex, more important to more people, and more difficult. When the risk or cost of making an error increases, subsequently increasing the value of *preventing* an error, the role of investigation in geodesign becomes as much to avert the worst from happening as to come to the best solution. During investigation, the study of history and precedent become more analogous to its role in the sciences. The designer begins to recognize that the future can only be built upon the activities of the past. Directing change into the future is not done with a free hand.

The roles of history and precedent take a somewhat different form in this investigative frame of mind. Understanding the history of the place, with a social and environmental perspective, becomes more important. The history that is important is the history of values, of life processes, of indigenous physical solutions, and in general, of things which are seen as stable over the long run. The problems (i.e., the need for changes) are also what we first hope to understand. Another role for history and precedent in investigation lies in the study of methods for analyzing and resolving problems. Clearly this is one of the major purposes of this book. I firmly believe that methodological breakthroughs are possible but the idea that a designer is

not rooted within a long intellectual and methodological history seems fatuous.

Most designers tend to mix intuition, emulation, and investigation, but if pressed, would probably identify more closely with one of these over the others. In all three there is an essential and indispensable role for the study of history and precedent. Simply stated, geodesign cannot function in ignorance of the past. But how shall we incorporate the study of history and precedent into our educational programs? I can distinguish six different ways, all of which may have their place, but some of which I value more highly.

The first is to emphasize a professional history: the history of geodesign, or of its practitioners, or of their methods. I personally do not believe that this is a fruitful path. The important work of geodesign will increasingly be influenced and altered by society at large, technological innovation, and the work of other fields. A focus on "professionalist history" seems premature.

The second approach is a focus on "time periods," an approach commonly used in schools of architecture and departments of history. In my view, geodesign's long history makes this an inefficient approach for students to truly understand what has been attempted and accomplished. Furthermore, I do not believe that in this way we could identify those aspects which are most significant to the wide range of contemporary geodesign approaches and which are capable of being integrated into them.

Another approach is the study of history via heroes. I'm increasingly less taken by "the innovative great person" theory. I see the needs of complex institutional and organizational efforts as being far more important for effective geodesign action. While I greatly value the influential contributions made by the people whose work I know, admire, and have written about,[3] I also understand that none of their work could have been implemented without a much larger set of participants. I equally value the geodesign accomplishments of institutions such as the US National Park Service and the anonymous actions of many traditional cultures. Recognizing the accomplishments of individuals cannot be fully disregarded, but hero worship oriented towards an egocentric and idiosyncratic view of geodesign is not what is needed to solve the truly complex and difficult problems confronting us.

Three organizing principles that are highly valuable in the study of history and precedent are place, prototype, and situation. Place is a particularly effective way of introducing a geodesign study area, be it a one-acre residential project or a regional watershed. The history of its social, environmental, economic, and physical development is necessary for the understanding of how a design "fits." Even a design that is proposing a radical change can only be measured against the precedents of the place. As I have stated before, there is substantial benefit of knowing the roots of the geographic study area within which one is working.

Another potentially effective organizing principle focuses around the idea of content-prototypes, be they linear parks, new cities, conservation strategies, flood control programs, or efficient commercial distribution networks. Tying the historical study to the content of the problem being addressed, and to its possible solutions, is a common approach in the design professions. One learns about biaxial symmetry by studying the buildings of Rome, and one learns about new towns by studying twentieth century London. One can learn about floodplains by studying the Yangtze River, and so on. Broadening a common vocabulary and deepening the case memory are the end objectives, and along the way, we learn which aspects are of value to emulate, adapt, or reject.

Another approach and one which I value highly focuses on the situation. In a sense, this could be called "the case study approach." The organizing principles could well be a problem to be solved, an analysis of the study area, the issues, the principal actors, the processes of analysis, the solutions proposed, the decision and its implementation, and a retrospective of its effect. The last, "What actually happened," is an especially important component of a good case study. This approach holds the greatest attraction to me, and it is evident in the important role of case studies in this book.

## The study of failures[4]

In choosing content for curricula, and in the style of presentation among the design professions, there is an overwhelming focus on "successes." This may be only slightly less so in the sciences. Most people prefer to base their view of the past on accomplishment and other outcomes for which they can be proud. This positive focus is easy to understand, but *is this good*, particularly when one realizes that case memory is as much about things to avoid as things to emulate or adapt?

I strongly encourage us to study "failures" as well as "successes," for several reasons. To begin, they exist as part of the heritage of proposed and accomplished action. Failures are more numerous than we like to admit, especially when one considers how many designs that were once considered "cutting edge" and highly positive became viewed over time as highly negative, even relatively soon after implementation. Plus, change is an important "constant." Geodesign is not fixed in time but must be adaptable to unpredictable change, frequently in the social context of its geography. The analysis of failures

demands an overall sense of history as its context, even more so than does the history of success.

The study of failures offers the study of cautions; of limits on the range of possibility for social, economic, technical, and other reasons; and a "Let's not repeat the mistakes of the past" attitude. I believe that creative freedom exists within the sphere of what experience tells us *not* to do. The study of failure points out the caveats, but within the "envelope of possibility" we are free to design and to act. Indeed, we must find "the best solution."

How shall we organize for the study of failures in geodesign? I suggest an interpretation of a classification of failures proposed by the military historians Eliot A. Cohen and John Gooch.[5] Their book, *Military Misfortunes, The Anatomy of Failure in War* (1991), is an analysis of different kinds of failure throughout military history and has instructive parallels that are applicable to geodesign. I have added some categories and examples:

- failure to learn: rebuilding in the floodplain, building on barrier beaches, building in an avalanche zone;
- failure to anticipate: building in an earthquake zone, fire suppression in national parks, introducing rabbits into Australia;
- failure to adapt: one crop agriculture (monoculture), water gardens in the California desert;
- aggregate failure: filling wetlands, salting on highways, cutting of hedgerows, and as ecologist William E. Odum (1942–1991) applied to ecological degradation, "the tyranny of small decisions;"[6]
- catastrophic failure: groundwater depletion, desertification, the dust bowl;
- failures of technology: cheap hand labor to costly machinery, cheap energy to costly, damming rivers to nutrient deprivation;
- failures of leaving out key factors: unlit, and thus unsafe and unused parks;
- failures of prediction: premature subdivisions, over-extended infrastructure, speculative agriculture;
- failures of social organization: the landscape of slavery, the landscape of atomic bomb defense;
- failures of adaptation: highly specialized buildings, rapid demographic changes; and
- failures of physical form: why grids have diagonals, why symmetry breaks down, why diversity is more sustainable, etc.

The acknowledgment and study of failure is not comfortable to the ego. It does not create heroes. Instead it relies on criticism and our ability to engage in considerably more comparative research upon which to base that criticism. To say that the product of geodesign is a success demands a concept of failure, and valid models of and metrics for evaluation. And the selection of failures (or successes) cannot be value free. One is always acting in the realm of values, but this demands a commitment to value judgments. Are we prepared to do this?

I have found that the preparation, presentation, and comparison of case studies is a particularly effective, robust, and useful device for geodesign-related teaching. For decades I have used this approach, with case studies prepared by students, as part of my "theories and methods" course. Each student selects a study or project from the current or historical literature or personal experience, prepares a research paper, digitally adapts the case's methods to a current class-wide problem, delivers an illustrated 30-minute lecture (including question time) to the class, and at the end of the course participates in a lengthy class discussion comparing the cases and the methods that were applied.

For those who engage in design, there are many important lessons to be found in these case studies, including the interaction between the study of successes and failures. But in my view, case study failures are the most important precedents to understand for those engaged in geodesign.

# Toward curricula for geodesign[7]

What are the implications of the framework for geodesign-related education for practice? From an academic perspective, I believe that the framework that is the basis of this book can and should be applied to different levels of geodesign-related education (figure 11.1). This illustrates how the six questions and the necessary levels of education could interact, a step towards envisioning learning objectives that can be integrated into the existing curricula of the geographic sciences, information technologies, and design professions.

For entry level undergraduate or pre-professional students, the emphasis is on the basics of both theory and method, a conservative path through the six questions. A master's level or post-professional approach is more likely to be speculative, recognizing diversity of methods and the need to fit the geodesign approach to the problem. The emphasis here would include the design of the study methodology, and the need to make the choices *upwards* through the six questions. At the most advanced doctoral level, research, critical scholarship, and creative practice may begin with an iconoclastic attitude towards the current state of theory, methods and practice. From this perspective, any of the six questions is an appropriate starting point or focus.

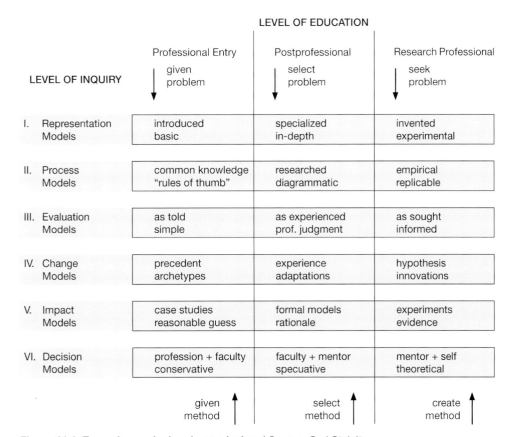

LEVEL OF EDUCATION

| LEVEL OF INQUIRY | Professional Entry \| given problem ↓ | Postprofessional \| select problem ↓ | Research Professional \| seek problem ↓ |
|---|---|---|---|
| I. Representation Models | introduced basic | specialized in-depth | invented experimental |
| II. Process Models | common knowledge "rules of thumb" | researched diagrammatic | empirical replicable |
| III. Evaluation Models | as told simple | as experienced prof. judgment | as sought informed |
| IV. Change Models | precedent archetypes | experience adaptations | hypothesis innovations |
| V. Impact Models | case studies reasonable guess | formal models rationale | experiments evidence |
| VI. Decision Models | profession + faculty conservative | faculty + mentor speculative | mentor + self theoretical |
| | given method ↑ | select method ↑ | create method ↑ |

**Figure 11.1: Toward a curriculum in geodesign.** | Source: Carl Steinitz.

Of course, geodesign theory, methods, and practices are themselves subject to change. The models associated with each level of inquiry can be clarified, expanded, added to, or replaced. Sometimes implementation results in a built project that alters theory via professional or public interest. All aspects of geodesign are subject to change via our expanding knowledge. As a frequent attendee and contributor to conferences focused on research in the design professions, and especially landscape architecture and planning, I increasingly see research being focused around several themes, most of which are directed at larger, regional scales:

- a content-problem seen over scale, such as suburban sprawl, cultural landscapes, river restoration, etc.;
- a decision model and its implications, such as public participation at regional scales;
- a comparative study of landscape processes and the complexity of the models to consider these, such as visual preference, landscape ecology, etc.;
- a design method and its applications, such as agent-based modeling;
- visualization methods such as realistic visualization or real-time animation; and
- history as discussed above.

New technologies, such as the iPhone or Android mobile devices, crowd-based sources of data, 3D visualizations, supercomputers, etc., also drive a steady stream of research and development with regards to geodesign applications.

However, the scale, size, and direction of these research themes are not equal. More of it seems to trace influences from the larger issues to the smaller. It can be assumed that much of the research effort is caused by a sense that these larger research themes are important as well as being of personal and/or societal interest, and that they will be of use in the improvement of geodesign methods and their outcomes.

## A master's level curriculum in geodesign

The people who will collaborate in geodesign activities will necessarily come from diverse academic backgrounds and with varied personal experiences. I am most interested in the education of the individuals who will organize and then conduct geodesign teams. In my view, these will be people who will need both a broad experience and also considerable depth in at least one aspect required for geodesign. As I have previously said, "They will need to know a little about a lot and a lot about a little." I think that the appropriate level of geodesign education for such people

is at a master's level, in an academic program that is structured to support and foster collaboration among diverse contributors, and at a scale of "problem" for which this is necessary.

I have lectured and taught workshops in many universities over my long academic career and am aware of the great diversity of objectives and assets in universities, from a global perspective. Many excellent students cannot attend university on a full-time basis. I therefore propose here a master's level curriculum in three versions: one for full-time students, one for part-time commuting participants, and one which is Internet-based. The curriculum is structured by my framework for geodesign (figure 11.2).

All students, regardless of the version of the program in which they are participating, should contribute something of importance to it based on their past academic and/or professional experience. Applicants would be expected to be proficient in at least one of the model types of the framework. Thus for example it should be expected that an information technologist or GIS specialist would be proficient in data management and representation; a geographically-oriented scientist such as a hydrologist, ecologist, or geologist would be proficient in both process and impact models; a sociologist would understand evaluation; an architect, landscape architect, urban planner or civil engineer would be proficient in change models; and a lawyer, banker, economist, political scientist or an elected official such as a mayor would understand decision models. Geographers might have expertise in several of these areas, depending on whether they had focused on physical or human geography, or on information technologies, during their studies and professional practice.

The program should be taught by a faculty which reflects the collaborative nature of the required teaching. It is not likely to be rooted in any single department or even a particular school in the university, but rather it would be drawn broadly from across the campus. At many institutions, this may require administrative creativity. Faculty on the teaching (and likely research) team must find ways for their activities and achievements to be recognized and valued by their institutional programs of promotion and tenure. While critical issues as these must be thought through ahead of time, they are not unfamiliar ones in higher education. The value of interdisciplinary teaching and research is increasingly common and recognized as essential in addressing the real problems of the world.

The curriculum in this master's program should consist of three kinds of courses: history/case studies, courses directed at the six questions of the framework and their associated model types, and applied studios. The history/case studies course should be organized with an appropriate balance between significant examples from the theoretical and applied literature, as well as cases relevant to the regional locale of the university, with which many of its students may be familiar. In every situation, the cases should emphasize how the study was organized, its methods, and the success or failure of its outcomes. In some circumstances, this course might also be an undergraduate general education course and serve as a test for admission into the master's program.

Courses that focus on models require considerable judgment in balancing academic assets, the capabilities of the students, and time available. In this curriculum proposal I make the simplest of assumptions: that there will be at least one course for each of the question and model types: representation, process, evaluation, change, impact, and decision. A second option might be to pair-up the model types based on their necessary interrelationships into three different classes: decision and evaluation, impact and process, and change and representation. Students would be expected to take the course in each of the model types.

The curriculum proposes three collaborative studios. Their geographic contexts and problem-issues should in all cases be real and authentic ones. In the first, collaboration could be within a small team of from three to five people led by one or more members of the core faculty, with other faculty members available as consultants and reviewers. There might be several such teams in one studio, each studying the same issue but possibly in a different way. The second studio would be a much

larger group of students having to work together as a "team of the whole," possibly from 10 to 15 people, managed by the students themselves and guided by the faculty.

The third and final studio would be the equivalent of an applied thesis and organized in a very different way. Each student would be expected to prepare, organize and design a real, applied geodesign study in the prior semester, working with a team of collaborators who are not necessarily associated with the program, and then conduct the study in the last semester or longer if needed.

The curriculum can be organized to accommodate different schedules, as shown in figure 11.3.

|  | FULL TIME ADMISSION | PART TIME COMMUTING ADMISSION | INTERNET-BASED INDIVIDUALIZED |
|---|---|---|---|
| YEAR 1 | history/cases<br>1 course  studio 1<br>2 course<br>3 course  studio 2 | history/cases<br>1 course<br>2 course<br>studio 1 | history/cases<br>ADMISSION<br>1 course<br>2 course |
| YEAR 2 | 4 course  prep<br>5 course  for<br>6 course  thesis<br>studio 3 | 3 course<br>4 course<br>5 course<br>studio 2 | studio 1<br>3 course<br>4 course |
| YEAR 3 |  | 6 course  prep<br>for<br>thesis<br>studio 3 | studio 2<br>5 course  prep<br>6 course  for |
| YEAR 4 |  |  | thesis<br>studio 3 |

Figure 11.3: Scheduling for a curriculum for geodesign. | Source: Carl Steinitz.

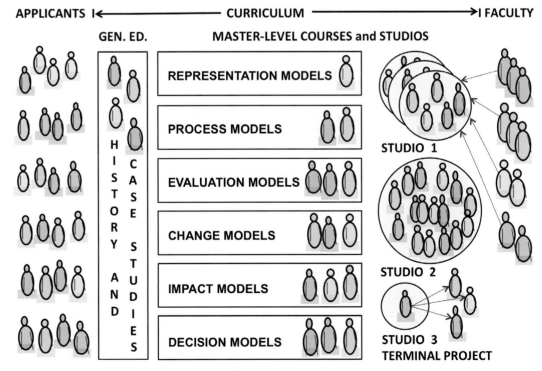

APPLICANTS |◄—————— CURRICULUM ——————►| FACULTY

GEN. ED.                    MASTER-LEVEL COURSES and STUDIOS

HISTORY AND

CASE STUDIES

REPRESENTATION MODELS

PROCESS MODELS

EVALUATION MODELS

CHANGE MODELS

IMPACT MODELS

DECISION MODELS

STUDIO 1

STUDIO 2

STUDIO 3
TERMINAL PROJECT

Figure 11.2: A curriculum for geodesign. | Source: Carl Steinitz.

A full-time sequence of courses would take two years to complete under the assumption that the academic year consists of two semesters of full-time residence. The part-time sequence assumes that the equivalent academic work would take three or four years for students who are otherwise employed or for whatever reason are unable to engage in full-time study.

In addition to residential programs, I fully expect that within a short period of time, several universities will propose Internet-based curricula in geodesign. These are likely to require more individualized variations in how students schedule and participate in the various aspects of the curriculum, but online instruction also presents opportunities for more flexible experimentation and exploration by students. For example, it might be that an initial course focused on history and case studies is made easily available to anybody who is interested in participating, and that this might result in a very large number of people taking the course as they consider whether they want to proceed further or not. Formal admission into the master's program might then occur only after students have completed this course and at least one other, with admission based both upon their success within those courses as well as any other admissions criteria.

An Internet–based curriculum in geodesign would present the additional challenge of how one teaches a collaborative studio where the student and faculty participants are remote from each other but connected electronically. I have personally had three such experiences in which my students at Harvard University were linked with student and faculty colleagues at other universities and were integrated in a single collaborative studio. This way of teaching is different in its personal relationships and affects the dynamics of instruction, but it *can* be successful and there is no doubt that the technologies are improving rapidly toward making remote collaboration easier and more effective.

I now reiterate a comment that I made in the preface of this book: I am not interested in creating people called "geodesigners" or producing something called "a geodesign." Rather I propose this curriculum to promote the educational collaboration among people from multiple design and scientific backgrounds and interests, since this is essential for geodesign to work well. Participants in such a program will gain a much broader perspective and a much more effective capability for collaboration, and especially for leadership in that collaboration. They can and should achieve this without losing their previous (and future) professional identities.

## Notes

1.  Adapted from C. Steinitz, "Educating Conductors vs. Training Soloists," in Proceedings, Council of Educators in Landscape Architecture Conference, 1984.

    Revised as "Conductors vs. Soloists." *Studio Works 4: Approaches,* (Graduate School of Design, Harvard University, 1996), 87–88.

2.  Adapted from C. Steinitz, "On the Roles of Precedent: A Personal View" (Conference on Teaching the History of Landscape Architecture, Graduate School of Design, Harvard University, April 8–9, 1974).

3.  C. Steinitz. "Landscape Planning: A History of Influential Ideas." *Journal of the Japanese Institute of Landscape Architecture*. (January 2002): 201–8. (In Japanese.)

    Republished in *Chinese Landscape Architecture* 5: 92–95 and 6: 80–96. (In Chinese.)

    Republished in *Journal of Landscape Architecture (JoLA)* (Spring 2008): 68–75.

    Republished in *Landscape Architecture* (February 2009): 74–84.

4.  Adapted from C. Steinitz, "On the Need to Study Failures As Well As Successes" (Conference on Teaching The History of Landscape Architecture, Graduate School of Design, Harvard University, April 8–9, 1974).

5.  E. A. Cohen and J. Gooch, *Military Misfortunes: The Anatomy of Failure in War* (New York: Vintage Books, 1991).

6.  W. E. Odum, "Environmental Degradation and the Tyranny of Small Decisions," *BioScience* 32, no. 9 (1982): 728–29.6.

7.  Adapted from C. Steinitz, "On Teaching Ecological Principles to Designers," in *Ecology and Design: Frameworks for Learning,* eds. B. Johnson and K. Hill. (Washington, D.C.: Island Press, 2001).

CHAPTER **12**

# A future for geodesign

## A future for geodesign education

Persistently changing conditions, in the world and in higher education, have profound implications towards the future of geodesign. It does not seem reasonable to attempt to do everything related to geodesign at an equal level. There will always be the temptation to specialize, to draw our energy inward and to focus on one or a just a few combinations of scale, problem types, decision processes, and methods. Most academic design programs in the world begin in and focus on smaller scale projects (on the left side of figure 12.1), and with well-defined clients, simpler process models, and traditional design methods. This is clearly a safe path and has been the basis for a long tradition in design-teaching and practice, including the sharpening of distinctions among architecture, landscape architecture, and urban planning.[1] At the same time, a parallel to this educational specialization is taking place in the geographic sciences, one that is more typically focused on systems that are larger, involving studies that rely on more complex processes and more algorithmically-based methods.

Given these recognized and persistent differences, having geodesign curricula focus at the scales and sizes at which collaboration is most likely to be needed and effective may produce the best outcomes (figure 12.2). Students' prior preferences and experiences will have influenced their disciplinary knowledge, and their practices are most likely to continue along disciplinary lines as they continue to learn later in life. Education will be most effective if *all* students have some organized collaborative experiences among designers and scientists, and this should be in the overlapping sizes and scales where collaboration seems easiest and most appropriate (again, figures 12.1 and 12.2). This perspective requires enough available opportunities so that students can then find their own wider path through an increased set of choices. It also requires

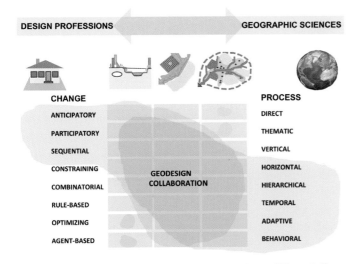

**Figure 12.1:** Designers and scientists come from different directions. The territory of most effective geodesign collaboration is likely to be where they overlap. | Source: Carl Steinitz.

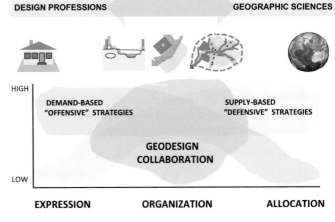

**Figure 12.2:** Focus first on collaboration, then specialization. The overlap area with its sizes and scales of projects and several major influences is where geodesign collaboration is likely to be most needed and effective. | Source: Carl Steinitz.

considerable further development of integrated information technologies, the media which underpin the entire process of collaboration in geodesign, as was shown in figure 10.4.

In practice, the roles of scientists and designers will not be the same, and their influence will vary among the six questions and the stages of working through the framework, as hypothesized and shown in figure 12.3. No one need fear that collaboration in geodesign will lead to uniformity or loss of professional identity. For students as well as experienced designers and scientists, geodesign collaboration will broaden the participants' sense of the whole, in that everyone who contributes brings their own specialized knowledge to the table and in the process will learn many more things in general. They will intensify their "working knowledge" capabilities and broaden their understanding and "talking knowledge" of the others' contributions.

## A future for geodesign practice

The practice of geodesign is changing rapidly and will continue in this manner, due largely to changes in political attitudes and in information technologies. For example, consider the implications of what is happening in Europe with regards to planning, something which may become a worldwide model. In Florence in October 2000, the 47 member countries of The Council of

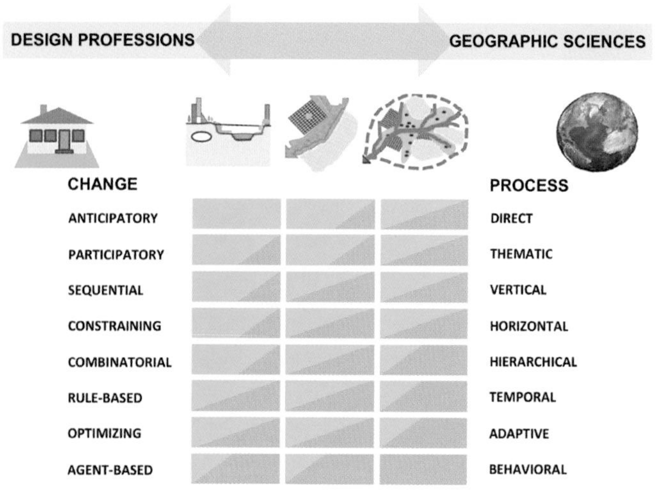

Europe adopted The European Landscape Convention[2]. The Action Plan of the European Landscape Convention was adopted by the Heads of States and Governments of the member states in Warsaw, on May 17, 2005. This treaty has been ratified and is law in most but not all of the member states. As an international treaty, it supersedes national law in its field. As such, the European Landscape Convention of the Council of Europe offers a very useful model for geodesign.

The principal provisions of the European Landscape Convention's Action Plan are in Article 5.

In Article 5 General Measures, each Party undertakes to

a. recognize landscapes in law as an essential component of people's surroundings, an expression of the diversity of their shared cultural and natural heritage, and a foundation of their identity;

b. establish and implement landscape policies aimed at landscape protection, management and planning through the adoption of the specific measures set out in Article 6;

c. establish procedures *for the participation* of the general public, local and regional authorities, and other parties with an interest *in the definition* and Implementation *of the landscape policies* mentioned in paragraph b above (italics mine);

d. integrate landscape into its regional land town planning policies and in its cultural, environmental, agricultural, social and economic policies, as well as in any other policies with possible direct or indirect impact on landscape.

The European Landscape Convention is already having an increasingly profound effect on geodesign-related practice, as it requires these activities as part of the treaty's legal obligations. It is also having a major impact on geodesign-related education throughout Europe, and indirectly in the rest of the world. Because it codifies the need for stakeholder input *into the beginning of defining any future policy or design,* the design team is then required to organize its work to produce such materials for public review and decision making. The people of the place are not just considered geodesign clients, but are active members of the geodesign team. I believe that this will ultimately transform how geodesign is practiced, and it will force us to rethink some of our educational processes.

**Figure 12.3:** Balances of influence between scientists and designers will shift depending of the specific methods used in a geodesign study. | Source: Carl Steinitz.

I have argued throughout this book the geodesign is necessarily a collaborative enterprise. This is different from the individualistic assumptions underpinning the majority (but not all) of education in the design professions. The model of practice implied by traditional design practice is that there is a client (at the head of the table) and a single designer (albeit often supported by "staff") who will help make the design (figure12.4).

Recognizing the collaborative nature required to deal with the obvious complexities of geodesign contributed to this geodesign framework being structured as it is, as I have described it in detail in this text. The stakeholder group has its necessary roles in input and decision making, while the technical team of designers and scientists and information technologists has the responsibility of carrying out the study (figure12.5).

The European Landscape Convention broadens the responsibility of the people of the place and stakeholders and legitimizes their direct and deeper involvement with the design team (figure12.6).

In the case studies presented in this book, there is at least one example of direct stakeholder involvement in each of the six fundamental questions of the framework.

1. How should the study area be described? In the Idyllwild fire modeling study, Mike Flaxman obtained his large property-based data set directly within his study area. The Bermuda dump study was based entirely on data collected in the study area by my students, guided by residents of Bermuda.

2. How does the study area operate? The economic process models which underlay the La Paz and Telluride cases were derived from records produced directly from the personal stakeholder actions of buying and selling property.

3. Is the current study area working well? In several of the case studies (Camp Pendleton, Bermuda, Cagliari, Padova, La Paz, and Telluride), an advisory group of approximately 30 people, broadly representative of the study areas, guided the geodesign teams in the definition of their respective issues. While recognizing that interests within the advisory group were not uniform and that disagreements existed, this guidance typically focused on the protection of positively valued aspects, and change of those negatively evaluated aspects of the region as directly expressed by residents and/or tourists.

4. How might the study area be altered? The Osa case study in Costa Rica is a compelling example of the ability of ordinary people who know the study area region to make a design expressing their views of what a desirable future should be.

5. What differences might the changes cause? In the La Paz and Telluride regions, the visual landscape is a central component of the attractiveness of the area for tourism and

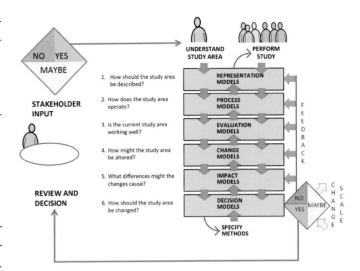

**Figure 12.4: The client and the designer.** | Source: Carl Steinitz.

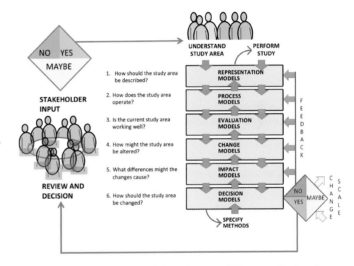

**Figure 12.5: The people of the place and the geodesign team.** | Source: Carl Steinitz.

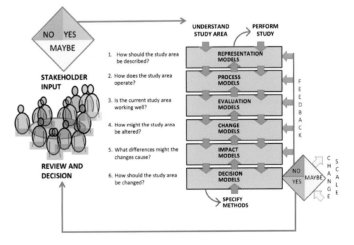

**Figure 12.6: Deeper direct involvement by the people of the place.** | Source: Carl Steinitz

recreation, and maintaining its high visual preference under conditions of change is critical to the future economy. In both of these studies (and many more in which I have participated), surveys of residents and tourists were the basis of the visual preference models. These facilitated our comparing the alternative futures produced by the scenarios that the studies simulated.

6. How should the study area be changed? The case studies in this book present several decision models. Camp Pendleton is a military hierarchy, the industrial zone of Padova has a board of directors, the city of Cagliari has a mayor and council, the Telluride foundation has a director responsible to a board, Idyllwild has many independent residents, and the history of West London is the work of many independent developers. Perhaps most compelling is what happened in Bermuda, where the Prime Minister decided that the electorate should directly decide which of the three designs they preferred.

Each of the above illustrates direct stakeholder participation in geodesign. Each of the cases also had a major public communication effort, aimed to enable the people of the place and the stakeholders to make better informed decisions leading to implementation of what they considered their best alternative for the future.

The question must be asked, "Why shouldn't the people of the place take over the whole process of geodesign?" (figure 12.6). After all, it's their place and among them they surely know more than the other members of the geodesign team. Why shouldn't they take responsibility for changing their own geography, as they see fit? There are several obvious and limiting reasons. They may not have any of the relevant experiences, or any interest beyond their own (if that), or the time and energy to devote to what is frequently a long and difficult set of integrated tasks. Especially in a large region, self-guided geodesign would undoubtedly be a very inefficient and unwieldy process. Both the professional literature and the cases herein show direct involvement *in the parts* but not *in the whole* linked process of geodesign.

However, I have no doubt that the next generation of people in geodesign will see increasing public participation in all aspects, including direct management of the process by the people of the place. I expect a reversal of an important social relationship. Typically, the geodesign team of design professionals, scientists, and information technology specialists work as a team separately from the people of the place. While we meet regularly with stakeholder representatives and communicate on a question-by-question basis during the course of conducting the study, ultimately the process is not a wholly democratic and entirely participatory one. I expect future geodesign studies

to involve much more frequent and real-time participation and communication. The extent of that direct participation will vary, principally as a function of size and scale. Smaller projects and simpler methods enable more direct participation (figure 12.7), while larger studies with more complex methods require more significant roles by the design professionals and scientists (figure 12.8). The roles of the "conductor" (as discussed in the previous chapter) will become even more central to geodesign, as will the needs for wider and more efficient communication.

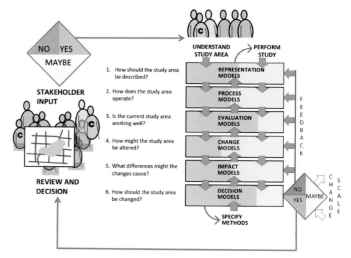

**Figure 12.7:** The people of the place will have a greater role in smaller geodesign studies, whose geographic scale and scope of the project is more limited and manageable. Projects of smaller size and scale may also require less technical expertise. "Conductors" are indicated with the letter C on their shirts and will be needed both on the geodesign team and also from among the stakeholders. | Source: Carl Steinitz.

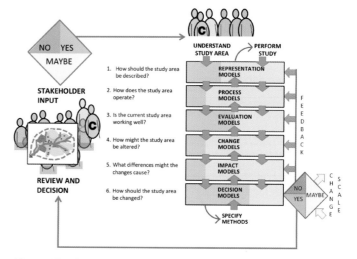

**Figure 12.8:** In the future, larger size geodesign projects will also have greater involvement from the people of the place, but there will be a need for more technically competent people and they will have to take a more active role. | Source: Carl Steinitz.

When we consider the research our more advanced students are conducting, and today's technology-driven development, we can see an emerging pattern for geodesign that will develop rapidly in this century. We will be living in a world where major geodesign decisions will be made simultaneously and interactively at several sizes and scales. We will be managing the process (as best we can). Or, in worst case scenarios, we all will be managed by some combination of uninformed decisions and anarchy. There is every likelihood that the students we are teaching today will be practicing in a world where they will have an overload of data and methodological options, and where they will have to choose even much more wisely than we do today. The balance of activity among design professionals and geographic scientists in applying the framework for geodesign will shift as a function of study area size and scale. The collaborative activities will also see shifting influences among the four essential participating groups as a function of where they are in the framework. However, one thing should not change, and that is the responsibility of the people of the place to make the final decision, to change their context-geography by "*WHAT, WHERE, and WHEN.*"

During the many decades that I have been active in this field, I have observed that we are getting better at understanding the geographies in which we are designing, with improved data and models. In democratic processes, environmental politics are getting more open and complicated, and designs are as well. Anyone even mildly observant will become aware of a future of climate change, desertification, over-population, water crises, and other potentially catastrophic changes. If we are in an increasingly serious environmental crisis, and I think we are, it is very important for people to understand the situation and their options, or they will not make vital changes. This may be our greatest challenge, to make geodesign more broadly and readily understandable in order to increase public participation and closer collaboration among the stakeholders, the geographic sciences, information technologists and the design professions. The objectives are clear: to enable better designs and to improve communication towards decision making that supports a more adaptable and equitable future.

## Notes

1. C. Steinitz, "Matters of Scale," *Landscape Architecture* (September 2010): 206–8.

2. Council of Europe. Council of Europe Treaty Series no. 176—The European Landscape Convention. Florence, October 20, 2000.

## Some last words

*Geodesign (like all design) depends on judgment.*

*It is not a science but it depends on science.*

*There are no perfect formulae but there are methods.*

*There is no universal tool kit but there are many tools.*

*You cannot copy an example but you can gain experience by joining the collaborative activities of geodesign and changing geography by design.*

C. S.

2012

# Bibliography

Adams, C. W., and C. Steinitz. "An Alternative Future for the Region of Camp Pendleton, CA." In *Landscape Perspectives of Land Use Changes,* edited by U. Mander and R. H. G. Jongman, 18–83. Advances in Ecological Sciences 6. Southampton, UK: WIT Press, 2000.

Batty, M. "Cellular Automata and Urban Form: A Primer." *Journal of the American Planning Association* 63 (1997): 266–74.

———. *Cities and Complexity.* Cambridge, MA: MIT Press, 2007.

———. "A Digital Breeder for Designing Cities." In *Architectural Design,* 79, no. 4 (2009): 46–49.

———. "Generating Cities from the Bottom-Up: Using Complexity Theory for Effective Design." *Cluster* 7 (2008): 150–61.

Bermuda, Department of Planning. *The Pembroke Marsh Plan, 1987.* Bermuda: Department of Planning, Government of Bermuda, 1987.

Brandford, V., and P. Geddes. *The Coming Polity: A Study in Reconstruction.* London: Williams and Norgate, 1917.

Buhmann, E., S. Ervin, D. Tomlin, and M. Pietsch, eds. *Teaching Landscape Architecture.* Proceedings, Digital Landscape Architecture, Anhalt University of Applied Sciences. Dessau, Germany, May 2011.

Chrisman, N. *Charting the Unknown: How Computer Mapping at Harvard Became GIS.* Redlands, CA: ESRI Press, 2006.

Cohen, E. A., and J. Gooch. *Military Misfortunes: The Anatomy of Failure in War.* New York: Vintage Books, 1991.

Council of Europe. Council of Europe Treaty Series no. 176—The European Landscape Convention. Florence, October 20, 2000.

Crain, W. C. *Theories of Development.* New Jersey: Prentice-Hall, 1985.

Dale, V. H., and H. M. Rauscher. "Assessing Impacts of Climate Change on Forests: The State of Biological Modeling." *Climatic Change* 28 (1994): 65–90.

Environmental Awareness Center of the University of Wisconsin, with Steinitz Rogers Associates. *Interstate 57 Corridor Selection Study.* Madison, WI: Environmental Awareness Center of the University of Wisconsin, 1970.

Ervin, S. "A System for Geodesign." In *Teaching Landscape Architecture,* edited by E. Buhmann, S. Ervin, D. Tomlin, and M. Pietsch, 145–54. Proceedings, Digital Landscape Architecture, Anhalt University of Applied Sciences. Dessau, Germany, May 2011.

Escritt, L. B. *Regional Planning: An Outline of the Scientific Data Relating to Planning in the United Kingdom.* London: George Allen & Unwin, 1943.

Fagg, C. C., and G. E. Hutchings. *An Introduction to Regional Surveying.* Cambridge, UK: The University Press, 1930.

Finney, M. A. "FARSITE: Fire Area Simulator—Model Development and Evaluation." Research paper. RMRS-RP-4. Ogden, UT: US Department of Agriculture, Forest Service, Rocky Mountain Research Station, 2004.

Flaxman, M. "Multi-scale Fire Hazard Assessment for Wildland Urban Interface Areas: An Alternative Futures Approach." D. Des. diss., Graduate School of Design, Harvard University, 2001.

Flaxman, M., C. Steinitz, R. Faris, T. Canfield, J. C. Vargas-Moreno. *Alternative Futures for the Telluride Region, Colorado.* Telluride, CO: Telluride Foundation, 2010.

Forman, R. T. T., and M. Godron. *Landscape Ecology.* New York: Wiley, 1986.

Forshaw, H., and L. P. Abercrombie. *County of London Plan, 1943.* Westminster, England: Town Planning and Improvements Committee, 1944.

Galileo Galilei. *Dialogues Concerning Two New Sciences.* Translated by Henry Crew and Alfonso de Salvio. New York: McGraw Hill Book Co., 1914.

Geddes, P. *Cities in Evolution: An Introduction to the Town Planning Movement and to the Study of Civics.* London: Williams & Norgate, 1915.

Haddon, W., Jr., 1970. "Escape of Tigers: An Ecologic Note." *Technology Review* 72 (1970) : 44–53.

Hall, P. G. *London 2001.* London: Unwin Hyman, 1989.

Hammond, K. J. "Case-Based Planning: A Framework for Planning from Experience." *Journal of Cognitive Science* 14 (1990): 385–443.

Howard, E. *Garden Cities for Tomorrow.* London: S. Sonnenschein & Co., Ltd., 1902.

Kohlberg, Lawrence. *The Philosophy of Moral Development.* New York: Harper & Row, 1981.

———. *The Psychology of Moral Development.* New York: Harper & Row, 1984.

Kunzmann, K. R. "Geodesign: Chance oder Gefahr?" In Planungskartographie und Geodesign. Hrsg.: Bundesforschungsanstalt fur Landeskunde und Raumordnung. *Informationen zur Raumentwicklung* 7 (1993): 389–96

Lewis, Philip H., Jr. *Tomorrow by Design: A Regional Design Process for Sustainability.* New York: Wiley, 1996.

Lowry, Ira S. "A Short Course in Model Design." *Journal of the American Institute of Planners* 31 (May 1965), 158–165.

Lukacs, J. "The Stirrings of History: A New World Rises from the Ruins of Empire." *Harper's* (August 1990): 41–48.

Lyman, D., Jr. *The Moral Sayings of Publius Syrus, a Roman Slave.* Cleveland, OH: L. E. Barnard & Company, 1856.

Lynch, K. "Environmental Adaptability." *Journal of the American Institute of Planners* 14, no. 2 (1958):16–24.

———. *The Image of the City.* Cambridge, MA: MIT Press, 1960.

———. *A Theory of Good Urban Form.* Cambridge, MA: MIT Press, 1981.

MacEwan, R. "Reading Between the Lines: Knowledge for Natural Resource Management." In *Landscape Analysis and Visualisation: Spatial Models for Natural Resource Management and Planning,* edited by C. Pettit, W. Cartwright, I. Bishop, K. Lowell, D. Pullar and D. Duncan, 19–27. Berlin: Springer, 2008.

Mairet, P. *Pioneer of Sociology: The Life and Letters of Patrick Geddes.* London: Lund Humphries, 1957.

Manning, W. H. "A National Plan Study Brief." *Landscape Architecture* 13 (July 1923): 3–24.

McHarg, I. L. *Design with Nature.* Garden City, NY: Natural History Press, 1969.

Mueller, A., R. France, and C. Steinitz. "Aquifer Recharge Model: Evaluating the Impacts of Urban Development on Groundwater Resources (Galilee, Israel)." In *Integrative Studies in Water Management and Land Development Series. Handbook of Water Sensitive Planning and Design,* edited by R. L. France, 615–33. London: CRC Press, 2002.

Murray, H. A., and C. Kluckhohn. *Personality in Nature, Society, and Culture.* New York: Knopf, 1953.

Niemann, B., P. Lewis, and C. Steinitz. *Interstate 57 Corridor Selection Study.* Madison, WI: Environmental Awareness Center, University of Wisconsin, 1970.

Nyerges, T. L., and P. Jankowski. *Regional and Urban GIS: A Decision Support Approach.* New York: Guilford Press, 2010.

Odum, W. E. "Environmental Degradation and the Tyranny of Small Decisions." *BioScience* 32, no. 9 (1982): 728–29.

Rapaport, A. "Cross-Cultural Aspects of Environmental Design." In *Human Behavior and Environment,* edited by I. Altman, A. Rapaport, and J. F. Wohlwill. Vol. 4. Human Behavior and Environment. New York: Plenum Press, 1980.

Repton, H. *Observations on the Theory and Practice of Landscape Gardening: Including Some Remarks on Grecian and Gothic Architecture, Collected from Various Manuscripts, in the Possession of the Different Noblemen and Gentlemen, for Whose Use They Were Originally Written; the Whole Tending to Establish Fixed Principles in the Respective Arts.* London: Printed by T. Bensley for J. Taylor, 1805.

Rogers, P., and C. Steinitz. *Qualitative Values in Environmental Planning: A Study of Resource Use in Urbanizing Watersheds.* Waltham, MA: Harvard University, Department of Landscape Architecture Research Office and US Army Corps of Engineers, New England Division, 1969.

Schwarz-v.Raumer, H-G., and A. Stokman. "Geodesign—Approximations of a Catchphrase." In *Teaching Landscape Architecture,* edited by E. Buhmann, S. Ervin, D. Tomlin, and M. Pietsch, 106–15. Proceedings, Digital Landscape Architecture, Anhalt University of Applied Sciences. Dessau, Germany, May 2011.

Simon, H. A. "Designing Organizations for an Information-Rich World." In *Computers, Communication, and the Public Interest,* by M. Greenberger. Baltimore, MD: The Johns Hopkins Press, 1971.

———. *The Sciences of the Artificial.* Cambridge, MA: MIT Press, 1969.

Smith, R. A. "Beach Resorts: A Model of Development Evolution." D. Des. diss., Graduate School of Design, Harvard University, 1990.\

———. "Beach Resorts: A Model of Development Evolution." *Landscape and Urban Planning* 21, no. 3 (1991): 189–210.

Stanilov, K., and M. Batty. "Exploring the Historical Determinants of Urban Growth through Cellular Automata." *Transactions in GIS* 15, no. 3 (2011): 253–71.

Steinitz, C. "Alternative Futures: Development, Environment, and Economics in Hangzhou, China." Proceedings Harvard-ASCI Conference on Transportation, Land Use, and the Environment: China and India. Hyderabad, 2004.

———. *Defensible Processes for Regional Landscape Design.* Landscape Architecture Technical Information Series vol. 2, no. 1. Washington, D.C.: American Society of Landscape Architects, 1979.

———. "The DELMARVA Study." Proceedings, Council of Educators in Landscape Architecture, St Louis, MO, July 1968.

———. "Design Is a Verb; Design Is a Noun." *Landscape Journal* 4, no. 2 (1995): 188–200.

———. "Educating Conductors vs. Training Soloists." In Proceedings, Council of Educators in Landscape Architecture Conference, 1984.

Revised as "Conductors vs. Soloists." *Studio Works 4: Approaches,* 87–88. Graduate School of Design, Harvard University, 1996.

——. "Estudio de Paisage Visual de la Comunitat Valenciana/A Study of the Visual Landscape of the Autonomous Community of Valencia." In *La Nueva Politica de Paisage de la Comunitat Valenciana* by A Munoz-Criado, 11–42. Valencia: Generalitat Valenciana, 2009.

Also published in Steinitz, C., and A. Munoz-Criado. "The Visual Assessment of the Autonomous Community of Valencia, Spain." *Chinese Landscape Architecture*, 2 (2011):168–85. (In Chinese and English.)

——. "A Framework for Theory Applicable to the Education of Landscape Architects (and Other Environmental Design Professionals)." *Landscape Journal* 9 (1990): 136–43.

Revised version in *Process Architecture* 127 (1995). (English and Japanese.)

Revised version in *GIS Europe* 2 (1993): 42–45.

Revised version in *Planning* (2000). (Chinese.)

Revised version in *Environmental Planning for Communities: A Guide to the Environmental Visioning Process Utilizing a Geographic Information System (GIS).* Cincinnati, OH: US Environmental Protection Agency Office of Research and Development, 2002.

Revised version in chapter 3 of *Alternative Futures for Changing Landscapes: The San Pedro River Basin in Arizona and Sonora* by C. Steinitz, H. Arias, S. Bassett, M. Flaxman, T. Goode, T. Maddock, D. Mouat, R. Peiser and A. Shearer. Washington, D.C.: Island Press, 2003.

——. "From Project to Global: On Landscape Planning and Scale." *Landscape Review* 9, no. 2 (2005): 117–27.

——. "Introduction." World Conference on Education for Landscape Planning special issue of *Landscape and Urban Planning,* edited by C. Steinitz.13, no. 5/6 (1986): 329–32.

——. "Landscape Planning: A History of Influential Ideas." *Journal of the Japanese Institute of Landscape Architecture.* (January 2002): 201–8. (In Japanese.)

Republished in *Chinese Landscape Architecture* 5: 92–95 and 6: 80–96. (In Chinese.)

Republished in *Journal of Landscape Architecture (JoLA)* (Spring 2008): 68–75.

Republished in *Landscape Architecture* (February 2009): 74–84.

——. "Matters of Scale." *Landscape Architecture* (September 2010): 206–8.

——. "Meaning and the Congruence of Urban Form and Activity." PhD diss., Massachusetts Institute of Technology, 1965.

——. "Meaning and the Congruence of Urban Form and Activity." *Journal of the American Institute of Planners* 34, no. 4 (July 1968): 223–47.

——. "On Scale and Complexity and the Need for Spatial Analysis." Specialist Meeting on Spatial Concepts in GIS and Design; Santa Barbara, California; December 15–16, 2008.

——. "On Teaching Ecological Principles to Designers." In *Ecology and Design: Frameworks for Learning,* edited by B. Johnson and K. Hill. Washington, D.C.: Island Press, 2001.

——. "On the Need to Study Failures As Well As Successes." Conference on Teaching the History of Landscape Architecture, Graduate School of Design, Harvard University, April 8–9, 1974.

——. "On the Roles of Precedent: A Personal View." Conference on Teaching the History of Landscape Architecture, Graduate School of Design, Harvard University, April 8–9, 1974.

——. "Simulating Alternative Policies for Implementing the Massachusetts Scenic and Recreational Rivers Act: The North River Demonstration Project." *Landscape Planning* 6, no. 1 (1979): 51–89.

——. "Teaching in a Multidisciplinary Collaborative Workshop Format: The Cagliari Workshop." In *2010 FutureMAC09: Alternative Futures for the Metropolitan Area of Cagliari, The Cagliari Workshop: An Experiment in Interdisciplinary Education / FutureMAC09 : Scenari Alternativi per l'area Metropolitana di Cagliari, Workshop di Sperimentazione Didattica Interdisciplinare,* by C. Steinitz, E. Abis, V. von Haaren, C. Albert, D. Kempa, C. Palmas, S. Pili, and J. C. Vargas-Moreno. Roma: Gangemi, 2010.

——. "Tools and Techniques: Some General Notes but Precious Few 'Hard' Recommendations." In Proceedings, Council of Educators in Landscape Architecture Conference, 1974.

——. "Toward a Sustainable Landscape Where Visual Preference and Ecological Integrity are Congruent: The Loop Road in Acadia National Park." *Landscape and Urban Planning* 19, no. 3 (1990): 213–50.

——. "The Trouble with 'A Strong Concept, Fully Worked Out.'" *Landscape Architecture* (November 1979): 565–67.

Steinitz, C., ed. *An Alternative Future for the Region of Camp Pendleton, California.* Cambridge, MA: Graduate School of Design, Harvard University, 1997.

——. *Alternative Futures for Monroe County, Pennsylvania.* Cambridge, MA: Harvard University Graduate School of Design, 1994.

——. *Alternative Futures for the Bermuda Dump.* Cambridge, MA: Graduate School of Design, Harvard University, 1986.

——. *Alternative Futures in the Western Galilee, Israel.* Cambridge, MA: Graduate School of Design, Harvard University, 1998.

Steinitz, C., ed., with A. Rahamimoff, M. Flaxman, and T. Canfield. *Coexistence, Cooperation, Partnership: Alternative Futures for the Region of Beit She'an Jenin and Northern Jordan.* Cambridge, MA: Graduate School of Design, Harvard University, 2000. [ K. A. Connelly, D. Ford, S. Hurand, S. Kennings, S. Khanna, H. Kozloff, L. MacAulay, J. Mayeux, R. el Samahy, S. Siegel, S. A. Shapiro, E. D. Shaw, C. Teike, J. P. Weesner]

Steinitz, C., H. Arias, S. Bassett, M. Flaxman, T. Goode, T. Maddock, D. Mouat, R. Peiser, and A. Shearer. *Alternative Futures for Changing Landscapes: The San Pedro River Basin in Arizona and Sonora.* Washington, D.C.: Island Press, 2003.

In Chinese, C. Steinitz, et al. "Alternative Futures for Changing Landscapes: The Upper San Pedro River Basin, Arizona, and Sonora." Beijing: Construction Bookstore/Building Society, 2008, translated by Cheng Bing.

Also in C. Steinitz, et al. "Alternative Futures for Landscapes in the Upper San Pedro River Basin of Arizona and Sonora." US Department of Agriculture, Forest Service, Pacific Southwest Station, General Technical Report #PSW-GTR-191, Bird Conservation Implementation and Integration in the Americas: Proceedings of the Third International Partners in Flight Conference, vol. 1, June 2005, 93–100.

Steinitz, C., M. Binford, P. Cote, T. Edwards Jr., S. Ervin, R. T. T. Forman, C. Johnson, R. Kiester, D. Mouat, D. Olson, A. Shearer, R. Toth, and R. Wills. *Landscape Planning for Biodiversity; Alternative Futures for the Region of Camp Pendleton, CA.* Cambridge, MA: Graduate School of Design, Harvard University, 1996.

In Japanese, C. Steinitz, et al. "Chiri-Joho-Shisutemu ni yoru Seibutu-tayosei to Keikan-Pulan-ningu (Biodiversity and Landscape Planning with GIS). Kyoto/Tokyo: Resident Shobo, 1999, translated by Keiji Yano and T. Nakaya.

Steinitz, C., H. J. Brown, P. Goodale with P. Rogers, D. Sinton, F. Smith, W. Giezentanner, and D. Way. *Managing Suburban Growth: A Modeling Approach. Summary.* (Of the research program entitled The Interaction between Urbanization and Land: Quality and Quantity in Environmental Planning and Design.) National Science Foundation, Research Applied to National Needs (RANN) Program Grant ENV-72-03372-A06. Cambridge, MA: Landscape Architecture Research Office, Graduate School of Design, Harvard University, 1978.

## With technical documentation as follows:

Bloom, H. S., and H. J. Brown. *The Interaction between Urbanization and Land: Quality and Quantity in Environmental Planning and Design: The Land Value Model Technical Documentation.* Cambridge, MA: Harvard University Graduate School of Design Landscape Architecture Research Office, 1979.

Giezentanner, W., and C. Steinitz. *The Interaction between Urbanization and Land: Quality and Quantity in Environmental Planning and Design: The Legal/Implementation Model Technical Documentation.* Cambridge, MA: Harvard University Graduate School of Design Landscape Architecture Research Office, 1978.

Goltry, D., R. Ewing, H. Wilkins, and H. J. Brown. *The Interaction between Urbanization and Land: Quality and Quantity in Environmental Planning and Design: The Industrial Model Technical Documentation.* Cambridge, MA: Harvard University Graduate School of Design Landscape Architecture Research Office, 1979.

Held, K., H. Wilkins, and H. J. Brown. *The Interaction between Urbanization and Land: Quality and Quantity in Environmental Planning and Design: The Commercial Model Technical Documentation.* Cambridge, MA: Harvard University Graduate School of Design Landscape Architecture Research Office, 1979.

Kirlin, J., and H. J. Brown. *The Interaction between Urbanization and Land: Quality and Quantity in Environmental Planning and Design: The Public Fiscal Accounting Model Technical Documentation.* Cambridge, MA: Harvard University Graduate School of Design Landscape Architecture Research Office, 1979.

Kirlin, J., and H. J. Brown. *The Interaction between Urbanization and Land: Quality and Quantity in Environmental Planning and Design: The Public Expenditure Model Technical Documentation.* Cambridge, MA: Harvard University Graduate School of Design Landscape Architecture Research Office, 1979.

Rogers, P., and R. S. Berwick. *The Interaction between Urbanization and Land: Quality and Quantity in Environmental Planning and Design: Water Quantity and Water Quality Model.* Cambridge, MA: Harvard University Graduate School of Design Landscape Architecture Research Office, 1978.

Rogers, P., and P. McClelland. *The Interaction between Urbanization and Land: Quality and Quantity in Environmental Planning and Design: The Solid Waste Management Model Technical Documentation.* Cambridge, MA: Harvard University Graduate School of Design Landscape Architecture Research Office, 1979.

Rogers, P., and P. McClelland. *The Interaction between Urbanization and Land: Quality and Quantity in Environmental Planning and Design: The Air Quality Evaluation Model Technical Documentation.* Cambridge, MA: Harvard University Graduate School of Design Landscape Architecture Research Office, 1979.

Smith, F. E. *The Interaction between Urbanization and Land: Quality and Quantity in Environmental Planning and Design: The Vegetation and Wildlife Model Technical Documentation.* Cambridge, MA: Harvard University Graduate School of Design Landscape Architecture Research Office, 1979.

Steinitz, C., and D. Allen. *The Interaction between Urbanization and Land: Quality and Quantity in Environmental Planning and Design: The Recreational Model Technical Documentation.* Cambridge, MA: Harvard University Graduate School of Design Landscape Architecture Research Office, 1979.

Steinitz, C., and C. Barton. *The Interaction between Urbanization and Land: Quality and Quantity in Environmental Planning and Design: The Conservation Model Technical Documentation.* Cambridge, MA: Harvard University Graduate School of Design Landscape Architecture Research Office, 1978.

Steinitz, C., C. J. Frederick, and P. Goodale. *The Interaction between Urbanization and Land: Quality and Quantity in Environmental Planning and Design: The Data Base Model Technical Documentation.* Cambridge, MA: Harvard University Graduate School of Design Landscape Architecture Research Office, 1978.

Steinitz, C., and K. Haglund. *The Interaction between Urbanization and Land: Quality and Quantity in Environmental Planning and Design: The Historical Resources Model Technical Documentation.* Cambridge, MA: Harvard University Graduate School of Design Landscape Architecture Research Office, 1978.

Tyler, M., and S. Cummings. *The Interaction between Urbanization and Land: Quality and Quantity in Environmental Planning and Design: The Transportation Model Technical Documentation.* Cambridge, MA: Harvard University Graduate School of Design Landscape Architecture Research Office, 1979.

Vidal, A. C., and H. J. Brown. *The Interaction between Urbanization and Land: Quality and Quantity in Environmental Planning and Design: The Public Institutions Model Technical Documentation.* Cambridge, MA: Harvard University Graduate School of Design Landscape Architecture Research Office, 1979.

Way, D. S. *The Interaction between Urbanization and Land: Quality and Quantity in Environmental Planning and Design: The Soils Model Technical Documentation.* Cambridge, MA: Harvard University Graduate School of Design Landscape Architecture Research Office, 1978.

Way, D. S. *The Interaction between Urbanization and Land: Quality and Quantity in Environmental Planning and Design: Land Use Descriptors Model Technical Documentation.* Cambridge, MA: Harvard University Graduate School of Design Landscape Architecture Research Office, 1978.

Wilkins, H., and H. J. Brown with J. Kirlin, M. Li, and K. Vardell. *The Interaction between Urbanization and Land: Quality and Quantity in Environmental Planning and Design: The Housing Model Technical Documentation.* Cambridge, MA: Harvard University Graduate School of Design Landscape Architecture Research Office, 1979.

Steinitz, C., L. Cipriani, J. C. Vargas-Moreno, and T. Canfield. *Padova e il Paesaggio-Scenarui Futuri peri il Parco Roncajette e la Zona Industriale / Padova and the Landscape—Alternative Futures for the Roncajette Park and the Industrial Zone.* Cambridge, MA: Graduate School of Design, Harvard University, Commune de Padova and Zona Industriale Padova, 2005. [A. Adeya, C. Barrows, A. H. Bastow, P. Brashear, E. S. Chamberlain, K. Cinami, M. F. Spear, S. Hurley, Y. M. Kim, I. Liebert, L. T. Lynn, V. Shashidhar, J. Toy]

Steinitz, C., and R. Faris. "Uncertain Futures? Commentary, Part B." *Environment* 48, no. 1 (2006): 41.

Steinitz, C., R. Faris, M. Flaxman, K. Karish, A. D. Mellinger, T. Canfield, and L. Sucre. "A Delicate Balance: Conservation and Development Scenarios for Panama's Coiba National Park." *Environment: Science and Policy for Sustainable Development* 47 (2005): 24–39.

Steinitz, C., R. Faris, M. Flaxman, J. C. Vargas-Moreno, T. Canfield, O. Arizpe, M. Angeles, M. Carino, F. Santiago, and T. Maddock. "A Sustainable Path? Deciding the Future of La Paz." *Environment: Science and Policy for Sustainable Development* 47 (2005): 24–38.

In Japanese in *Landscape Research Japan* 69, no.1 (2005): 66–67.

Steinitz, C., R. Faris, M. Flaxman, J. C. Vargas-Moreno, G. Huang, S.-Y. Lu, T. Canfield, O. Arizpe, M. Angeles, M. Cariño, F. Santiago,T. Maddock III, C. Lambert, K. Baird, and L. Godínez. *Futuros Alternativos para la Region de La Paz, Baja California Sur, Mexico/Alternative Futures for La Paz, BCS, Mexico.* Mexico D. F., Mexico: Fundacion Mexicana para la Educación Ambiental, and International Community Foundation, 2006.

Steinitz, C., A. Figueroa, and G. Castorena, eds. *Futuros Alternativos para Tepotzotlan/ Alternative Futures for Tepotzotlan.* Mexico D.F., Mexico: Universidad Autonoma Metropolitana, 2010. [S. Y. Lu, A. Cervantes, L. Margolis, J. C. Vargas-Moreno, K. Brigati, I. S. Ramirez, F. Timoltzi, W. Trimble, D. P. Barranco, A. Rivera, C. A. Ortiz, J. Lagarde, J. L. Torres, M. B-Valedon, J. B. Segon, M. Keating, R. Kaufman, P. Curran, A. G. Mendoza, B. B. Sierra, R. Tubon, A. Robinson, J. C. Cruz, E. Schneider, C. L-Chuvala, D. G. Juarez, B. Pons-Giner, G. U. Acevedo, B. Stigge, J. A. Rendon, A. A. Mora, B. Sanchez, I. Gaitan, J. U. Uribe]

Steinitz, C., and S. McDowell. "Alternative Futures for Monroe County, Pennsylvania: A Case Study in Applying Ecological Principles." In *Applying Ecological Principles to Land Management,* edited by V. H. Dale and R. A. Haeuber, 165–193. New York: Springer, 2001.

Steinitz, C., T. Murray, P. Rogers, D. Sinton, R. Toth, and D. Way. *Honey Hill: A Systems Analysis for Planning the Multiple Use of Controlled Water Areas.* Cambridge, MA: Harvard University, Graduate School of Design, Landscape Architecture Research Office, 1971.

Steinitz, C., P. Parker, and L. Jordan. "Hand Drawn Overlays: Their History and Prospective Uses." *Landscape Architecture* 66, no. 5 (1976): 444–55.

Steinitz, C., R. Pasini, M. Golobic, and T. Canfield. *Pensare il Verde a Cesena//Envisioning the Landscape of Cesena (Italy).* Cambridge, MA: Harvard University Graduate School of Design, 2004. [H. H. Chan, C. C. Chang, N. DeNormandie, A. Fargnoli, M. Horn, K. Hoyt, G. Huang, M. Kametani, S. Y. Kao, H. L. Liu, S. Y. Lu, J. Merkel, E. O-Douglas,D. Sears, H. Stecker]

Steinitz, C., and P. Rogers. *A Systems Analysis Model of Urbanization and Change: An Experiment in Interdisciplinary Education.* Cambridge, MA: MIT Press, 1970. [N. Dines, J. Gaffney, D. Gates, J. Gaudette, L. Gibson, P. Jacobs, L. Lea, T. Murray, H. Parnass, D. Parry, D. Sinton, S. Smith, F. Stuber, G. Sultan, T. Vint, D. Way, B. White]

Japanese edition, Tokyo: Orion Press, 1973.

Steinitz Rogers Associates, Inc. *Interstate Highway 84 in Rhode Island from I-295 to Connecticut State Line, Draft Environmental Impact Statement.* Vols. 2 and 3, Appendices. Providence, RI: Department of Transportation, State of Rhode Island and Providence Plantation, 1972.

———. *The Santa Anna Basin Study: An Example of the Use of Computers in Regional Plan Evaluation.* Fort Belvoir, VA: US Army Corps of Engineers, Institute for Water Resources Research, 1975.

Steinitz Rogers Associates, Inc., and Environmedia, Inc. *Natural Resources Protection Study and Airport Development Area Study.* St. Paul, MI: Metropolitan Council of the Twin Cities Area, 1970.

Sullivan, A. L., and M. L. Shaffer. "Biogeography of the Megazoo." *Science* 189 (1975): 13–17.

Thucydides. *History of the Peloponnesian War.* New York: Penguin Books, 1954.

Toth, R. "Theory and Language in Landscape Analysis, Planning and Evaluation." *Landscape Ecology* 1, no. 4 (1988): 193–201.

US Department of Energy, Western Area Power Administration. "Quartzite Solar Energy Project EIS." Scoping Summary Report, Phoenix, Arizona: Western Area Power Administration, 2010.

Vargas-Moreno, J. C. "Participatory Landscape Planning Using Portable Geospatial Information Systems and Technologies: The Case of the Osa Region of Costa Rica." D. Des. diss., Graduate School of Design, Harvard University, 2008.

———. "Spatial Delphi: Geo-Collaboration and Participatory GIS in Design and Planning." Specialist Meeting on Spatial Concepts in GIS and Design; Santa Barbara, California; December 15–16, 2008.

Wallace-McHarg Associates. *Plan for the Valleys.* Prepared for the Green Spring and Worthington Valley Planning Council, Inc. Philadelphia, PA: Green Spring and Worthington Valley Planning Council, 1964.

Werthmann, C., and C. Steinitz, eds. *El Renacar del Rio Tajo—Reviving the Tajo River.* Toledo, Spain: Fundacion +SUMA and Communidad de Castilla La Mancha, Espana, 2008. [A. Abdulla, R. Garg, M. J. Hsueh, J. Im, N. Johnson, E. Oettinger, S. Park, A. Peterson, Q. Riano, L. Shi, A. Sponzilli, J. H. Yoo]

Werthmann, C., and C. Steinitz, eds., with J. C. Vargas-Moreno. *Un Futuro Alternativo Para el Paisaje de Castilla-La Mancha/ An Alternative Future for the Landscape of Castilla La-Mancha (Spain).* Toledo, Spain: Foro Civitas Nova, 2007. [K. Bunker, C.-W. Chang, D. Joseph, K. Lucius, S. Melbourne, A.Phaosawasdi, A. Pierce-McManamon, J. Ridenour, R. Silver, J. J. Terrasa-Soler, A. Vaterlaus, J. Watson]

White, D., et al. "Assessing Risks to Bio-diversity from Future Landscape Change." *Conservation Biology*, 11, no. 2: 349–60.

Williams, S. K. "Process and Meaning in Design Decision-making." In *Design + Values* 1992 Council of Educators in Landscape Architecture Conference Proceedings, edited by Elissa Rosenberg, 199–204. Landscape Architecture Foundation/Council of Educators in Landscape Architecture. 1993.

Wright, F. L. "A Conversation with Frank Lloyd Wright." By Hugh Downs, "Wisdom," NBC News, May 8, 1953.

Zipf, George Kingsley. *The Psychobiology of Language.* Boston: Houghton-Mifflin, 1935.

# About the author

CARL STEINITZ is the Alexander and Victoria Wiley Professor of Landscape Architecture and Planning, Emeritus, at the Graduate School of Design, Harvard University. In 1967, Steinitz received his PhD degree in City and Regional Planning, with a major in urban design, from the Massachusetts Institute of Technology (MIT). He also holds the Master of Architecture degree from MIT and a Bachelor of Architecture degree from Cornell University. In 1965 he began his affiliation with the Harvard Graduate School of Design as a research associate in the Laboratory for Computer Graphics and Spatial Analysis. He has been Professor of Landscape Architecture and Planning at the Graduate School of Design since 1973.

Professor Steinitz has devoted much of his academic and professional career to improving methods to analyze large land areas and make design decisions about conservation and development. His applied research and teaching focus on highly valued landscapes that are undergoing substantial pressures for change. Professor Steinitz has directed studies in as wide ranging locales as the Gunnison region of Colorado; the Monadnock region of New Hampshire; the Snyderville Basin, Utah; Monroe County, Pennsylvania; the region of Camp Pendleton, California; the Gartenreich Worlitz in Germany; Muskau in Germany and Poland; the West Lake in Hangzhou, China; the Upper San Pedro River Basin in Sonora and Arizona; Coiba National Park in Panama; the regions of La Paz and Loreto in Baja California Sur, Mexico; Cagliari, Italy; the Tajo River and Henares River corridors in Spain; and the regions of Castilla La Mancha and Valencia in Spain.

In 1984, the Council of Educators in Landscape Architecture (CELA) presented Professor Steinitz with the Outstanding Educator Award for his "extraordinary contribution to environmental design education" and for his "pioneering exploration in the use of computer technology in landscape planning, especially in the areas of resource management and visual impact assessment." In 1996 he received the annual "Outstanding Practitioner Award" from the International Society of Landscape Ecology (USA). In 2002, he was honored as one of Harvard University's outstanding teachers.

Professor Steinitz is principal author of *Alternative Futures for Changing* Landscapes (Island Press 2003). He has received several honorary degrees. Professor Steinitz is currently the External Academic Adviser to the European Union funded LE:NOTRE program to rationalize landscape education in Europe and Honorary Visiting Professor at the Centre for Advanced Spatial Analysis at University College London.